The Brazilian Photographs of Genevieve Naylor, 1940–1942

The Brazilian Photographs of Genevieve Naylor, 1940–1942

Robert M. Levine

Duke University Press   Durham and London 1998

© 1998 Duke University Press
All rights reserved
Printed in the United States of America
on acid-free paper ∞
Designed by Mary Mendell. Typeset in Galliard
The publication of this book was generously supported
by the Brazilian Consulate in Miami.

Library of Congress Cataloging-in-Publication Data
appear on the last printed page of this book.

to Barbara H. and Stanley J. Stein,
and to the anonymous Brazilians photographed
by Genevieve Naylor (and the millions more
who lived out of range of her lens)

Contents

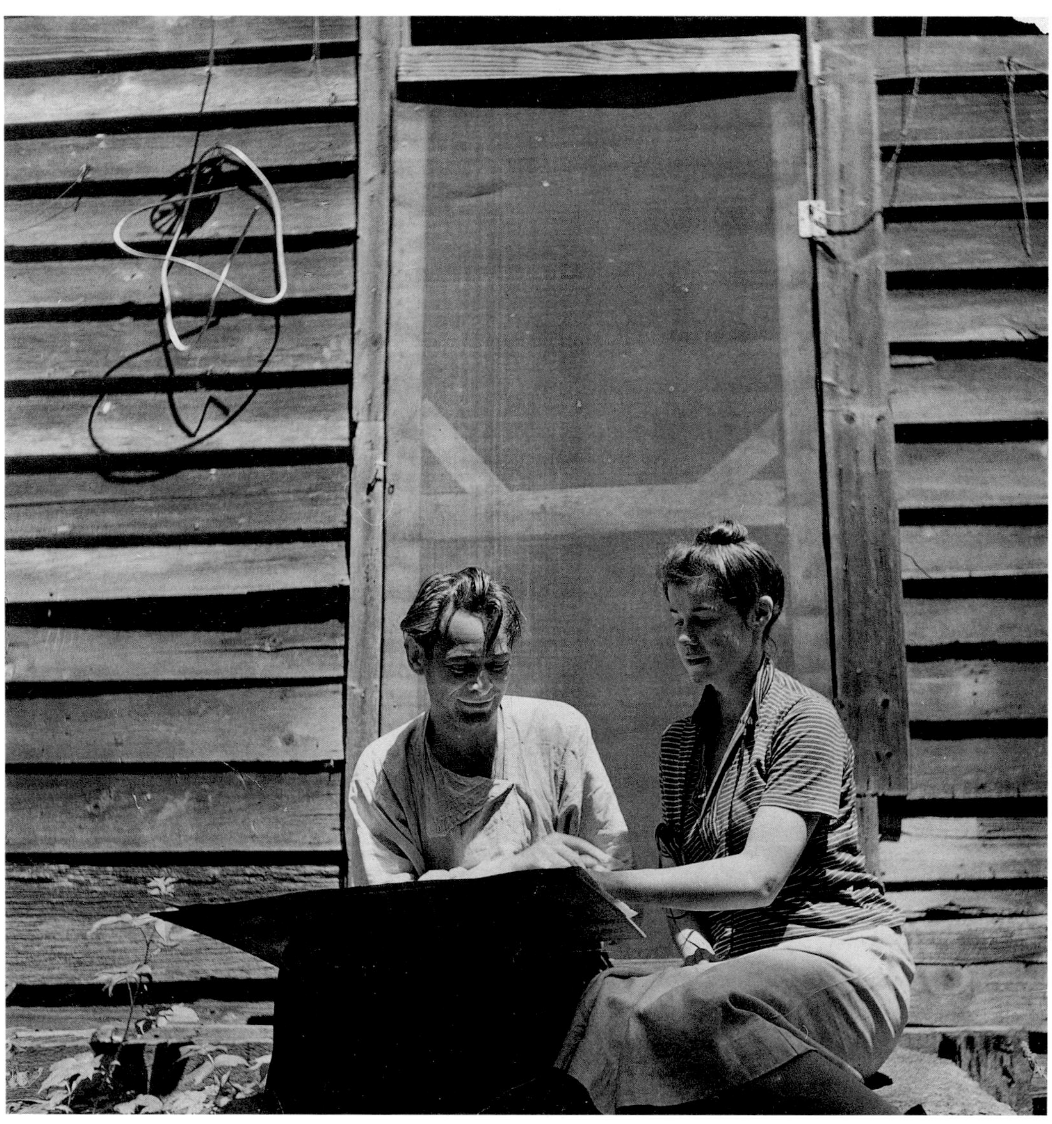

Genevieve and Misha.

Acknowledgments

Many persons kindly helped make this book a reality. Roberta M. Delson put me in touch with Genevieve Naylor's son Peter Reznikoff when she learned about the surviving collection of prints and negatives from Brazil. Peter needed someone to talk to about Brazil, and I had published a book on Latin American photography. I flew to New York, and on an icy day in February trekked up to Peter's apartment on West End Avenue to see the photographs. Within a few hours we decided to tackle several projects: an exhibition of Naylor's photographs at Columbia University, a jointly written article for the Organization of American States magazine, *Americas*, a videotaped documentary narrated by Peter, to be submitted to the Arts and Entertainment Network's History Channel, and a full-length book. Little did we know that all of this would happen within a very short period of time.[1]

On my second trip to New York to continue preparations, Peter invited Catherine Benamou to stop in. Benamou, now at Duke University, was the executive producer of the re-creation of Orson Welles's 1940s Brazilian-made film *It's All True*, and a sensitive critic of things photographic and on film. Kenneth P. Maxwell and Donzelina Barroso of the Camões Center arranged for the showing of Naylor photographs at Columbia University's Low Library and kindly invited me to New York for still another visit to speak at the opening. Jordan Young, an old Brazil hand who was there during the Second World War, not only put us in touch with important contacts but allowed himself to be interviewed on tape to provide context and background. Young's Princeton neighbors, Barbara and Stanley Stein, who resided in Brazil from 1941 to 1942 and again in 1948 to 1949 and 1951 to 1952, graciously reviewed the Naylor photographs and offered comments based on their experiences; Stanley, my doctoral adviser at Princeton, also provided useful comments on the draft manuscript. Antônio Pedro Tota offered wise counsel, as did Barbara Simpson.

Biographical material on Genevieve Naylor and Misha Reznikoff was provided by Peter Naylor, their nephew; Cynthia Gillipsie, Genevieve's sister; Eleanore Reznikoff, Genevieve's former daughter-in-law; and Peter and Michael Reznikoff, their sons.

Other helpful persons included the University of Wisconsin's Henry John Drewal, an art historian who specializes on Brazil; UCLA's Bill Summerhill; Rhodes's Michael LaRosa; the Washington, D.C., staff of *Americas* magazine; and, at the University of Miami, Michael Carlebach, Paul Blaney, Liliana Davidson Tower, Robin Bachin, Elza Rezende, and Cristina Mehrtens. Profuse thanks go to Brazil's consul in Miami, Ambassador Luiz A. Benedini, for his support of the book project.

All photographs, unless otherwise credited, are by Genevieve Naylor and are reproduced with the permission of Peter Reznikoff.

---

1   The earlier book was *Images of History* (Durham, N.C.: Duke University Press, 1989). See also Robert M. Levine and Peter V. Reznikoff, "Through the Lens of a Good Neighbor," *Americas* 47, no. 6 (November–December 1995), 16–23; "Genevieve Naylor's Brazil," videotaped documentary screened nationally on the A&E History Channel, March 24, 1997; and this book. The exhibit is discussed in the following text.

The Brazilian Photographs of Genevieve Naylor, 1940–1942

Introduction: Genevieve Naylor and Brazil

This book examines the photography of Genevieve Naylor in Brazil during the early 1940s, setting her work in the context of that country's history. During the middle and late 1930s Naylor had been one of the first photojournalists hired by the Associated Press, the leading national news agency, and she also worked for the U.S. government's Works Progress Administration (WPA). In 1940, she and her companion (and later husband) Misha Reznikoff, an artist, were sent to South America by Nelson A. Rockefeller's Office of Inter-American Affairs (OIAA),[1] the wartime agency organized to cultivate Latin American support for the allies. Independent-minded, Naylor balked at the mundane assignments given to her, and she spent a good deal of time finding ways to photograph outside the fashionable neighborhoods of Rio de Janeiro. Her more than 1,350 surviving photographs depict Brazil during those years in considerable detail. They are valuable not as creative works but as documents of everyday life. On her return from Brazil, Naylor had a successful one-woman show at New York's Museum of Modern Art in 1943, and some of her photographs appeared in wartime magazines, but save for exhibit catalogs her Brazilian work is not nearly as well known as the photography of her contemporaries who worked in the United States.[2] After the war the focus of her career changed. She became a leading fashion and reportage photographer for *Harper's Bazaar* and other Hearst and Condé Nast publications. It is her Brazilian work, however, that for historians holds inestimable value.

This study emphasizes what Naylor's experiences and output reveal about the photographer and about the country in which she worked. Her resistance of the limitations her superiors tried to impose on her and her sense of fascination with her subjects make her compositions valuable historical documents. Brazil during the early 1940s was a dictatorship, even if a mild one; magazines, newspapers, films, radio programs, and all other branches of the media were censored by the regime's propaganda ministry, the Departamento da Imprensa e Propaganda (DIP). The DIP worked closely with the OIAA, both agencies sharing the wartime view that carefully selected images could boost morale, foster good neighborliness, and, in the case of the Americans, aid the Allied war effort. DIP officials reported directly to president Getúlio Vargas and exercised enormous power. As a result, what we usually see from that era are images commissioned to show Brazil's progress toward becoming a modern nation. Naylor's images do this too, but they are often more spontaneous. They convey the excitement of a foreign observer for whom everything was fresh and alive. As a young woman during the Depression, she had sympathized with the artistic radicalism and bohemianism centered in New York City, although by taking a job with the mainstream Associated Press she showed that she was no radical herself. No shrinking violet either, Naylor confidently took up new challenges. The force of her personality drove her to photograph subjects of her own choosing, therefore enlarging the range of her subject matter and producing photographs that today hold more interest for us than had she shot only what she was told to shoot.

---

1   The agency's name changed from the Office for the Coordination of Commercial and Cultural Relations between the American Republics after July 30, 1941, to the Office of the Coordinator of Inter-American Affairs and again on March 23, 1945, until its termination on May 20, 1946, as the Office of Inter-American Affairs.

2   Her non-Brazilian work is included in Naomi Rosenblum's *A History of Women Photographers* (Abbeville Press, 1994).

Her style was unique, grounded in photojournalism but more concerned with composition than with reportage. Naylor combined spontaneity with meticulous concern for aesthetics. Her Brazilian work foreshadowed her subsequent career in high-fashion studio photography, a craft that combines elements of brazenness with an exquisite sense of composition. Naylor's job in Brazil was to create propaganda, to photograph the country in ways that would convey to Allied audiences the essence of Brazilian life, to educate Americans about Brazilians, to reassure Americans that Brazilians were reliable wartime partners. More than two years of shooting with limited supplies of film forced Naylor to consider her shots very carefully. "Film is being rationed to everyone," she wrote to her sister. "I don't have the luxury of shooting anything I want. I have to be damn careful, and choose my images with great care and hope my exposures are correct." The scarcity of film and the limitations of her equipment—she had neither flash gun nor studio lights, for example—shaped the way she executed her assignments in Brazil.[3] She had never had to face such constraints before: she was trained when film was cheap and plentiful. In the heyday of the national magazines, for example, *Life* photographers often shot hundreds of photographs for every one selected for publication. Wartime photographers did not have this luxury, especially Naylor, whose assignment to Brazil was minimally funded in the face of the vast war effort. Yet even with restricted supplies, she produced an archive that Emanoel Araújo, curator of São Paulo's Pinoteca de Estado, credited later with being one of the best surviving collections of images of Brazil from the early 1940s.

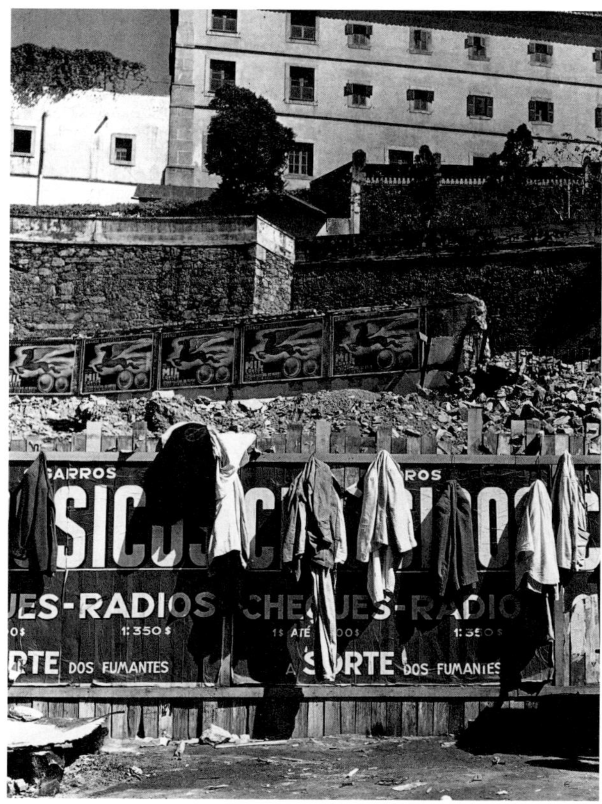

Clothes hanging to dry on a wall.

Visual Evidence

In their quest for more comprehensive understanding of the past, historians have turned to new forms of evidence on which to base analysis. "Visual history," in turn, offers a way to reconstruct how people defined their lives and the world in which they lived. We do not know exactly what they saw or how they reacted to visual signs, yet drawings, paintings, and, during and after the nineteenth century, photographs, offer a wealth of detail, including

---

3   Letter, Genevieve Naylor to her sister Cynthia, Rio de Janeiro, c. December 1941, courtesy of Cynthia Gillipsie.

the patterns and scale of spatial geography, human habitation, dress, physical appearance, and status.

To help understand these messages, experts have created grammars to explain culture, values, architecture, civic pageantry, and the theater of politics. But these languages are best suited to understand the affluent and the powerful. Ordinary people have been relegated to the category of the historically nameless. We know them only impersonally, within categories. From the 1880s through the 1940s, commercial picture agencies assigned their photographers to capture "types" because this is what customers were supposed to want to see. So the subjects of most commercial photographs live for us as anonymous members of groups: native peoples, African slaves, immigrants, indigents, human beasts of burden. They are stereotype bound, portrayed as docile exotics or as dangerous primitives. We know them as shadows, or ghosts. Social values contributed to this legacy. "Servus non habet personam" (servants do not have personalities) went the saying. Residents of *favelas*, shantytowns crowding the hillsides of Rio de Janeiro, one of the most photogenic cities in the world, were depicted as aimless ne'er-do-wells even though a study of one of the major favelas, conducted by Vargas's own government, showed that only 10 percent of favela residents in 1942 were unemployed; the large majority worked for a living.[4]

Although the opportunity to inspect visual records provides a way to decipher the material culture of the past, the exercise is risky. Photographs offer not a window on "reality" but a record of the shorthand cultural conventions deployed by the photographer, which reflect social values and perceptions. Thus, ambiguities remain. Do the gestures, body language, clothes, and mannerisms of the posed subjects depict accurately the drama of everyday life? Or do they just tell us about stock symbols engaged to facilitate identification?

Seeking "objective" or "pure" visual sources that bypass conventional symbols is illusory. Historical photographs capture postures that reinforce time-honored cultural and moralizing social conventions. Photographers brought their subjects into their studios but dressed them as if they were outdoors. Others used canvas backdrops to create the illusion of natural settings, posing subjects carefully to achieve "spontaneity." In the nineteenth century, especially in the decades immediately following the invention of the daguerreotype in France in 1839, photography was considered an objective science, capturing in minute detail the workings of nature. Few understood that the angle of the lens, or the quality of the light, or the backdrop selected by the photographer could completely change the mood and therefore the message conveyed by the photograph. Only after the invention of faster lenses, cheap films, and, after 1888, when the first Kodak camera was sold, did photography come to enjoy the versatility that transformed it not only into an amateur pastime but into a tool to manufacture images suitable for magazines and newspapers, as well as studio art, advertising, and scientific measurement.

Photojournalism came into its own at the end of the nineteenth century as one of the waves of this revolution. The principle was to document subjects in clear, uncluttered ways, to capture everyday experiences and to con-

---

4   "Apuração do Censo Realisado na Favela Largo da Memória," Rio de Janeiro, 1942, cited by Julio César Pino, "Family and Favela: The Reproduction of Poverty in Rio de Janeiro, 1940-69," manuscript, 2, with the permission of the author.

vey them with the intention of revealing life in an unvarnished, not choreographed, manner. Photographers increasingly had access to smaller cameras and faster film, permitting shots that were (or seemed to be) unposed. This technology gave photographers the freedom to play detective, to ferret out visual information. They probed the intimacy of daily life and editorialized, using visual conventions, about human relationships. Examples in the United States include reformist Jacob Riis's independent documentation of immigrant tenement life in New York City and to Lewis Hine's Progressive-era photography for the National Child Labor Committee. Photographers began to be able to make a living as freelance professionals, selling their work to magazines, displaying it in galleries, or using it in advertising. Distinct styles emerged. Photographers no longer said with their pictures, "This Is What It Looked Like," but "This Is How I Saw It."[5] The best of the new photographers grouped their subjects in ways that would reveal emotion; photographs became intimate, sometimes to the point of embarrassment or, when they went too far, voyeurism. The best of the subjective photographers—Edward Steichen, Edward Weston, Georgia O'Keefe, Diane Arbus, Henri Cartier-Bresson, Dorothea Lange, among many others (including the Brazilian Marc Ferrez)—probed beneath the surface of their subjects, producing work that startled, that forced observers to look harder, to consider in depth what was being presented to them. Many of the most talented photographers were women, perhaps because photographers had the freedom to work in the field anonymously, without the constraints imposed on other more traditional journalists during decades when barriers to hiring women in almost every profession were high.

Photojournalism's ascension was spurred by the Great Depression, which drove millions of Americans out of work and into conditions of dire hardship. Many photojournalists, especially those hired by the newsmagazines and for New Deal agencies that assigned them to chronicle the lives of ordinary citizens, shot photographs that responded emotionally to pressing national social difficulties. They were advocates and they fought for causes, even if their editors and other superiors attempted to restrain them. They were instructed to find out as much as possible about the places they visited and to interview their subjects before taking pictures.[6] W. Eugene Smith, one of the great photo essayists, explained his outlook:

> My station in life is to capture the action of life, the life of the world, its humor, its tragedies, in other words life as it is. A true picture, unposed and real. There is enough sham and deceit in the world without faking life and the world about us. If I am shooting a beggar, I want the distress in his eyes, if a steel factory I want the symbol of strength and power that is there. . . . I no longer take pictures for the pure joy of taking them, but like many of the old masters of the paints, I want them to be symbolic of something.[7]

From 1937 to 1945 Brazil lived under the Estado Novo, a dictatorship backed by the armed forces. The Estado Novo did not permit reformism, although the state itself

---

5   Kathy Ryan, "The Subjective Eye," *New York Times Magazine* (June 9, 1996), 52.

6   F.[orrest] Jack Hurley, *Portrait of a Decade: Roy Stryker and the Development of Documentary Photography in the Thirties* (Baton Rouge: Louisiana State University Press, 1972), 58; Glenn G. Willumson, *W. Eugene Smith and the Photographic Essay* (New York: Cambridge University Press, 1992), 2.

7   Letter, W. Eugene Smith to his mother, c. 1938, cited in Willumson, *W. Eugene Smith*, 25.

promoted social change it considered good for the population, along the lines of like reforms in Mussolini's Italy and Salazar's Portugal. With the media and press completely censored, there was little opportunity for advocacy or independent expression.

Photojournalistic efforts to record people's lives in Brazil and in the United States span a broad spectrum anchored on one end by the DIP photographs and on the other by the Farm Security Administration (FSA), founded by New Deal brain truster Rexford Tugwell to "rehabilitat[e] poor people and poor land."[8] There was a contradiction in the way the American photojournalists set out to capture life during the Depression. On the one hand, they thought of themselves as clinical observers, committed to a "direct, unmanipulated recording of contemporary events."[9] On the other hand, almost all the photographers retained by the Roosevelt administration empathized deeply with the men and women whose tragic lives they were recording. More than anything else the American photojournalistic projects, as far back as Riis and Hine, were efforts to alert the better-off to the problems of the poor in order to alleviate these problems, although the resulting images stopped far short of revealing the depths of squalor and misery that existed both in turn-of-the-century urban America or in rural America during the Depression. Documentary photographers were muckrakers, but they dealt with suffering at arm's length.[10] The DIP's theatrical images of smiling, hardworking poor people basking in achievement and thankful to the government were, of course, elements of the Brazilian government's efforts to orchestrate emotion

and to promote the attitude that it knew all.

Kathy Ryan, the photography editor of the *New York Times Magazine*, contends that photographic subjectivity emerged in the 1950s, once cameras were lighter, film speeds faster, and lenses more able to bring the photographers closer to their subjects.[11] I disagree emphatically. The portability of even a 4 x 5 Speed Graphic camera, and after the 1920s of the subminiature 35-millimeter Leica, which weighed less than a pound, permitted their users to get as close as they needed. Lenses of the best pre–World War II cameras were extremely sharp, and photographers—who often developed their own film and did their own printing—produced black-and-white prints that were usually crisper and more technically dazzling than today's automated color prints. Using the zone system of exposure and knowing intimately the characteristics of their lenses, film, and printing paper permitted equally as much subjectivity as today, at least until the advent of digitalized image manipulation.

Beginning as early as the late nineteenth century, professional photography branched into new specializations, each with its own characteristics. Advertising and fashion photography emphasized glamour and the apple-pie quality of American life. Photographers employed by the great civic expositions—Chicago's "White City" at its 1893 Columbian Fair, the Pan-American Exposition, the 1939 World's Fair—and hundreds of other photographers hired by municipalities, corporations, and private interests became photographic publicists, skilled in shaping images on demand. Photographers of still another specialty, studio-based community photographers like

---

8 Maren Stange, "The Record Itself," in Pete Daniel, Merry A. Foresta, Maren Stange, and Sally Stein, eds., *Official Images: New Deal Photography* (Washington, D.C.: Smithsonian Institution Press, 1987), 2.

9 James Curtis, "The Contemplation of Things as They Are," in *Mind's Eye, Mind's Truth: FSA Photography Reconsidered* (Philadelphia: Temple University Press, 1989), 47.

10 Vicki Goldberg, "Looking at the Poor in a Gilded Frame," *New York Times*, April 9, 1995, sec. 2, p. 1.

11 Ryan, "The Subjective Eye," 52–53.

Harlem's James VanderZee, worked quietly for decades recording family rites of passage—births, religious ceremonies, weddings, funerals—capturing the texture of life, although the cumulative power of their work was often lost unless their negative archives were after many years, as in VanderZee's case, discovered and exhibited.

The Great Depression, of course, produced its own kind of specialization: photographs of the harshness of unemployment and despair. *Life* magazine, which started publication in the 1930s, combined an uplifting editorial policy with stark images produced by photojournalists such as Margaret Bourke-White, whose work had a profound influence on the young Genevieve Naylor. Who could have been more subjective than the New Deal's FSA photographers who set out to capture the tenacity of Americans in hardship, the ravaged earth, and the ironies of poverty in a nation proud of its affluence? Their goal was to use photography to heighten awareness of conditions, although the congressmen who appropriated the funds to hire artists, photographers, and writers probably saw their actions more as make-work measures than anything else. The outbreak of World War II, however, abruptly changed things. Wartime government censorship intruded on photographers' freedom. Coverage of the fighting dominated magazines and newspapers from the first days of the Nazi conquest of Poland in 1939, but few published images showed casualties or mass destruction, especially photographs of the Allied side. Rather, photography was employed to boost morale, emphasizing preparedness and patriotism. Genevieve Naylor, too, was hired by the OIAA to produce photographs of Brazil

that would strengthen the war effort by showing that Brazil was a hardworking, reliable ally. But she felt constrained by her instructions. Because her bosses could not control what she did in the field, her photographs—like the work of all the great Depression-era and wartime photographers—convey far more information and meaning than any stock publicity photograph could.

Photographs possess the capacity to speak eloquently, although they are two-dimensional and frozen in time. It remains for the viewer to grasp the photographer's meaning. This is difficult, because photographs disclose diversity and individuality to an astonishing degree. Yet a good photograph indeed is worth a thousand words or more, especially when it penetrates convention and shows the details of places, lives, or events that otherwise would never be preserved for scrutiny. Traditionally, photographs have been measured on the basis of their *nominal content*—genre, tonality, composition, and other aesthetic characteristics. For the social historian, photographs provide information about *effective content* as well. This category includes inventories of material culture, unexpected objects, and things not expected to be found.[12] Naylor's images contain both kinds of content, and for this reason they have left their mark not only as works of beauty but as sources of historical details.

Given that photographs are intrinsically subjective, we must resist imposing the standards of our day on the past. Critic Susan Sontag has criticized documentary photographers for exploiting the poor, "turning them into objects of dubious beauty."[13] During the Depression, many Americans felt an expanded sense of social responsibility

---

12   I am grateful to Max Kozloff for this insight.

13   Susan Sontag, cited in Goldberg, "Looking at the Poor," 39.

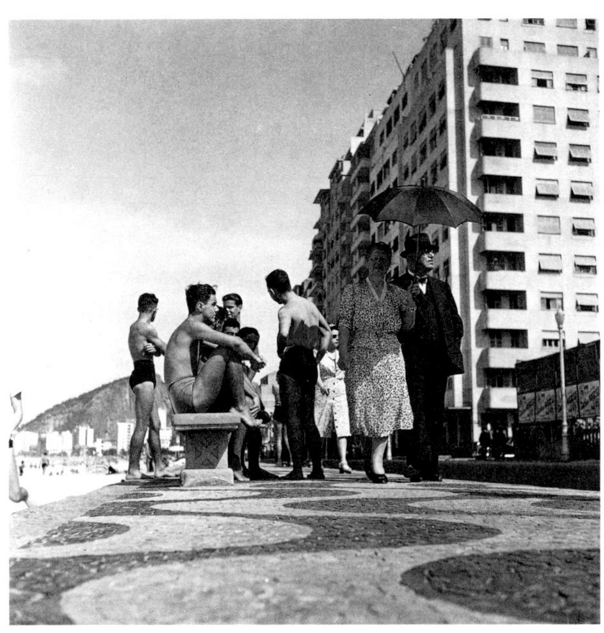

Copacabana.

their assignments. Naylor had a much more specific assignment, and the fact that she accomplished it successfully as part of the war effort makes us respect her all the more. She never patronized, never intruded, and never sensationalized. She managed, nonetheless, to capture the Brazil of the early 1940s, something that the dozens of DIP photographers failed to achieve because they were trying too hard to find what the bureaucracy wanted them to depict. She was also freer to do as she wanted: after all, a foreigner, especially an employee of the U.S. government holding a diplomatic passport, enjoyed far greater freedom than that of most Brazilian citizens during the dictatorship.

and, in some, a sense of common humanity; Dorothea Lange produced moving and compassionate photographs of migrants and rural workers in part because she "was confident that the audience shared her feelings."[14] This attitude was altered by the coming of the war, and it certainly was not heard in Brazil during the late 1930s and early 1940s. Genevieve Naylor's photographs, produced for a wartime agency under the further influence of the Brazilian government's propaganda agency, should not be compared with Lange's even if their photojournalistic styles had much in common. Nor did Naylor seek to copy what social activists Ben Shahn or Walker Evans did: championing "workers" and the "downtrodden" in

14 Ibid.

Genevieve Naylor and Misha Reznikoff arrived in Brazil ten years after the 1930 revolution, which had put Getúlio Vargas in power. The decade had seen far-reaching changes in Brazilian life. Committed to a modernizing nationalism at any cost and seeking to remain distant from American influence, lest his nation fall further into dependency on its giant North American neighbor, Vargas used authoritarian methods to remain in office, culminating in the Estado Novo coup of November 1937, which closed Congress and installed him as a dictator.

This act was committed in the name of national unity and to close ranks against foreign ideological penetration. Most Brazilians liked Vargas, though some made fun of his provincial mannerisms—attributes he cultivated for effect. Vargas used a combination of old-fashioned and modern methods to instill pride in being Brazilian. He reached out via radio and newspapers to ordinary Brazilians, millions of whom lived at the subsistence level or not far above it. Most of these people were illiterate, without a sense of citizenship in a country that had evolved from a great colonial plantation to a fragmented nation dominated by a few strong states. Vargas brought with him no natural base of political support, especially because his home state of Rio Grande do Sul bitterly objected to his emphasis on government centralization, so he courted white- and blue-collar workers, still a great minority within the population, for support. Later he would cultivate the backing of the working class, creating the national Labor Party as its instrument. But in the early 1940s he clearly reached out to the Brazilian people as a whole, although his programs ignored the chronically destitute rural poor (and a sizable portion of urban residents as well). The minimum rate of pay fixed by Getúlio Vargas, Stefan Zweig complained, "has not yet been able to penetrate to the interior, into the forests of Mato Grosso and Acre, parts of the world as far removed from a street as they are from a railway."[1] The poor did not participate in the market economy, were not consumers, and were mostly illiterate, unskilled, and struggling.

Historian Stanley J. Stein, who was in Brazil in 1942, adds his recollection:

> To a young man from the U. S. East Coast in 1942, *Brésil profonde* was profoundly conservative, with a simmering anti-British undercurrent widespread in the military, perhaps less so in the intellectual class. There was still no real danger in voicing what were essentially *integralista* [fascist] thoughts about the need for an organic society, Catholic, agrarian—tied to the social conscience of *rerum novarum* [papal encyclical, "On the Condition of Workers"]. At the same time there was both cultural nationalism (a reaction to the anglosaxonization of the First Republic) and recognition that the "social problem" was more than a matter for the police. The country was deeply conservative yet in some respects timidly reformist—only in this sense can we understand that brief period of radicalism that surfaced between 1944 and 1949.[2]

Under Vargas's leadership Brazil changed from a fragmented entity made up of disparate states linked by political ties—an archipelago, in Stein's words[3]—to a united country sharing pride in its flag and culture and appreciative of its head of state. Before Vargas, Brazilians felt that

---

1   Stefan Zweig, *Brazil: Land of the Future,* trans. Andrew St. James (New York: Viking, 1942), 150.

2   Letter, Stanley J. Stein to author, Princeton, N.J., April 4, 1997.

3   Interview, Stanley J. Stein, Princeton, N.J., March 1, 1997, with Peter Reznikoff.

they lagged behind other nations, holding a timid and apologetic self-image. Vargas and his advisers understood the need to overcome this conception. The stated rationale of the Liberal Alliance coup, which Vargas and Oswaldo Aranha somewhat brazenly called the "1930 Revolution," was to create not only a new national government but a new Brazilian patriotism, reducing the hegemony of the powerful states of the Center-South and their elites, now shaken by the collapse of coffee prices in the world market. The times called for far-reaching initiatives, and propaganda was the way to win popular support for them.[4]

Vargas created a national propaganda agency in 1931, only months after his successful coup d'etat. The Departamento Oficial de Propaganda (DOP) was in turn succeeded by the Departamento de Propaganda e Difusão Cultural (DPDC) in 1934. This agency was charged with exploring the use of films, "radiotelegraphy," and "other technological processes" to disseminate propaganda for the regime.[5] Two years later Vargas put into motion steps to create a nationwide patriotic radio program, the *Hora do Brasil* (Hour of Brazil), broadcast daily at 6 P.M. Vargas and other government figures addressed the nation regularly, seeking to bolster morale and to counter the psychological effects of the Great Depression, which hit Brazil hard. The radio program was the first event in Brazilian history to touch the lives of all Brazilian citizens, from the coast to the vast interior, regardless of their social status.

Vargas and the armed forces overthrew his own government in November 1937 and imposed the Estado Novo dictatorship. The event culminated more than two years of government by decree. Vargas now redoubled his propaganda efforts, first through the Departamento Nacional de Propaganda (DNP) in 1938 and a year later through the DIP. The second agency, substantially larger than its predecessors and responsible directly to the president, was given the power to impose a nationwide apparatus for censorship and to punish offenders.

For this and many other reasons, the early 1940s represented a watershed in the lives of Brazilians. A decade of Getúlio Vargas's rule had seen the construction of a powerful central government committed to nationalism and industrial self-sufficiency. Brazil was rapidly becoming transformed from a rural nation to one of burgeoning cities dominated by factories and commerce. Urban overcrowding caused by streams of rural migrants seeking jobs created the basis for a new populist style of mass politics that would emerge at mid-decade. "It seemed a matter of time," historian Arthur P. Whitaker wrote, "before popular pressures would break through the dikes, and bring in a flood of political and social changes."[6] New kinds of government were emerging throughout Latin America, led by politicians who "claimed to represent the people and [who] treated social and economic problems as fundamental."[7] In Brazil, Vargas asserted almost daily that the goal of his regime was to move the country forward. In response, most citizens came to regard him affectionately, so much so that in 1950 when he ran for the presidency he received the highest number of votes ever, even though he had been unceremoniously ousted from power five years earlier by the military command.

When outsiders (as well as most urban Brazilians)

---

4   See Robert M. Levine, *The Vargas Regime: The Critical Years, 1934–1938* (New York: Columbia University Press, 1970).

5   André L. F. Couto and Telma Bonniau Gitirana, "Fotografia e propaganda política: o Estado Novo em foco" (Rio de Janeiro: Centro de Pesquisa e Documentação, 1989), 11; Aristheu Achilles, "O Departamento Nacional de Propaganda," *Revista do Serviço Público* (Rio de Janeiro), 4, no. 1 (October 1938), 54–61.

6   Arthur P. Whitaker, cited in David Rock, "War and Postwar Intersections: Latin America and the United States," in David Rock, ed., *Latin America in the 1940s: War and Postwar Transitions* (Berkeley: University of California Press, 1994), 15.

7   Whitaker, cited in ibid.

thought about the country in the early 1940s they really had two places in mind: the coast—dominated by its major cities: Belém, Recife, Salvador, Rio de Janeiro, São Paulo, and Porto Alegre—and the "damp, iridescent vastness of the jungle," where, some believed, aboriginal tribes still practiced cannibalism.[8] There were 41 million Brazilians in 1940, the same number as French people in France. Brazil's population had jumped by more than 50 percent since the previous national census in 1920 and was increasingly located in cities and towns, not in the rural countryside. Manufacturing and commercial growth in coastal cities continued to draw migrants from the backlands, an occurrence facilitated by the construction of roads and the expansion of coastal shipping under Vargas. The interior, especially the forested states of Amazonas, Pará, Mato Grosso, and Goiás, was so sparsely populated that the arm of the government barely reached beyond the state capitals.

Brazil's stereotype abroad was one of a vast expanse of coffee plantations, bordered by rain forest, and peopled by swarthy-skinned people who danced at Carnival. Many Americans thought that Brazilians spoke Spanish, not Portuguese, and that Buenos Aires was the country's capital. In reality, the collapse of coffee prices during the Depression had relegated the value of coffee exports to less than 20 percent of the nation's foreign sales. Still, the old images persisted, heightened by the fact that upper-class Brazilians looked to Europe—and especially France—for cultural direction. As a result, some elites disparaged their country, especially the hinterland that stretched thousands of kilometers away from the coast. This way of seeing their own country as backward and primitive differed little from the way people in other countries thought about Brazil. There were few incentives to visit the interior to learn about its character and diversity.

Few knew what this world was like. Rural families eked out a living by working as farm laborers or renters in one of more than a dozen kinds of sharecropping arrangements that kept them a step above being a true peasantry but which at the same time mired them in debt and poverty. Before Vargas came to power there were virtually no public schools in the interior, and although he made education a major plank in his government's program the problem was so vast that most rural children during the 1940s received little or no schooling. Teachers were paid less than fifty dollars a month when they were paid at all, and facilities were crude and discouraging. Large producers of export crops such as coffee, cotton, and sugar profited, but were hampered by plunging prices during the Depression and by wartime shipping difficulties.

Poverty was concentrated among the nonwhite population. Consider Sir Harry H. Johnston's contemporary observation about land tenure and race in his book *The Negro in the New World*:

> The conditions regarding the acquisition of land (more especially Government land in new districts) require the possession of more or less ready money. The white man, therefore, acquires the land and surveys it at his own expense. Before he casts his eye over this likely estate it may already have been squatted on by negroes, negroids, or Indians. . . . [Rather than] the estate owner desiring to evict the

---

8 Zweig, *Brazil*, 5–6.

squatter, he is anxious to come to terms with him, because if he is harsh, the squatter with his invaluable labour will move off. . . . The unwritten law is that the squatter will pay for his rent and other benefits in labour. . . . Until the negro acquires capital . . . so long will the white man hold the political and social ascendancy in Brazil.[9]

Brazil's major cities were transformed during the second half of the nineteenth century into centers of commerce and government administration. Physically they burst their former boundaries, although until well after World War II the prime residential districts for the wealthy and for the emerging middle classes remained in the center of the cities. Urban growth and the availability of jobs attracted population, but the shortage of housing relegated migrants from the hinterland and working-class newcomers to the periphery, or, as in the case of Rio de Janeiro, the nation's capital, to the hills rising abruptly from the coastal shore. After the turn of the century, city administrations razed residential neighborhoods to build thoroughfares and required their inhabitants to relocate to the distant and undesirable suburbs.[10] Rather than having to live at great distances from their work sites, Rio's poor occupied privately held land, often on hillsides, and constructed shantytowns known as favelas. These favelas grew, their total population reaching at least a million by 1960. Of all the city's favelas two decades later, the largest number—some 44 percent of the total—started up in the years between 1940 and 1960.[11] Some working-class families did not live in favelas but in sweltering tenements carved out of old buildings and factories in outlying zones near railroad depots and the docks.

Middle- and working-class residents looked to Vargas warmly, and, in some cases, as a father figure. The neighborhoods of the very poor were usually ignored, even under Vargas's paternalistic regime. The exception was in Rio de Janeiro, where the government, under military intervenor Pedro Ernesto Baptista, sent agents who functioned as social workers to help the poorest residents, and the women's auxiliary of the fascist Integralist Party organized sewing classes and instructed women in hygiene and child-rearing practices.[12] In 1937, legislation prohibited the construction of new dwellings or the improvements of old ones in the favelas. Plans were also discussed to find ways to dissuade migrants from settling in the city and to convince them to return to the hinterland. In the early 1940s, Rio de Janeiro authorities coupled their continued efforts to tear down favelas with efforts to build low-income housing. In 1942, three large units opened, known as Parques Proletários, or "Workers' Parks." They were, as Robert Gay reminds us, designed not only to provide housing but to isolate and control the residents. Occupants were issued identity cards that had to be shown to get through the gatehouse, which was closed at 10 P.M. Housing officials also used loudspeaker systems to lecture residents on "issues of public morality."[13] In all, this public-housing policy failed: the government built too few units, and favelas continued to expand largely unchecked. Encouraged by the Roman Catholic Church hierarchy, the government after Vargas's ouster in 1945 now permitted favelas to be "urbanized," that is, they allowed such improvements as electric power, running water, and brick and mortar structures to be built in place of the jerry-built shacks that had been the norm.

---

9 Sir Harry J. Johnston, *The Negro in the New World*, 100–101, cited in T. Lynn Smith, *Brazil: People and Institutions*, 4th ed. (Baton Rouge: Louisiana State University Press, 1972), 301.

10 See June Hahner, *Poverty and Politics: The Urban Poor in Brazil, 1870–1920* (Albuquerque: University of New Mexico Press, 1986), 160–165; Victor V. Valla, *Educação e favela: política para as favelas do Rio de Janeiro* (Rio de Janeiro: Editora Zahar, 1986); Jeffrey Needell, *A Tropical Belle Epoque: Elite Culture and Society in Turn-of-the-Century Rio de Janeiro* (Cambridge: Cambridge University Press, 1987); Robert Gay, *Popular Organization and Democracy in Rio de Janeiro: A Tale of Two Favelas* (Philadelphia: Temple University Press, 1994), esp. 14–17.

11 Gay, *Popular Organization and Democracy in Rio de Janeiro*, 11, table 4.

12 Levine, *The Vargas Regime*.

If the visitors to Brazil under the OIAA and Good Neighbor Policy struggled personally with any issue in Brazilian life, it was the matter of race. The reactions depended on the individual. Many members of the U.S. Foreign Service were either genteel sons of well-placed families or from the American South or both; it was not uncommon to encounter among members of this group considerable prejudice not only against nonwhites but against Jews and Roman Catholics as well. Some foreigners in Brazil shared this outlook, whereas others did not. The matter of race—and the fact that Brazilians included a richer blend of racial mixtures than almost any other place—had always fascinated outsiders. Nineteenth-century travelers, fortified by their belief in white supremacy, used blunt terms that shock us today: "We are certain," wrote an anonymous reviewer of Richard F. Burton's *Exploration in the Highlands of the Brazil* in 1869,

> that the true civilization on the tropics will be effected only when a certain proportion of European women are imported, to form the nucleus of a future white population. This pure white population—"creole" in the literal sense of the word—will extirpate the atrocious "mixed breed" that now crawls like a disgusting reptile, over the fair face of the Brazil.[14]

Others, on the contrary, found Brazil's seemingly relaxed attitudes about race and the general ease by which people of all racial groups interacted to be exemplary. Genevieve Naylor felt this way, as did Orson Welles. Welles's fascination with Afro-Brazilian culture, in fact, led to conflict with Hollywood studio executives and set into motion events that ultimately were to prove instrumental in his downfall.

Welles was at the apex of his highly controversial career as a movie director, having recently completed *Citizen Kane*, which was universally taken to be a thinly veiled portrait of the newspaper tycoon William Randolph Hearst. Welles had come to Rockefeller's attention because the Rockefeller family owned a substantial share of RKO Pictures, for whom Welles worked under contract. Rockefeller suggested that Welles shoot a movie in Latin America and offered him protection against financial loss during its realization. Welles wanted to complete his anthology film *It's All True,* which he had started to make in Mexico, and he arrived in Brazil under an intense publicity barrage kicked off by his entrance into Rio de Janeiro at the head of a motorcade flanked by motorcyclists. He was received as a cultural idol. He threw his energy into his stay in Brazil, becoming a companion of many Brazilians, including diplomat Oswaldo Aranha, before his film production soured. When Foreign Minister Aranha signed Brazil's declaration of war against the Axis in 1942, the news photographs circulated around the world had Welles seated alongside him.

Welles's fascination with the city's favelas convinced him to concentrate his shooting in the shantytown slums of the capital, a turn that quickly wore out his welcome with his U.S. State Department escorts and members of the local social elite. He also lived extravagantly and ran up large cost overruns each week. Genevieve Naylor met him right after he arrived and showed him some of the places in the city, including Praça Onze, the square where blacks of modest economic standing practiced for Carni-

---

13   Gay, *Popular Organization and Democracy in Rio de Janeiro,* 16, citing Anthony and Elizabeth Leeds, *A sociologia do Brasil urbano* (Rio de Janeiro: Editora Zahar, 1978), 191–198; and Lucien Parisse, *Favelas do Rio de Janeiro: evolução e sentido* (Rio de Janeiro: Centro Nacional de Pesquisas Habitacionais, 1969), 66–77.

14   "Burton's Exploration in the Brazil," *Anthropological Review* 7 (April 1869), 170–176, quote on p. 175.

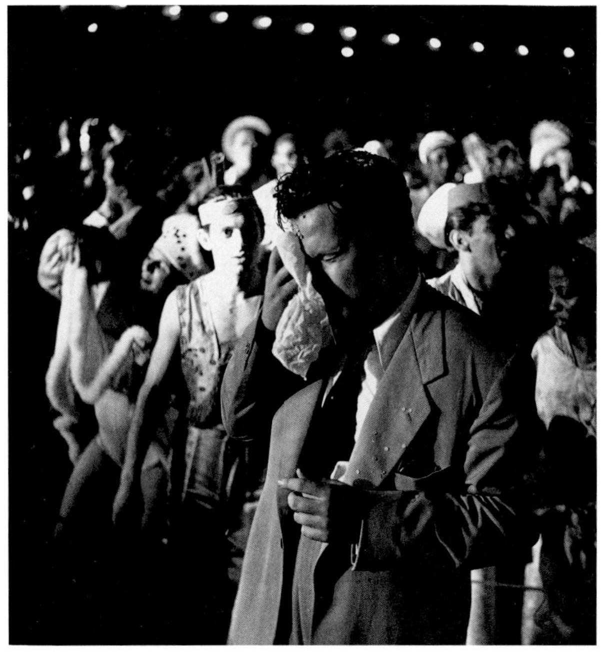

Orson Welles: The "boy wonder" actor and director.

again, the OIAA had come down on the side of prudence and noncontroversy.

The U.S. propaganda effort also subsidized anti-Nazi writers from other countries. In Cuba, Salvador Díaz Versón's anti-Nazi books were underwritten; the State Department helped the Austrian Jewish author Stefan Zweig settle in Brazil and encouraged him to write *Brazil: Land of the Future*, a book of friendly impressions that sold widely in the United States before Zweig's suicide from depression in 1943.[16] Interestingly, Zweig wrote eloquently about the need for racial and ethnic democracy (and about Brazil's rich racial mix), a subject that American authors often minimized or avoided, presumably to avoid offending the sensibilities of U.S. southerners. "Brazil," Zweig wrote, "has shown up in the simplest way the absurdity of the racial problem that is destroying our European world: by just ignoring its alleged validity," and he argued,

> Whereas our old world is more than ever ruled by the insane attempt to breed people racially pure, like race-horses and dogs, the Brazilian nation for centuries has been built upon the principle of a free and unsuppressed miscegenation, the complete equalization of black and white, brown and yellow.[17]

Zweig, however, tempered his enthusiasm with a dash of reality. "Far be it for me to pretend that conditions in Brazil today are ideal." He added:

> Many things are still in their infancy or in a state of transition. The standard of living of a large part of

val. An OIAA official sent a warning to Washington that Welles was offending local sensibilities, by which he meant the sensibilities of the Jockey Club set and the diplomats attached to the American Embassy. RKO, angered at Welles's demands to spend $150,000 to shoot one nightclub scene and embroiled with Welles over other studio problems, fired him. Shooting of *It's All True* was halted, although RKO had spent $1.2 million to that point.[15] Now that Welles was no longer working for RKO, Rockefeller withdrew his financial guarantee. Welles spent years trying, unsuccessfully, to have the film project revived, but by early 1945 he abandoned it. Once

---

15   Fifty years later, in 1995, a team of film historians reconstructed *It's All True* from outtakes discovered in a film storehouse and made it available to the public.

16   See Salvador Díaz Versón, *El nazismo en Cuba* (Havana: Obrapia, 1944); Zweig, *Brazil*.

17   Ibid., 8.

the population is still far below ours. The technical and industrial achievements of these fifty million people can still only be compared with those of a minor European State.[18]

Rio de Janeiro and São Paulo, the two largest and most important cities, differed in the racial composition of their residents. São Paulo, which over the decades had attracted not only mixed-race migrants from the rural interior but large numbers of European immigrants—principally Italians, Spaniards, Portuguese, and Japanese—was approximately 40 percent nonwhite (*negro* and *pardo* [brown] according to census categories), but, as a city of neighborhoods, was strictly segregated residentially. About half the residents of the city of Rio de Janeiro fell into the intermediate racial categories of *mulatto, caboclo*, and so on. Rio had a far greater number of favelas perched on hillsides around the city, mostly occupied by blacks. São Paulo's slum districts were made up of decaying tenements; favelas in that city were not present until the 1950s. Neighborhoods and parts of neighborhoods in both cities, and in every city in Brazil, were demarcated for nonwhites, who also were segregated into their own samba schools, soccer clubs, dance halls, and places of worship (especially such centers for Afro-Brazilian spiritist cults as *candomblé* and *umbanda*).[19]

How one felt about the Brazilian regime depended upon one's vantage point. Progressive intellectuals faced persecution for their beliefs, and leftists faced police-state brutality. Industrialists and business owners grumbled about the government's rhetoric but applauded Vargas's nationalistic thrust and his efforts to modernize the economy. Brazil's calculated decision to back the allies meant the nationalization of German-owned airlines, the closing of German schools in the South, the replacement of British and French influence by American investment (and popular culture), and the creation of the country's first steel mill at Volta Redonda—its workers' housing a dramatic experiment in social engineering. The wartime years saw the publication of the *Reader's Digest* in Portuguese, wary relations with Argentine dictator Juan Perón, naval battles in the south Atlantic, a general reform of the educational system, and exploitation of Brazil's great untapped natural resources for the war effort. The government seized newspapers unfriendly to it (including *A Noite* in Rio de Janeiro and the *Estado de São Paulo*).[20] Cronies of Vargas's dominated his government behind the scenes, including Lourival Fontes and his canny friend J. S. de Maciel Filho, the editor of *O Imparcial*, and, during the second half of Vargas's public career, Vargas's right-hand man. Under Vargas, Brazil enacted one of the highest tariffs in the world to protect its heavily regulated and increasingly centralized economy.[21]

On June 11, 1940, three days after the fall of France to the Nazis, Vargas made an address aboard a Brazilian warship that frightened the Americans more than ever. "We march towards a diverse future," he said; "the age of liberalism has passed."[22] The U.S. State Department moved into high gear, anchored by intense exchanges of communications between Ambassador Jefferson Caffery, a veteran of U.S. diplomacy in Cuba, and Undersecretary for Latin American Affairs Sumner Welles. Other Americans practiced their own kind of diplomacy: the actor Errol Flynn, sponsored by the DIP, visited Vargas at the

---

18   Ibid., 10–11.

19   The little research that has been done on the subject of residential racial segregation appeared in the late 1980s. See Michael George Hanchard, *Orpheus and Power: The Movimento Negro of Rio de Janeiro and São Paulo, Brazil, 1945–1988* (Princeton, N.J.: Princeton University Press, 1994), esp. 28–29.

20   "Free form" commentary on the 1940s courtesy of Lawrence Hallewell.

21   Rock, "War and Postwar Intersections," 16; George Wythe, *Industry in Latin America* (New York: Columbia University Press, 1945).

22   Cited in Antonio Pedro Tota, "Americanização no condicional: Brasil nos anos 40," *Perspectivas* (São Paulo), 16 (1993), 198.

Catete Palace four days after Vargas's speech. Flynn wrote to Franklin D. Roosevelt from the Copacabana Palace Hotel, telling him of the warm reception he had been given "by hundreds of happy, smiling, friendly faces." He gave a nationwide radio address broadcast over the DIP's *Hora do Brasil*. "Perhaps the very hope for the world's future," he told his audience, "may lie in Pan Americanism."[23]

Although it was in many ways mutually distasteful, both Washington and Rio de Janeiro took pains to accept the fiction that Brazil under Vargas's Estado Novo was a democracy. Brazil, in reality, was a police state, albeit a mild one for most citizens. Members of the armed forces high command openly sympathized with the European fascists, the local German and Italian colonies were vocally supportive of the European dictators, Franco's and Salazar's dictatorial regimes in Spain and Portugal, respectively, enjoyed close relations with Rio de Janeiro, and as late as January 1942 Vargas had not yet indicated whether he would choose the side of the Allies or the Axis. W. Guest, an official of the U.S. Foreign Service, in a letter to Nelson A. Rockefeller in 1941 warned that "we are sitting atop a volcano which can erupt at any moment." He added, "From the vantage point of the U.S., we believe that there are a whole bunch of friendly democracies to the South. When we look more closely, though, we see that they are neither friendly nor democratic," and, even more ominously, "All of the members of the [Brazilian] government are openly pro-Nazi except President Vargas and Oswaldo Aranha."[24] Aranha, an old crony of Vargas's (and the man considered the architect behind Vargas's 1930 coup), had himself been edged aside in 1937 by the military because he had refused to go along with the imposition of a fascist-style dictatorship.

For years, some historians have argued that Vargas, true to his authoritarian nature, privately favored the Axis cause. Based on the publication in 1995 of his edited secret diaries and on other new research, it seems more likely that he—like most of the members of Brazil's elite—did not favor fascism; rather, he believed that by allying with the United States he would doom Brazil to permanent dependency. Given that economic independence and national sovereignty were Vargas's foremost goals, it is credible that he delayed breaking with the Axis for as long as he did. When the German Navy sank several ships of the Brazilian merchant marine in 1942, Vargas had to enter the war on the Allied side. By then the Nazi offensive had become bogged down, and it was safe to assume that the free nations among the Allies would not be overrun as had been France, the Low Countries, and central-eastern Europe. This interpretation also explains the tense reception given by the Brazilians to aspects of Washington's Good Neighbor Policy. Ostensibly that policy was a two-way street of cultural exchange, but to Vargas and many Brazilians it meant that American culture would enter Brazil unchecked, threatening Brazil's heritage. They feared that after the war Brazil would emerge as an economic appendage of the United States, just as Brazil has been dominated by Great Britain in the previous century.[25]

---

23   Letter, Errol Flynn to Franklin D. Roosevelt, June 15, 1940, PPF-6697, FDR Library, Hyde Park.

24   Letter, W. Guest to Nelson Rockefeller, cited in Carlos Guilherme Mota, "A fotógrafa e o pintor: Genevieve Naylor e Misha Reznikoff no Brasil, 1940/43: a política da boa vizinhança," in *Genevieve Naylor, Faces and Places in Brazil/ Misha Reznikoff, Monstros da Guerra*, catalog of show at Pinoteca (São Paulo), November 1994, 10. We now know that only Aranha believed the United States to be Brazil's natural ally; Vargas was more ambivalent. See Ricardo Antônio Silva Seitenfus, *O Brasil de Getúlio Vargas e a formação dos Blocos: 1930–1942* (Rio de Janeiro: Companhia Editora Nacional, 1985), 430.

25   See Robert M. Levine, *Father of the Poor? Vargas and His Era* (Cambridge: Cambridge University Press, 1997).

Washington responded to the Axis threat posed to the hemisphere by establishing the Office of Inter-American Affairs. Formed out of several smaller entities, the OIAA was formally founded in the summer of 1940. This was a dark time, following the fall of France and the Low Countries, the defeat of British forces on the Continent, and Nazi advances to the east. South and Central American countries provided many needed raw materials to the Axis powers. Large communities of German nationals lived in the hemisphere, organized into tightly knit groups directed from Berlin, potentially linked to other seditious groups formed of Italians, Japanese, Spanish Falangists, Poles, and others. German propaganda attacking the United States and Jews was disseminated through German banking houses, airlines, shipping companies, athletic clubs, cultural centers, subsidized radio stations, and press agencies.[1] The propaganda was skillfully crafted and cloaked in cultural goodwill, and in many Latin American circles it proved effective.

Beginning in 1936, the United States began to counter fascist influence and to use Pan-Americanism as a vehicle to promote inter-American solidarity. Foreign ministers met in Lima in 1938 and again in Panama (1939) and Havana (July 1940), to discuss hemispheric defense and refugee issues as well as safeguards for trade and transportation. An Inter-American Development Commission was formed in June 1940 to coordinate economic efforts and to provide for loans. Washington also took steps to supply foreign exchange for hemispheric nations whose economies had become strained to the breaking point: it was estimated that markets for 40 percent of the normal exports from Latin America were lost due to the war.[2] The United States proposed to stockpile raw materials and strategic materials that formerly had been sold to Europe, especially Chilean copper but also cotton, wool, rubber, nitrates, and wax, if they were not consumed by wartime needs. Brazil was given priority for several reasons. The U.S. Army knew that Brazil's proximity to West Africa would make it a logical target for invasion were North Africa to fall. State Department officials felt more comfortable with Brazilians, who lacked the anti-American edge present in many Latin American countries, especially Mexico and Argentina.

An influx of dollars, Washington bureaucrats argued, would permit Latin American republics to purchase more manufactured goods from the United States and "prevent discontent and disorder and thus eliminate a fertile field for Nazi propaganda." Roosevelt set things into motion with a memorandum to his cabinet explaining the need for a hemispheric economic policy that would permit the U.S. to protect its international position through the use of economic measures that would be "competitively effective against totalitarian techniques." Among the wartime agencies brought into the planning process were the Rubber Reserve Company and the Metals Reserve Company.[3]

On August 16, 1940, the administration's new Latin American commercial and cultural agency was born. President Roosevelt, always disposed toward creating new agencies, separated its functions from those of the State Department, which was considered by Roosevelt's aides as too bound by its Brahmin traditions to innovate very much.[4] Diplomats from both Latin America and Washington reacted to the new agency realistically, see-

---

1   Donald W. Rowland, *A History of the Office of the Coordinator of Inter-American Affairs* (Washington, D.C.: Government Printing Office, 1947), 3.

2   OIAA memorandum, "Development of Economic Warfare," Rockefeller Archives.

3   Rowland, *History*, 4. Roosevelt memorandum in the Rockefeller Archives and the Roosevelt papers.

4   On the creation of the OIAA, see Cary Reich, *The Life of Nelson A. Rockefeller: Worlds to Conquer, 1908–1958* (New York: Doubleday, 1996), chaps. 13–14.

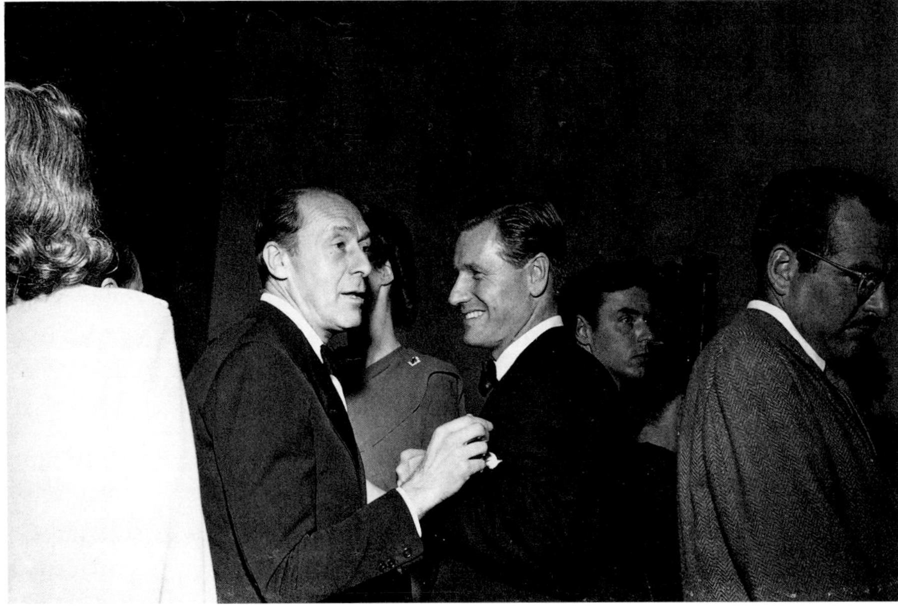

Nelson Aldrich Rockefeller. He is talking with Pavel Tchelitchew, a Russian-born American painter who was one of the leading exponents of the neoromanticist movement.

ing it as a vehicle for mutual self-interest. Even this was difficult. Americans impatiently expected the Latin American republics to fall into line and had trouble accepting what they considered foot dragging, an attitude that infuriated the Latin Americans. And only a few observers in the United States understood that cooperation with the Americans on the scale demanded by Washington would set back the Latin American nationalist governments' goals of economic independence and sovereignty.[5] Regimes all across the continent—Vargas's Estado Novo being one of the most nationalist—wanted nothing less than to lessen ties with North America, exactly at the point when Washington demanded that they join the war effort and increase their exports of rubber, food, minerals, and other needed products. Mexico's ex-propriation of European and United States petroleum contracts under Lázaro Cárdenas in 1938, which led to angry economic retaliation by the oil companies and their governments, fueled Latin American resentment and made governments more wary.

The executive order establishing the coordinator's office named Rockefeller as its director. Much of the impetus for creating the department had come from him. The assiduous Rockefeller had made several proposals to Tommy Corcoran and Benjamin Cohen of the president's staff, suggesting the creation of an inter-American program in which private business interests would work together with the government. Rockefeller, who was thirty-two years old in 1940, had just finished directing the project to build Rockefeller Center in New York. He also

---

5   Paul J. Carter, *Waldo Frank* (New York: Twayne, 1967), 116; Waldo Frank, *South American Journey* (New York: Duell, Sloan, and Pearce, 1943).

was serving as a trustee of the Museum of Modern Art.[6] The Rockefeller family had developed extensive ties in Venezuela and in the Caribbean, largely because of Standard Oil and the Chase Manhattan Bank's interests there, and the young Nelson gladly volunteered to serve as a dollar-a-year man.[7] He spoke passable Spanish and had first visited Venezuela in 1935, when he had helped set up a modern art museum. When he moved to the OIAA, several employees of the Rockefeller family enterprises in Caracas went along for the duration of the war. Rockefeller was a Republican but the effort, because it dealt with wartime priorities, was kept completely nonpartisan. Roosevelt, in a letter to Rockefeller, acknowledged that he hoped that the OIAA would aid "our long-term plan for carrying forward the Good Neighbor Policy."[8]

The OIAA reported to the Department of State but was closely linked to other wartime agencies. Because Latin America was considered in the first line of defense against possible Axis invasion of the hemisphere, the agency was tied organizationally to the Council of National Defense and also to the Navy Department, the Export-Import Bank, and the War Department. The agency was expected to achieve several goals. The public one was to foster goodwill and bring together the peoples of the hemisphere, a direct extension of Roosevelt's Good Neighbor Policy. Implied in this mission was the wartime message promoting the democratic way of life and countering Nazi influence. Not for public consumption was the need to observe the extent of Axis penetration and to report back to military intelligence on such issues as Nazi inroads among intellectuals and Axis sympathy among German, Italian, and Japanese immigrant groups and to enlist influential people to the allied cause. The OIAA, then, although not an espionage agency, collaborated hand in hand with the Office of Strategic Services (OSS), the forerunner of the Central Intelligence Agency (CIA). Two months before Rockefeller came to the OIAA, President Roosevelt had signed a directive permitting J. Edgar Hoover to plant covert FBI agents throughout Latin America. Rockefeller went along with the scheme—it was wartime, after all—and pledged to work closely with Hoover.[9]

Rockefeller's first "weapon" (in the words of the OIAA's official chronicler) was money. Funds were allocated to improve living conditions in the region and to promote social and economic welfare as a deterrent against international fascism. This was the first time the U.S. government had given this kind of aid.[10] Rockefeller's first undertaking in this area was initiated in the spring of 1942, with a massive effort to improve health and sanitation, especially in areas important to the production of war material, notably rubber. This was an extension of the long-term efforts by the Rockefeller Foundation to improve health conditions, but now incorporated into the OIAA's mission. Roosevelt increased the funding limit of the Export-Import Bank to $700 million and encouraged its officials to lend money to the American republics to "preserve internal stability" and to help adjust the republic's external debt.

The agency's wartime budget was $89,258,448 in Depression-era dollars. Additional congressional funds were appropriated for promotion, shipping, salaries, stipends, travel and printing costs. Corporations, including Stan-

---

6   See Geoffrey T. Hellman, "Best Neighbor: Nelson Rockefeller," *New Yorker* (April 18, 1942).

7   For the Rockefeller family's long role in Latin America, see Gerard Colby and Charlotte Dennett Colby, *Thy Will Be Done: The Conquest of the Amazon: Nelson Rockefeller and Evangelism in the Age of Oil* (New York: HarperCollins, 1996).

8   Letter, Roosevelt to Rockefeller, September 24, 1941, cited in Rowland, *History*, 60.

9   Reich, *The Life of Nelson A. Rockefeller*, 194–195.

10   Traditionally foundations and private agencies, notably the Rockefeller Foundation, had provided aid of this nature.

dard Oil, underwrote travel expenses and other costs involved in sending musicians, artists, dancers, and others recruited for specific cultural missions. Rockefeller's assistants hired 1,110 persons to work in the United States and 300 to be posted to Latin America. This was a small number of employees for a wartime bureau, but it was limited to a specific geographic area. In all, during its six years of operations it spent $140 million, the equivalent of nearly a half-billion 1998 dollars. Its broad cultural exchange program was centered on Rockefeller's extensive personal connections in Latin America. The agency sponsored the formation of binational committees in each of the twenty Latin American republics, made up of prominent cultural and social personages. This, it was thought, would lend prestige, especially among influential members of the upper classes and among intellectuals.

In the cultural sphere, radio, journalism, and the film industry received most of the agency's attention because of its mandate to counter Nazism. Many Latin American radio stations and networks faced bankruptcy because of the loss of advertising from foreign firms, and Rockefeller was especially anxious to reward those stations and networks that had voluntarily refused to accept revenue from Axis sources or to use Axis propaganda handouts. The agency also provided supplies ranging from trucks equipped with projectors to show films in public places to turntables, records, microphones, and anything else needed to keep radio programs on the air and newspapers on the newsstands.

The Brazilian office of the OIAA worked closely with Vargas's DIP. Some of the DIP's unsavory reputation was deserved. The DIP not only carried out censorship of Bra-

zilian and foreign-made films, radio programs, newspapers, and books, but also worked closely with Vargas's brutal police in harassing artists and intellectuals considered enemies of Brazil's right-wing regime. On the other hand, its handouts tended to be innocuous tracts urging Brazilians to respect their country and to cooperate with the government in achieving national unity and economic progress. Some of the DIP's publications were of fairly high quality (*Cultura Política* was one), and DIP-produced newsreels differed little in tenor from those produced in the United States and elsewhere during the 1940s, when millions of people went to the movies every week and were influenced by the fast-paced and always upbeat newsreels that preceded the main feature.

The OIAA was also a propaganda agency, even though it did not contain the word in its official title. Much of its involvement was kept behind the scenes, although few efforts were made to hide its function.[11] One activity the agency did not admit to, however, was the launching in August 1941 of *En Guardia*, a slick photo magazine modeled on *Life*, assisted by *Life* editors, and wholly financed by Rockefeller. Further, the agency's information program was subject to the controls of the Office of Censorship and the Army and Navy departments. Officials bent over backward to rationalize the mission of the OIAA. In 1945, Nelson Rockefeller testified before Congress in response to the question of whether his agency had always told the truth. "We consider it an information program," he replied,

> the objectives being to explain what is going on in a military way the world over, and the significance

---

11 The Brazilian War Ministry issued an invitation to Genevieve Naylor to attend the Independence Day parade in 1941 with the typed-in explanation that she had been assigned by the American Embassy to work "a serviço da propaganda do Brasil nos Estados Unidos (reportagem fotográficas)," literally, "creating propaganda about Brazil for use in the United States through photographic assignments."

of the battle, the objectives of our enemies, our own objectives, that is, the preservation of freedom and the way of life which we have believed in as a nation from the beginning."[12]

A formal censorship apparatus, of course, had been imposed on Brazil in 1937, five years before the country's declaration of war against the Axis. It was used to control expression and minimize dissension in Brazilian society as well as to manipulate public opinion and impart values to the population that would allow the government to achieve progress while maintaining strict control. Censorship in the United States was reactive, not proactive, and only operated in wartime. Information program officials accentuated the positive, selecting those issues deemed useful to convey, "with unfavorable subjects admitted but not stressed."[13] Then again, censorship is censorship and propaganda is propaganda, wherever they occur.

The agency's Press Division supplied information to more than 1,250 newspapers, magazines, and radio stations throughout the hemisphere. Every day, radio news was beamed via shortwave, illustrated features (including cartoon and cartoon strips), and an average of more than 7,000 photographic prints monthly. Agency journalists sent out an average of 25,000 to 30,000 words every day, usually using as their sources the three major wire services, the Associated Press, United Press, and International News Service. Every week supplementary materials were sent via air (mostly using Pan American Airway's Clipper Ship Latin American routes), on economics, health, and sanitation topics. "Exclusive features" were shipped to leading newspapers. Posters, news maps, translations of twenty magazine articles per week, feature newsletters, pamphlets (nearly 6 million in all on twenty-five subjects), and a labor service were mailed to sixty labor publications, most of which, in Latin America, were tightly controlled by their governments. The binational coordination committees in each country supervised distribution of all these materials. To ease shortages, the Press Division subsidized the cost of buying and shipping newsprint to Latin America, borrowing from President Roosevelt's Emergency Fund in 1942 and then receiving appropriations from Congress thereafter.

As mentioned earlier, the Press Division published a biweekly fifty-six page pictorial magazine, *En Guardia* (On Guard) to be distributed in Spanish, French, and Portuguese to Latin America (and to Spanish-speaking areas in the southwestern United States and in Florida). McGraw-Hill agreed to handle the magazine with cooperation from Henry Luce's *Life*. Although the State Department decided to distribute it for free, in many cases news vendors charged whatever they felt like to buyers in the street. Within a year, more than 550,000 copies of each issue were circulated. The magazine was not without its critics, some of whom felt that it was aimed too high, to an exclusively upper-class audience; others argued that the slick publication would contrast too obviously with Latin American magazines. The Press Division dispatched writers and photographers to cover stories of particular interest to Latin Americans, including, for example, the Brazilian Expeditionary Force in Italy. The agency brought working journalists from Latin America to the United States. By the end of the war, more than

---

12 *Hearings, H.R. 1945*, pt. 1, 924–925.

13 Rowland, *History*, 42.

140 editors and publishers from Latin America had visited during twelve separate trips.

More than 125 employees worked for the agency's Radio Division. At the outset, staff members confronted problems: a shortage of radio receivers in the Latin American republics and a poor news tradition—as the Americans saw it—of monotonously read dispatches without any flair. In response, the agency created its own news service, which was broadcast via long- and shortwave equipment imported from the United States. This program ultimately expanded into the World Wide Broadcasting Network, in use throughout the war's duration. Beyond news, the agency sent commentaries, drama, and musical shows as well as thousands of phonograph recordings ranging from opera to swing.

Banker John Hay Whitney, who financed the film *Gone With the Wind*, headed the OIAA's Motion Picture Division. It supervised the production of no fewer than 288 full-length feature films—some on the war, some on the "American Way of Life," the rest on topics dealing in some way with Latin America—as well as 722 16-millimeter short features and weekly newsreels for the entire period from 1941 to 1945. In January 1941 Whitney organized the first of a series of trips to Central and South America by producers, actors, writers, and directors. In 1941 the agency sponsored a goodwill tour by Douglas Fairbanks Jr. and Walt Disney, along with a large staff from the Disney Studio. The agency spent $70,000 for the tour and guaranteed $150,000 against loss for a series of a dozen film projects to be undertaken by Disney's workers. Such guarantees were common-

place during the war, but in the case of the Film Division no funds had to be paid out. The film division was responsible for *The Life of Simón Bolívar*, Walt Disney's animated feature *Saludos Amigos*, and the comedy *The Road to Rio*—films of questionable quality but which nonetheless delivered the message that the Americans were paying attention to the lands south of their border. The most successful film was *Victory for the Americas*, about American war production and made by Paramount with the cooperation of major film distributors. It was seen by more Latin Americans than even Disney's cartoons.

The newsreels probably had the greatest impact. Three hundred projection trucks were shipped to areas lacking commercial theaters; audiences in these places received steady doses of war news and stirring (and sanitized) versions of the Allied advances: few newsreels during the war showed casualties. Donald W. Rowland summarizes the attitude that went into planning the weekly newsreels:

> Newsreel content was also arranged to indicate that the United States was affected by shortages in common with the rest of the hemisphere and, to combat Axis rumor propaganda circulated in Latin America, included scenes showing that Mexican workers in the United States were adequately housed, and that there was no discrimination in regard to Brazilian troops training in United States Army camps.[14]

Such efforts not only influenced Latin American public opinion during the duration of the war but served to Americanize Latin American popular culture, to the chagrin of local intellectuals (but to the delight of American

---

14   Ibid., 77.

diplomatic and business interests). Rockefeller encouraged the *New York Times* to develop an overseas edition and helped *Newsweek* magazine publish a Spanish-language edition. Both publications became permanent fixtures in Latin America and were joined by many other U.S.-based magazines, newspapers, and network radio and television programs in later years.

Following a suggestion by the FBI, Rockefeller's organization designated Brazil as a test case for opinion surveys conducted by George Gallup to measure the reaction of audiences to the OIAA's cultural programs and to gauge "the communication habits of Brazilians throughout the country and of all walks of life."[15] The survey also attempted to measure the extent to which Axis propaganda had worked. The surveys were carried out by local operatives, so as not to be linked in the public mind with the U.S. Embassy or other American agencies. In all, surveys were taken in eight Latin American countries, reporting on editorial policy of newspapers, circulation figures, popularity of radio programs, and the reception given to individual American films.

The agency contracted with writers to translate English-language books into Spanish and Portuguese, and it donated funds to libraries. Some $80,000 in federal money was allocated for Roosevelt scholarships for Latin American youths to study in the United States. Importation of art exhibitions and symphonic orchestras were arranged, along with archaeological digs and sporting events. Specialists were sent to offer advice on sanitation, agriculture, transportation, and economic health. The Tropical Institute was inaugurated, concentrating on problems of agriculture. In 1942 a Chilean ski team was invited to the United States for a six-month tour, and in the following year other skiers from the region were brought for Red Cross and army training in ski rescue and patrolling. The OIAA funded twenty "City of New York Scholarships" by which one student from each of the twenty Latin American republics could come to New York to study for a year. Microfilm copies of scientific and medical journals were made and sent free of charge to Latin American universities and libraries. The Inter-American Educational Foundation was chartered in 1943 to coordinate these activities and to provide textbooks, manuals, and other teaching materials for Latin American schools, especially, in the case of Brazil, in rural areas. The OIAA's Public Health and Sanitation department sent agents into the Amazon to work on rubber production.

Entrepreneurs who on their own already had forged links with Latin America took advantage of the heightened awareness about Latin America to increase the level of their activities. Carmen Miranda—the ebullient entertainer with her fruit-filled hats and the embodiment of Brazilian samba—who had been invited to New York by the Broadway impresario Lee Schubert, became an instant smash in roles based on Hollywood's stereotype of Brazilian culture. When she returned to Brazil at the end of 1940, she was ostracized by the elite, which was embarrassed by her popularization of samba, considered something that "belonged in the favela."[16] A masterful 1995 documentary, Helena Solberg and David Meyer's *Carmen Miranda: Bananas Is My Business*, claims that Miranda was "cynically exploited" by the OIAA "as part of

---

15 Memorandum, "Types of Information Being Gathered by the Export Information Bureau," n.d., cited in Rowland, *History*, 84. The J. Walter Thompson Company conducted similar surveys in Argentina.

16 Arnaldo Jabor, "Carmen foi do getulismo ao capitalismo," *O Globo* (Rio de Janeiro), August 8, 1995, 6.

its good-neighbor policy toward Latin America, whose natural resources it needed to fight the war."[17] In the 1990s, left-wing Brazilians, including many academic specialists on popular culture, disparaged the OIAA as the "DIP-OIAA" and complained that Rockefeller's incursion represented no less than the imperialist "destruction of [Brazilian] culture" and the first step in the insidious "Americanization" of Brazil itself.[18]

The problem with many of the efforts to foster inter-American understanding, in fact, was that some of them, from the North American side, were ignorant and patronizing at best and insulting at worst. Hollywood producers who released the film *Down Argentine Way* in 1941 typecast Latin Americans "as either slimy gigolos or amiable buffoons," and Argentine characters were portrayed by actors speaking with Mexican accents. Whitney and Rockefeller personally demanded that the producer reshoot $40,000 of scenes that were particularly offensive, and from that point on, as Cary Reich observes, the OIAA wielded its influence to the point of imposing censorship.[19]

During wartime, however, most government actions that would normally raise protests were overshadowed by the grim reality that democracy was dangerously threatened by the Axis. Many Americans assigned to the OIAA, and to the U.S. military stationed in Brazil, beyond their primary missions were instructed to report on subversive activities, especially evidence of German or Japanese influence or infiltration.

Most agency activities, however, were uncontroversial. In addition to appointing Naylor, Rockefeller assigned two other photographers to Brazil, one an architectural photographer and the other assigned to document public health projects, mainly in the Amazon. Roosevelt personally asked sculptor Jo Davidson to visit ten republics and make portrait busts of the presidents. The sculptures were ultimately cast in bronze and displayed at the National Gallery of Art in Washington. Many cultural institutions were enlisted by Rockefeller to participate in exchanges or to tour. The Yale Glee Club toured South America in the summer of 1941. The Pan American Union was invited to produce a catalog of Latin American musical materials in its possession and in the Library of Congress, and recordings of folk music were exchanged. The Press Division paid for the translation and publication of guidebooks to the countries of the Americas—a project not unlike the famous, WPA-produced series on the forty-eight American states. Efforts were made to stimulate the teaching of English in Latin America. The Guggenheim, Carnegie, and Rockefeller foundations were asked to cooperate in setting up exchange programs for students and educators. The OIAA helped fund the development of the Benjamin Franklin Library in Mexico City under the direction of the New York Public Library. Funding was provided for the creation of four institutes for the study of trade and culture, two to be situated in North America and two in Latin America. These institutes were to train young manufacturers, salesmen, and exporters in "all phases of commerce and industry on a regional basis,"[20] but they never came into existence.

In the summer of 1941 Lincoln Kirstein brought his forty-member New York–based American Ballet Caravan

---

17 Stephen Holden, *New York Times*, July 5, 1995, B5.

18 Tota's argument is more subtle: he suggests that American culture did not push out Brazilian culture; rather, it drove it in new directions. See Tota, "Americanização," 191–212.

19 Reich, *The Life of Nelson A. Rockefeller*, 216.

20 Rowland, *History*, 95. Samuel Flagg Bemis of Yale University and Isaiah Bowman, the president of the Johns Hopkins University, were consultants for this project, which was initially submitted by Walter B. Pitkin of Columbia University.

on a twenty-eight-week tour of Latin America. Rockefeller was a friend of Kirstein; they had worked together in behalf of the Museum of Modern Art, where Rockefeller sat on the Board of Directors. Kirstein had developed the idea of hiring American artists to paint murals for an exhibition at the Museum of Modern Art in 1932, and when the final works shocked the conservative Rockefeller Center board (Ben Shahn, for example, painted a depiction of the Sacco and Vanzetti trial, and another work implied that John D. Rockefeller Jr., Henry Ford, and other capitalists were cronies of gangster Al Capone), the twenty-five-year-old Nelson, John D.'s son, backed Kirstein, although he abandoned the plan to display the murals permanently at the Rockefeller Center. Not to be intimidated, Kirstein hired other muralists, including the Mexican Diego Rivera, then an active communist, and the Ukrainian-born Misha Reznikoff to work on the RCA Building. Rivera's designs scandalized the Rockefeller Center backers as much as the American artists had, and Rivera was fired. Nelson Rockefeller ordered the mural smashed, with its portrait of Lenin, but he continued to befriend Kirstein.[21]

Unencumbered by their artistic disagreements, when Kirstein arrived to Brazil he received Rockefeller's strong personal backing. In a "friendly, very loose, and rather unbusinesslike arrangement," in the words of Anatole Chujoy, Rockefeller guaranteed to pay the minimum expenses of the company for a six-month Latin American tour and to underwrite any deficits that might occur. Production costs would have to be borne by the American Ballet.[22] Kirstein then enticed George Balanchine to

set aside his Hollywood and Broadway commitments and to choreograph several new ballets for the tour. The artistic results were mixed: one of them, William Dollar's *Juke Box* (set to music by Alec Wilder) was a flop, and another, *Pastorela*, based on Mexican folklore, "was calculated to please the patriotic sense of Latin American spectators,"[23] a gesture considered patronizing by some Latin Americans. This was the last activity of the American Ballet before it became reorganized into the New York City Ballet. Kirstein by this time had developed an animosity toward everyone in the dance world not directly connected with his company and school, and as a result the atmosphere was charged with tension.

When the ballet troupe arrived, American Embassy staffers showed umbrage at having been instructed by Rockefeller's staff members to do whatever Kirstein and Ballanchine requested. Such requests meant dealing with Brazilians to expedite red tape, a process that was very tricky and which the American diplomats considered beneath them. The staffers bridled at what they considered to be requests that they run errands. Ballanchine, for example, demanded that the Municipal Theater's paper sets, which he considered fire hazards, be replaced virtually overnight. The episode exposed the strains between career State Department personnel, symbolized by the patrician Undersecretary of State Sumner Welles—like Roosevelt a graduate of Groton School and Harvard and the epitome of an American aristocrat—and the "amateurs" appointed to wartime posts the careerists considered superfluous. At the same time, Rockefeller's goal, to

---

21 See Reich, *The Life of Nelson A. Rockefeller: Worlds to Conquer,* 95–111.

22 Anatole Chujoy, *The New York City Ballet* (New York: Knopf, 1953), 132–133.

23 Ibid., 134.

send art and culture to Latin America "to show our southern neighbors that our art as well as our industry was exportable," seemed transparent to Latin American elites, some of whom disparaged American culture. Kirstein's tour, then, never received the glamorous reception, for example, that the Ballet Russe de Monte Carlo had won the summer before. The American dance programs were less traditional and more experimental than those of the Europeans, and not as well received.[24]

New York's Museum of Modern Art dispatched curators and officials to Brazil and also helped Rio's Modern Art Museum, which was designated as a sister institution. It was this arrangement that led to the Brazilian museum's decision to acquire popular art, a category that prior to the arrival of the American experts was not considered to be worthy of collecting by Brazilian institutions. American influence also changed the way Brazilians behaved: young women invited to dances at the American air bases up and down the coast learned GI slang and, in many cases, freed themselves from the strictures set by a system that traditionally used chaperons for all unmarried females of "good" families. Foreign films became wildly popular, with the result that the average Brazilian was more likely to recognize Charlie Chaplin or Tom Mix than Brazil's politicians and leaders. This fact was not lost on the elite and would contribute to an anti-American backlash after the war.

The Brazilians accepted all of this because they knew that by entering the war on the Allied side they would be expected to make the same kinds of public relations gestures as the Americans. In the days before video, when ra-

dio and newsreels were still for the affluent, most Brazilians had no notion of the United States or of American culture. This would change, of course, after the war, with the incursion of mass advertising, and, after 1970, national television. Part of Brazil's later infatuation with Hollywood can be traced back to the wartime efforts of Walt Disney and the steady stream of feature films cranked out to raise public morale.

Vargas, on the other hand, attempted to alter the ways Brazilians saw themselves and their country's role in the world. In many ways, he succeeded. Brazilians rallied emotionally to the Allied cause, especially when Vargas entered the war after the sinking of several Brazilian merchant ships. The Americans were pleased by this, and they considered their efforts in Brazil among the most successful of their programs in the hemisphere. In his testimony to Congress in 1945, with the war nearing its end, Nelson Rockefeller explained what his agency had attempted to achieve:

> We attempt to bring them an understanding of this country, honestly portraying life in the United States. We try to picture for them our appreciations of spiritual and cultural values, so that they might understand us better and recognize that—in common with them—we have similar aspirations, share the same sense of decency and the same desire to create opportunities for all to better themselves through their own efforts.[25]

The DIP promoted the Estado Novo's message through a massive nationwide campaign of public rela-

---

24   Ibid., 137.

25   *Hearings, H.R., 1945*, pt. 1, 924–925.

tions disseminated by five functional divisions that covered patriotic education, radio, cinema and theater, tourist information, and the press. Not only did Vargas speak regularly; Labor Minister Marcondes Filho delivered more than 200 radio talks in cooperation with DIP officials. The DIP used radio broadcasts, publications, planted newspaper articles, films, and a host of other devices to portray positively the bland head of state, a man who had always shied from the limelight, as the *pai dos pobres* (father of the poor) and as the "nation's benefactor."

Every Brazilian town celebrated Vargas's birthday with parades of children dressed up in their school uniforms, bands, and gaiety. Flag-festooned rallies, held in gigantic soccer stadiums, rang with speeches and martial music, all carefully orchestrated to boost the president's popularity. Via radio, Vargas reached his largest audience, speaking frequently on the daily *Hora do Brasil*, a compendium of music, general news, uplifting speeches, and tips on farming, nutrition, child-rearing, agriculture, and anything else deemed appropriate by the DIP. Vargas reserved his major speeches for holidays (Christmas and New Year's as well as Independence Day and May Day). He always used uncomplicated language and straightforward examples to explain the issues of the day; he became a calming, familiar presence in the lives of most Brazilians, something new for a national leader. Estado Novo intervenors—officials appointed by Vargas to administer the states—invented their own programs on the national model. There were, for example, "production parades" in which workers and employers marched through the streets together, music provided by the army or police bands. These events were aimed at the mass public, even though those without work gained no benefits from the state. Whenever Vargas made a public appearance, it was filmed so that the scene could be repeated across the country via newsreels.

Knowledgeable Brazilians, of course, understood that much of this was a façade. Privately, jokers called Vargas the "father of the poor and the mother of the rich."[26] Wartime DIP-sponsored broadcasts had the Orwellian ring of truthspeak: on his 1944 Independence Day broadcast, Vargas assured the nation that he had brought freedom to Brazil through the Estado Novo, which he termed a "functional democracy." In his New Year's message he assured his audience that Brazil had entered the war to preserve liberty and to fight for "the Christian traditions of family." Marcondes Filho called Brazil's workers "the producers of Brazil's wealth"; workers, he said, "were producing a new Brazil with fuller rights, social justice, and human dignity." Daily, for ten minutes, Marcondes Filho addressed the nation over the radio on the *Hora do Brasil*, starting with the phrase "Boa noite trabalhador" (Good evening, worker), reaching the hearts of the listeners in ways never heard before in the country's history.[27]

Vargas's willingness to explain the need to impose dictatorship in 1937 on the basis of the communist threat and on a thinly veiled anti-Semitic plot entirely fabricated by his own intelligence service revealed his callow side. This coincided exactly with efforts by Washington and its allies to woo Brazil to join the Allied cause or, at least, not to

---

26   Frank, *South American Journey*, 12, 58; Dulce Chaves Pandolfi, *Pernambuco de Agamenón Magalhães: consolidação e crise de uma elite política* (Recife: Fundação Joaquim Nabuco, 1984), 54; Michael A. Ogorzaly, *Waldo Frank: Prophet of Hispanic Regeneration* (Lewisburg, Pa.: Bucknell University Press, 1994), 135. Lourival Fontes and Felinto Müller were removed from office in 1943 as a gesture to the Allies. On the subject of Vargas's radio broadcasts: Franklin D. Roosevelt, who also used the radio to great advantage, spoke less frequently. During the dozen years of his presidency, Roosevelt averaged less than three fireside chats each year.

27   Marcondes Filho's quotes from *A nova política do Brasil* and *Hora do Brasil*, cited in Joel Wolfe, *Working Women, Working Men: São Paulo and the Rise of Brazil's Industrial Working Class, 1900–1955* (Durham, N.C.: Duke University Press, 1993), 96; interview with Segadas Viana, cited in Valentina da Rocha Lima, *Getúlio: Uma história oral* (Rio de Janiero: Ed. Record, 1986), 258.

side with Nazi Germany and the European fascist states, for whom there was great sympathy among members of the conservative elite and in the high armed forces command. Vargas knew more than ever that he must rebuild his image through propaganda, so much so that he tossed aside his usual reluctance to be cast in the role of patriotic hero. He permitted his poker partner Lourival Fontes to command his propaganda agency and gave it sweeping powers. "Fontes," Guest wrote to Décio de Moura, Aranha's personal secretary, "is an enthusiastic reader of Goebbels."[28]

Vargas's officials paid close attention to the activities of fascist regimes around the world. As early as 1935, Felinto Müller, the chief of the federal police, enjoyed close personal relations with high officials of the German Reich and on one occasion paid an official visit to Berlin. General Francisco Franco was very popular among officials of the Roman Catholic hierarchy, and newspapers and magazines on the Right, especially (but not exclusively) the print media of the Brazilian fascist Integralist movement, devoted extensive coverage to the achievements of Benito Mussolini, Antonio de Oliveiro Salazar, Francisco Franco, Jozéf Klemens Pilsudski, and the German Nazis.[29] Brazilian diplomats in Washington were wooed by the Department of State, which sent a series of ambassadors to Brazil who were staunchly conservative in their political leanings. Jefferson Caffrey was posted to Brazil after helping force out General Gerardo Machado in Cuba in 1933, essentially turning the country over to Fulgencio Batista and his military and civilian cronies; Hugh Gibson not only failed to protest the abrupt cessa-

tion of civil liberties under Brazil's state of siege in 1937 but cooperated fully with the Brazilian police in tracking down alleged communist agents.

The DIP took up the task not only of selling Vargas as the father of the Brazilian people but of instructing Brazilians to be hard-working, family-centered, moral, and loyal citizens. Photographic portraits of Vargas were distributed to the most remote corners of the country (see photo 1). They hung in every government building and school, in post offices, in banks, in businesses, and in homes. Vargas addressed the nation frequently by radio, speaking to ordinary Brazilians and telling them that their labor and hard work were necessary to build the country and to make Brazil a modern nation. Perhaps because Vargas was personally self-effacing and preferred to stay out of the limelight, attention toward him never turned into a cult of personality, in contrast to the wartime European dictatorships or to the regime of Juan Perón in neighboring Argentina. But the DIP's publicity efforts were wide ranging, and they helped bring to Brazil a sense of being one nation. Vargas's programs reduced psychological distances in a country subcontinental in scope.

Within its first year of operation, the DIP adopted procedures and methods less borrowed from abroad than products of the Estado Novo environment. It took up its task of censoring print and broadcast media. It required all books, films, and scripts of theater productions to be submitted for prior censorship, although it demonstrated reasonably broad latitude in what it considered acceptable. Newspapers and magazines were subject to retroac-

---

28   Letter, W. Guest to Décio de Moura, cited in Mota, "A fotógrafa e o pintor," 11.

29   Recent scholarship in Brazil claims that Nazi sympathizers in Brazil were a smaller and less influential group than earlier thought. See René E. Gertz, "Influência alemã no Brasil na década de 1930," *Estudios Interdisciplinarios de América Latina y el Caribe* (Tel Aviv), 7, no. 1 (January–June 1996), 85–105.

tive censorship: DIP officials could seize any printed materials deemed objectionable after they were printed, thus forcing publishers to censor their own output in fear of economic loss. This method worked as well as any and was much less confrontational than, for example, the censorship systems imposed in fascist Europe and in Stalin's Soviet Union.

The DIP organized ceremonies, exhibitions, pageants, parades, and a host of popular events to disseminate the message that the Estado Novo sought to unify Brazil and to bring about progress based on a satisfied and hard-working citizenry.[30] Problems of distribution were massive, and materials did not get disseminated evenly. Most of the distribution of materials was initially done by the Agência Nacional, the state book distribution agency. In the past, the Agência had handled books for an elite audience. Now, given the DIP's mandate to reach out to the Brazilian people, its resources were stretched to the breaking point.

How did Brazilians react to all of the programs? Many remained ambivalent, even suspicious, of the Good Neighbor Policy and its cultural forays. To elites historically oriented toward Europe, Americanization was seen as a threat, especially its commercialized popular culture. Modernists, as well, after all, had spent two decades rediscovering indigenous Brazilian culture to substitute for European influences, and now Brazilian culture seemed vulnerable before the onslaught of imported American movie stars and the insensitive way Hollywood turned Carmen Miranda into an embarrassing caricature of Brazil and Brazilians. Critics smarted at the creation of Disney's Zé Carioca, an empty-headed parrot who essentially is a fool. Others attacked the Good Neighbor Policy's tendency toward puritanism and imposed morality—although Vargas's Estado Novo more or less shared the same outlook.[31]

Photography and the Estado Novo

In any case, the task of producing and distributing still photographs illustrating the accomplishments of the regime formed an important part of the DIP's mission. Photographers were hired to document Getúlio Vargas's daily activities: ribbon-cutting ceremonies, presidential visits, rallies, mingling with the elderly, holding babies, smiling at children, signing decrees, and receiving the adulation of the masses. Dozens of photographs of the chief of state were sent to newspapers and news agencies and weekly magazines. The DIP explained its basic motives in no uncertain terms:

> The data and the photographic images we present speak for themselves. They are so clear that no one can deny or not be aware of the benefits brought to Brazil by the fertile administrative activity, by the patriotism, and by the profound vision of President Getúlio Vargas.[32]

DIP publications emphasized what Vargas called the "new Brazil." They were published not only in Portuguese for national distribution but (through the Tourism Department) in English, to be shipped abroad. Famous foreign authors (including Stefan Zweig), as well as professional photographers, were invited to record their im-

---

30   See Aline Lopes de Lacerda, "A 'Obra Getuliana' ou como as imagens comemoram o regime," *Estudos Históricos*, 14 (July–December 1994), 241–263.

31   See Tota, "Americanização," 191–212.

32   *Brasil Novo* 3, no. 6 (January 1941), 1, cited in Lopes de Lacerda, "Obra," 245.

pressions. Many of the photographers were Germans who had taken refuge in Brazil, including Peter Lange, Erich Hess, and Peter Stille, who were put to work photographing Brazil's architectural and cultural heritage. In 1943, the French photojournalist Jean Manzon, who had fled Occupied France, helped redesign the feature magazine *O Cruzeiro*.[33]

Old-style "official" photographs were to be supplemented by a new kind of friendly image produced by local photographers under contract, portraying Vargas as a family man, a man of the people, an always-smiling father figure whose portrait adorned every public room, the eyes watching with a mixture of paternalism and encouragement.[34] For the first time ever, the chief of state was projected into the lives of ordinary people, deflecting the reality of the Estado Novo dictatorship by manipulating the emotions of patriotism and national pride. This emphasis had a decidedly anti-intellectual character. It was considered important to act on Education Minister Gustavo Capanema's directive to take back the "roots of Brazilian nationalism" from the formal and "superficial erudite culture" that had captured it during the 1920s and 1930s.[35] Capanema's Education and Health Ministry, in fact, shared with the DIP the task of molding opinion, being responsible for the school system as well as for programs in adult education and literacy training. In 1940, Capanema took on the task of producing an encyclopedic commemorative album to document all of the Vargas government's achievements between 1930 and 1940. The book was never published, but it was completed in layout. All but 151 of its 646 photographs were the work of

German cameramen who had taken refuge in Brazil.[36] The photographs were triumphalist, showing handsome public works; smiling, cheerful citizens; and the fruits of Brazil's readiness in military defense and hard work.

Officials handled the issue of race very gingerly. On the one hand, the Estado Novo was the first Brazilian government in history to advocate that Brazil should be a country for all races. On the other, it tiptoed around the matter of interracial contact and studiously avoided any hint that blacks and browns were in any way less favored in society. DIP photographers depicted all shades of Brazilians, as long as they seemed happy and moral and reflected the values the Estado Novo was trying to foment. The DIP's guidelines to OIAA photographers clearly emphasized "safe" subjects: architecture, elegant urban districts, public works. Genevieve Naylor, as we will see, not only photographed these subjects but her decision to photograph *mostly* people from the lower classes yielded, in turn, a much higher proportion of images of racially mixed Brazilians. More than anything, she captured Brazil's dearth of racial tension, one that fostered an atmosphere of human dignity present in few places in the world then or since.

---

33 See Silvana Goulart, *Sob a verdade oficial: ideologia, propaganda e censura no Estado Novo* (São Paulo: Marco Zero, 1990); Lopes de Lacerda, "Obra," 250–251.

34 Lopes de Lacerda, "Obra," 244.

35 See Simon Schwartzman, Helena Bomeny, and Vanda Maria Ribeiro Costa, *Tempos de Capanema* (Rio de Janeiro: Editora Paz e Terra, 1984), 80.

36 Of the 646 photographs selected for the album, 122 fell into the category *Production*; 106, *Education and Health*; 95, *Army*; 88, *Communication*; 67, *Work*; 63, *Navy*; 32, *Aviation*; 23, *Commerce*; 22, *Tourism*; 14, *Justice*; 11, *Public Administration Agency*; and 3, *Urbanism*.

Genevieve Hay Naylor was born in Springfield, Massachusetts, on February 12, 1915. Her father, Emmett Hay Naylor (1884–1938), was a trade association lawyer who divided his time between New York, Boston, and Springfield. Born in the Midwest, he came east to study at Dartmouth, then at Harvard for a master's degree, and finally at Columbia Law School before settling in western Massachusetts. Genevieve's mother, Ruth Houston Caldwell (1889–1978), tried to break rank and tradition after graduating from Vassar in 1911 with plans to go to New York and become a journalist, but her father, a paper mill tycoon, forbade it because he did not want the community to think that he could not support his daughter. Emmett and Ruth married on January 17, 1914.

Genevieve, who was given the middle name Hay to carry forward the family's lineage from John Hay, President Abraham Lincoln's personal secretary and poet laureate of the United States, was educated at Miss Hall's School in Pittsfield, Massachusetts, and at an arts school, the Music Box, founded by Emmett Naylor in the nearby town of Cummington. Miss Hall's was more of a finishing school than anything else; there, and at home, Genevieve was trained to be a lady. Her parents divorced in 1925, however, an act that in the 1920s raised eyebrows and was considered socially unsuitable. Emmett remarried but quickly succumbed to alcoholism. Six years later he would divorce again, and in 1938 he would drown accidently in the family swimming pool. During her sophomore year at Miss Hall's, in 1931, when she was sixteen, Genevieve began to study painting at the Music Box, pouring herself into her new avocation probably because of her need to escape her stifling, broken family life.

Her teacher was Misha Reznikoff. Misha had come to the United States from the small village of Kabilia, near Kiev, with his parents in 1921. His family settled in Providence, Rhode Island, where he had a difficult childhood struggling with learning English and a restrictive home life. As a teenager he found solace at the Museum of Rhode Island, where in time he began to sketch. With the help of a curator and a letter of recommendation from S. J. Perelman, he won a scholarship to the Rhode Island School of Design, and he also took courses at Brown University. When he told his father that he wanted to become an artist, the two of them fought and Misha left the house. He eventually roomed with fellow student Arshile Gorky (1904–1948), later a major figure in American art. In 1929, now married, Misha went to New York with an introduction to Stuart Davis.

Beginning to establish contacts, Misha did odd jobs, frequented art galleries, and in 1931 was hired as an art instructor at the Music Box, Genevieve's school. She was sixteen years old when Misha started teaching her in 1931, and two years later they were in love. She was an upper-class society girl; he was a chain-smoking, hard-drinking man with a rough, heavily accented manner of speaking, and he threw himself into his work with exuberance. He fled back to New York in late 1933 and soon afterward was joined by Genevieve. Relishing New York City, he became one of the adepts of the "bohemian" art and jazz world of Greenwich Village. He taught at the Art Students' League, and, in 1934, sold one of his paintings, "The End of the Horse," to New York's new Museum of Modern Art.[1]

In *The Treasury of Jazz*, Richard Gehman described

---

1   Mota, "A fotógrafa e o pintor," 10.

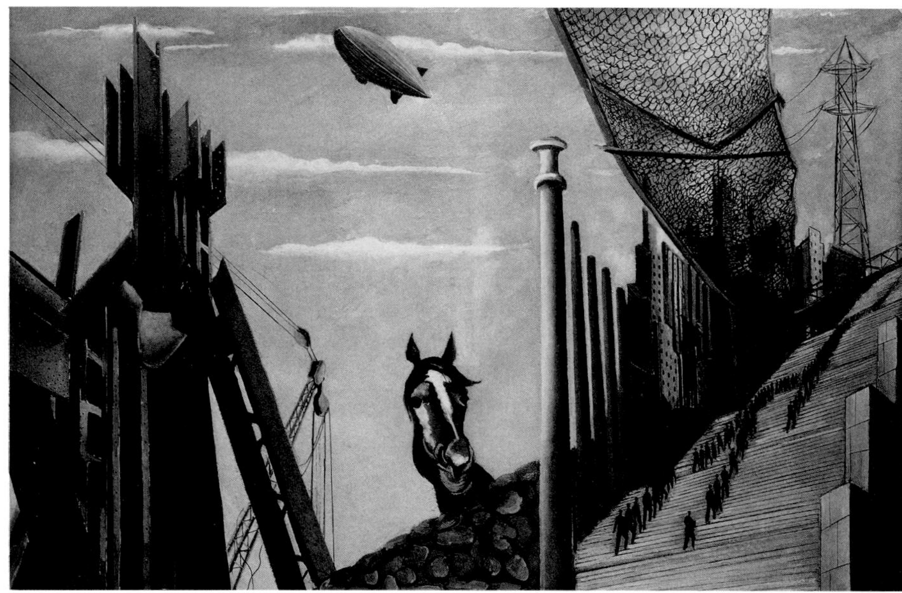

"The End of the Horse"
by Misha Reznikoff.

Misha and Genevieve's studio apartment on East Sixty-ninth Street, a huge converted stable. "The ground floor is one vast room," he wrote,

> in the front third of which Miss Naylor takes her studio shots. The rear two thirds looks as though it was designed for sizeable parties, which was indeed the case. It is decorated with Misha's huge abstract paintings and some statues he has constructed from coat hangers and whisky-bottle tops, and with hundreds of Parliament cigarette boxes on which he has drawn curious angular faces. . . . There is an upright piano in one corner, and near it the microphone for Misha's tape recorder. Inspired by Misha's booze, perhaps even stimulated by his wildly colored paintings, and unfettered by night-club audiences, the boys stand about, and improvise chorus after chorus of the old, nearly forgotten tunes, such as "Nobody Knows and Nobody Cares," "Peggy," and even, sometimes, "Wild Man Blues or Grandpa's Spells." Other musicians and singers or devotees may arrive, and the sessions have been known to go on for days. One Friday morning a friend of mine and I arrived at five A.M. At nine, I staggered out into the blazing sunlight. Next evening, the party was still going strong. My friend did not leave until the following Sunday afternoon at four.[2]

This experience thrust Genevieve into the midst of

---

2 Comments by Richard Gehman, in Richard Gehman and Eddie Condon, eds., *Eddie Condon's Treasury of Jazz* (New York: Dial, 1956), 13–14.

New York City's radical politics and into interracial friendships. Misha befriended blacks, especially jazz musicians who were beginning to perform in Greenwich Village as some jazz clubs integrated. One of his close friends, Zutty Singleton, a jazz drummer who recorded with Louis Armstrong, with his wife shared a summer house with Misha and Genevieve in Rocky Tavern, New York. Misha's lifestyle did not endear him to Genevieve's parents, but she moved into the apartment with him after Misha divorced his wife, Rochelle Springer, who then married Stuart Davis.

Misha became a member of the Tenth Street movement that later would form the nucleus of abstract expressionism. He was a regular patron of the Cedar Street Bar, drinking and brawling with Willem de Kooning, Jackson Pollack, and Frank Kline. With Davis's help, Reznikoff was named an instructor at the Art Students' League. Struggling to make a living as the Great Depression deepened, he got work as a WPA painter and muralist and was hired to paint some of the Rockefeller Center murals.

The fact that Misha was half-Jewish, ten years older than Genevieve, married (although divorcing), and a bohemian artist so infuriated her wealthy grandmother, Fanny Caldwell, that for ten years after the couple started living together they had to hide the fact from Genevieve's family, even when they went together to Brazil. Fanny Caldwell, in fact, was paying Genevieve's New York tuition and bills—and there was a real threat that had she found out, Genevieve would have been disinherited. Emmett Naylor, who himself had moved to New York City, tried to squelch the romance in 1933, when

Genevieve was still a student, by taking his daughter to Europe in the summer. On their return, she reached a compromise with her father: she would break off with Misha provided that the family would support her career decision. Emmett agreed but Genevieve tricked him, maintaining her clandestine relationship with Misha for ten years, until they returned from Brazil in 1943. Her father never found out, although at one point he hired detectives in New York City to follow his daughter and spy on her.

Her infatuation with Misha Reznikoff drew her into the bohemian life of music and art, but breaking away from her family and her class did not mean abandoning her impeccable manners. She moved with purpose and poise, with erect posture, and she sat with her legs crossed at the ankles. Like Misha, she was a heavy smoker, but she did so with style. When she exhaled, she would exhale in such a way that the smoke traveled in two distinct thin streams, first up, then down. This was done to keep eye contact with her conversational partner and to minimize facial movement. The hand holding the cigarette was always kept to the side, arm bent, close to the body. Being socially proper did not mean, however, that she was dull or prudish. She laughed heartily at bawdy jokes, often told by the black musicians who formed a social nucleus around her and Misha. She felt comfortable in the presence of expressive people with accessible personalities. This may be one of the reasons why she was later so taken by Brazil and the warmth of its people.

She started out in New York by continuing her lessons in painting. In 1934, after seeing an exhibit by Berenice Abbott at the Julien Levy Gallery alongside Eugene Atget and Henri Cartier-Bresson, Naylor switched to photography. She then enrolled in Abbott's classes at the New School for Social Research in 1934. Women (Abbott, Margaret Bourke-White, Imogen Cunningham) were beginning to make names for themselves in photography, and Naylor was especially attracted to Abbott's work. Her professional relationship with Abbott lasted from 1935, when she became Abbott's apprentice, until Naylor's death.[3] She also became caught up in some of the left-wing causes of Depression-era New York: social justice, racial integration, antifascism, and avant-garde culture. Indeed, New York City and the New School for Social Research, in particular, played crucial roles in forging a connection between artistic modernism and political radicalism in the 1930s. Maturing as an artist in this heady atmosphere, Naylor became adept at photographing persons up close, a difficult task that required a good deal of nerve to win the trust of her subjects. Although she retained the air of her high-society upbringing, her personality changed when she was behind a camera; it liberated her, and she displayed the aggressiveness necessary for assignments as a photojournalist.

In 1937, when Naylor was just twenty-two years old, Photo League photographers recommended her to Holger Cahill of the WPA. Early in 1938, Cahill gave Naylor her first professional job, assigning her to the Harlem Arts Center, the first federally funded program of its kind, and subsequently sent her to Maine and Vermont. She also worked for the WPA in New Hampshire, Pennsylvania, Washington, D.C., and New York, photographing blue-collar workers before turning to photojournalism with *Time*, *Fortune*, and the Feature Service of the Associated Press. She was one of the first women hired as a photojournalist by any American wire service. Her association with the Associated Press led to her hiring by the OIAA and her assignment to Brazil in October 1940.

By this time in her life—she was twenty-five years old when Rockefeller staff members invited her and Misha to go to Brazil—she was considered an extremely professional career woman who got along with her photo editors and superiors but at the same time was her own woman. Somewhat akin to an actor who is more comfortable when hiding behind the life of a character, Genevieve was more at ease when her concentration was focused on her photographic tasks. She appreciated her mentor, Berenice Abbott, as a splendid teacher in the mechanics of photography but even as her protégée, Genevieve struck out to craft her own style.

She was witty, very intelligent, and an avid reader of history and biography. She preferred art films to Hollywood productions; she loved classical music and jazz, especially the pianists Art Tatum, Fats Waller, James P. Johnson, and Bud Powell. She was shy among people, an attribute that sometimes gives the impression of aloofness. She did not mince her words, although in social settings she reverted to what her son Peter terms "her best Miss Hall's School behavior." Her lifestyle may have been bohemian but she dressed stylishly. Trousers, hats, sneakers, and gloves were not in her wardrobe. But when she was behind her camera and subjects froze up, she did not play the society girl. She would distract them with

---

3   Letters, Genevieve Naylor to Berenice Abbott, March 19 and May 2, 1989, courtesy of Peter Reznikoff. One of Genevieve's first projects was assisting Abbott in putting together Abbott's book *Changing New York*.

conversation, or music, or telling jokes whose punchlines, in Peter's words, included "a liberal dose of profanity."[4]

Succeeding in a career as a self-supporting woman was important to her. Her biggest fear, she confided to relatives, was to end up like her mother, unfulfilled and unhappy. Finding liberation in the bohemian lifestyle of Greenwich Village, she took delight in tweaking the sensibilities of her staunchly Republican family by announcing that she had cast her first vote for Franklin D. Roosevelt. Her infatuation with Misha offended her family and its values, but she refused to give him up or to retreat to the placid life of her parents.

Misha, through his association with Rockefeller Center, was hired by Rockefeller's office to work with Brazilian artists and to act as a goodwill ambassador. In 1941, Rio's Fine Arts Museum exhibited his abstract expressionist paintings in a show titled *Monsters of War*, evocative of Picasso's *Guernica*. He also lectured, exhibited his paintings in various American consular offices, and accompanied his wife on her trips through Brazil, going as far north as Pernambuco and the inner reaches of the São Francisco River and as far west as Minas Gerais and the interior of Bahia and the state of São Paulo. Genevieve's Russian-born companion was received with open arms in Brazil, in part because of his ebullient personality but also because his presence permitted left-wing intellectuals—who represented only a small fraction of Brazil's cultural world during the early 1940s—to lionize him as a link to the Soviet Union, now Brazil's wartime ally. It is telling that one of the friendliest overtures to his painting came

from Astrojildo Pereira, as a young man one of the founders of the Brazilian Communist Party in the early 1920s, and during the early 1940s a columnist for a leading Rio de Janeiro newspaper. He narrowly avoided persecution during wartime under the Estado Novo because of the Allied rapprochement with Joseph Stalin and the Soviet Union. Pereira wrote effusively of Misha's cyclopses and monsters, a "tangible reminder," he penned, of the "reality of a world cowering beneath the blows of furious human beasts."[5] Not only Soviet sympathizers greeted Misha warmly: similar reviews were published by poets Manuel Bandeira and Vinícius de Moraes, by writer Anibal M. Machado, by *O Imparcial*'s influential editor (and Vargas's friend) J. S. Maciel Filho, and several others.[6]

The couple also became close friends with several of Brazil's most accomplished intellectual figures. Their address book contained the names and addresses of modernist painter Tarsila do Amaral, writer and cultural icon Oswaldo de Andrade, and journalist Samuel Wainer. It also included the name and phone number of Carlos Lacerda, the charismatic young law student who later in his career would turn against his communist past and become a leading conservative newspaper publisher, mayor and then governor, and one of the supporters of the 1964 military-civilian coup. Misha and Genevieve both declined opportunities to "buy" favorable reviews, an assertion made by Carolina Durieux, a representative from New York's Museum of Modern Art and who was in Brazil as part of Nelson Rockefeller's entourage.[7] Affection for them was genuine.

---

4   Observations courtesy of Peter Reznikoff, February 26, 1997.

5   Astrojildo Pereira, "Laboratório Reznikoff," Rio de Janeiro, c. 1942 (no further identification, clipping in possession of Peter Reznikoff).

6   For example, see *A Manhã* (Rio de Janeiro), October 19, 1941, 5; April 30, 1942, 3; and April 10, 1943, 5.

7   Letter, Carolina Durieux to Olive Lyford, head of South American Art at the Museum of Modern Art, Rio de Janeiro, n.d., courtesy of Peter Reznikoff.

Naylor was drawn without ulterior motives to ordinary Brazilians in their own setting. Most of these men and women were dark complexioned, the descendants of the millions of Africans trafficked to Brazil as slaves from the early 1500s down to the 1850s. Her range of subjects included the very rich and the very poor, but her depictions of high society, in whose circles she and Misha mixed as befitting their assignment as goodwill ambassadors, are less arresting and penetrating than her photographs of ordinary people. Her images of the poor made some of her superiors upset. On more than one occasion she was warned to stop photographing "a preponderance of Negroes, Mulattos, Negro shacks, Negroes at Carnival, and various bric-a-brac." Her safe-conduct pass, signed personally by Lourival Fontes, stated that her job was to "take photographs of touristic sites" in Brazil.[8]

She stubbornly resisted attempts to limit her subject matter to handsome buildings and high society. Joseph Piazza, in charge of cultural relations at the U.S. Embassy

Travel pass.

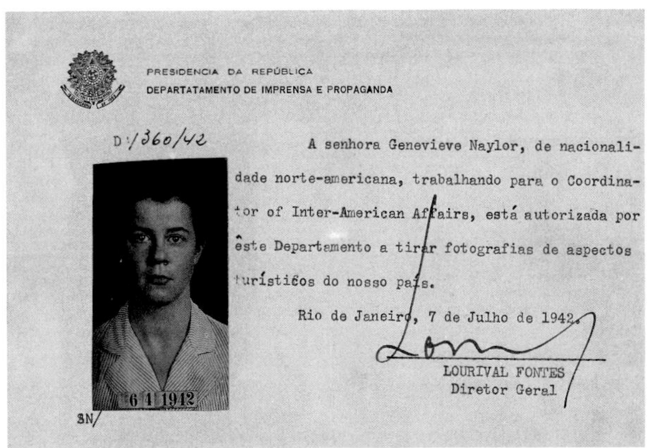

in Rio, became her closest ally. "Mr. Piazza," she wrote to her sister, "is a very cultured man who has more than once defended or maybe I would say, explained my artistic tastes to the big boys in Washington." Barbara Hadley Stein, a graduate student from Berkeley on an OIAA fellowship, also remembers Piazza as a "maverick," much more open than the other American diplomats.[9] Naylor refused to give in, and protected by Piazza, clung tenaciously to her vision of what was distinctive and important about ordinary Brazilians. She faced other obstacles. "Film is being rationed to everyone," she wrote. "I don't have the luxury of shooting anything I want. I have to be damn careful and pick and choose my images with great care and hope my exposures are correct." "What helps," she added, "is the absolute cooperation of the Brazilians. They are so natural in their demeanor, so giving and warm, that my camera just loves them."

Most of the Brazilian elite shared the State Department's view that Brazil's natural wonders, its handsome architecture, and the new factories and public works projects built under the auspices of Vargas's government were more appropriate than photographs of black Carnival dancers or rural peasants dressed in clothing that was clean but ragged. Brazilian critics who praised Naylor's (and Reznikoff's) work were those intellectuals who, like Naylor and Reznikoff, had been recruited to play the Good Neighbor game. Nonetheless, much of the applause seemed to be authentic. In an essay on the Good Neighbor Policy, critic and writer Aníbal Machado wrote that Naylor's decision to photograph ordinary people has helped reveal the "essential elements that comprise the physiognomy of our people."[10]

---

8   Document DG/360/42, Rio de Janeiro, July 7, 1942.

9   Interview, Barbara Hadley Stein, Princeton, N.J., March 1, 1997, with Peter Reznikoff. She had wanted to go to Peru, but the OIAA insisted that she go to Brazil.

10   Aníbal Machado, cited in Mota, "A fotógrafa e o pintor," 12.

Naylor's photographic vision produced images of Brazilian life for the American public that were considerably more nuanced than the stereotypes presented by most of the other American cultural figures the OIAA recruited. Looked at objectively and by present-day standards, much of the educational "culture" produced by the OIAA either trivialized or grossly insulted the peoples it depicted. Walt Disney's cigar-chomping parrot Zé Carioca is a case in point; movies like *Flying Down to Rio* another. Even Orson Welles's ill-fated film *It's All True*, produced for Rockefeller with the goal of telling the inter-American "story," patronized its subjects.[11] The film portrayed Latin Americans as exotic "types" no less insensitively than did the travel photographers, who since the 1840s had sold millions and millions of images of stereotyped photo cards to consumers in North America and Europe seeking vicarious knowledge about the world. As mentioned in the previous chapter, the roles forced on Carmen Miranda were so much of a self-parodying straitjacket that by the time she returned to Brazil from Hollywood at the end of the war her career was ruined.[12]

Naylor was assigned to Brazil at the height of the DIP's sway. The twenty-five-year-old photojournalist from New York arrived in Brazil in October 1940 with two cameras, a light meter, and a battered black wicker suitcase. She wrote to her sister Cynthia,

> My first striking visual sight was not the bustling energy of the Copacabana beach or the boulevards and slums, but a solitary young Negro girl sitting cross-legged in the center of a street, intensely focused on constructing a wooden flute. If there ever was a moment to have my camera! Unfortunately, the Brazilian authorities have confiscated my equipment while they scrutinize my background to make sure I'm not some fifth-columnist subversive![13]

Her assignment was part of the political jockeying between Washington and Rio de Janeiro. Once Vargas, after much prevarication (and substantial aid from the U.S. Lend-Lease program), entered the war on the Allied side, it became politically expedient for Rio de Janeiro and Washington to cooperate culturally, even if Brazil remained a dictatorship. Both the DIP and Rockefeller's OIAA assigned photographers to capture uplifting images, little more than thinly veiled propaganda. Three American photographers worked in Brazil: Naylor; G. E. Kidder Smith, who photographed architectural subjects (and whose work was dismissed as "boring" by the *San Francisco Examiner*); and Alan Fisher, assigned to the Public Health and Sanitation division of OIAA, who concentrated on medical subjects (and military installations) in the Amazon region.[14]

Unlike their photojournalistic counterparts in the United States, Naylor and her colleagues had little freedom. Roy Stryker, Rexford Tugwell's protégé and teaching assistant in economics at Columbia, shared a reformist attitude with the photographers he hired and encouraged them to editorialize with their camera, as it were. The photographers Stryker hired aggressively grasped the scope and interrelationships of problems because they wanted to bring about change.[15] The visual images they produced were therefore far more revealing than those

---

11 See Catherine Benamou, "*It's All True* as Document/Event: Notes towards an Historiographical and Textual Analysis," *Persistence of Vision* 7 (1989), 121–152.

12 See Stephen Holden review of *Carmen Miranda: Bananas Is My Business*, *New York Times*, July 5, 1995, B5.

13 Letter, Genevieve Naylor to Cynthia Gillipsie, Rio de Janeiro, n.d., in possession of Peter Reznikoff.

14 *San Francisco Examiner*, November 14, 1943. Alan Fisher's medical photographs are stored at the National Archives, Washington, D.C.

15 Karin Becker Ohrn, *Dorothea Lange and the Documentary Tradition* (Baton Rouge: Louisiana State University Press, 1980), 107.

likely intended by New Deal bureaucrats, who after all were signing on artists and photographers mostly to give them work.

Unlike Stryker's photographers, who were given free rein, Naylor received a full and detailed set of written instructions about what to photograph from the DIP when she arrived in Rio. One assignment sheet was divided into nine categories: modern architecture (mostly government buildings); homes in the affluent neighborhoods of Lagôa, Gavea, and Ipanema; residential interiors in specified apartment buildings and homes as well as a general instruction to do "certain modern and wealthy apartments in Flamengo"; Sunday beach and pool life in Copacabana and Ipanema; horseback riding at the elegant clubs; the two most exclusive golf courses; "yachts and beautiful girls" on Guanabara Bay; fashion establishments on Rua do Ouvidor, a downtown commercial street; and seven social assistance programs patronized by Vargas's wife Darcy: a sewing clinic, Christmas at the presidential palace, a shelter for the homeless, a school for children of fishermen, the newsboys' foundation, an orphanage, and a day care center.[16]

The OIAA, by contrast, cared little for depicting affluent touristic scenes and staged charities, although Naylor's superiors personally were concerned less about what she photographed than what would please the Brazilians. The agency's primary motivation was first and last to win sympathy for both the United States and the Allied cause. There was much less leeway during wartime; the OIAA had a job to do. Its officials sometimes had to look away from unpleasantries. Misha Reznikoff on one occasion was caught snooping in a place where he should not have

been—the OIAA asked its employees to "keep their eyes and ears open to fascist activities and report them," their son Peter recalls—and he was so severely beaten by Vargas's secret police that for a time he completely forgot how to speak English.[17]

Genevieve and Misha were housed in an apartment in the Zona Sul (South Zone) in Leme, atop the beach at the beginning of Avenida Atlântica.[18] The sand stretched from Leme through Copacabana and then wound around a point at Apoador to Ipanema and Leblón. The beachfront neighborhoods had risen during the 1920s, when a tunnel hewed through the towering granite hill that separated the Zona Sul from the main part of Rio de Janeiro permitted the development of the area for tourism and as a residential neighborhood for the well-to-do. There were plenty of poor people in the Zona Sul as well: men, women, and children who came down from their shantytown favelas perched on the hills above the beach, to work as janitors, handymen, laundresses, and maids. The district also developed into a major leisure center, with theaters, nightclubs, galleries, riding clubs, and hotels, anchored by the august Copacabana Palace Hotel in the center of Copacabana. The Zona Sul teemed with noise and music and human activity hemmed in between the sea and the hillsides, and Naylor loved it. She delighted in taking pictures on Copacabana that showed contrast: fisherman hauling in their nets alongside bathers; youths in scant bathing attire mixing with formally dressed older women and men conforming to the traditional standards of proper decorum. She dutifully photographed the buildings and clubs and civic monuments that her bosses expected she would emphasize, but when-

---

16 DIP, Divisão de Turismo, "Assuntos que devem ser fotografados no Rio de Janeiro," c. 1941, courtesy of Peter Reznikoff.

17 E-mail letter, Peter Reznikoff to Robert M. Levine, April 9, 1995.

18 See reference letter written for Genevieve Naylor by Prescott Childs, U.S. Consul, Rio de Janeiro, March 29, 1941, courtesy of Peter Reznikoff.

ever she could she snuck away, to the sectors of the city where the middle and lower classes lived, crammed into trolleys and suburban trains, congregating in social clubs located in wooden shacks, and otherwise dealing with their lives in ways almost entirely invisible to the upper-class elite.

The OIAA office was located downtown adjacent to the U.S. Embassy, about forty minutes from the Zona Sul by bus. Naylor and Reznikoff moved in prominent cultural circles, becoming friends with the architect Oscar Niemeyer (who a decade and a half later would design the new capital of Brasília). They also met many members of the younger generation of musicians. Naylor taught courses in photography and got to know Brazilians from a broad cross section of society.

Having arrived during the OIAA's first days in Brazil, Naylor and Reznikoff helped others who came later. Orson Welles asked Naylor to help him find the best streets and locations for the filming of *It's All True*. Welles knew the obvious spots, she wrote to her sister, "but he didn't know [that] in the Praça Onze a separate and almost exclusive Negro Carnival is staged."[19] They were described kindly by the Museum of Modern Art's representative, Caroline Durieux:

> Reznikoff and Naylor found out through their Brazilian contacts that it is possible to "buy" favorable articles in magazines. It is a practice they have declined to pursue, and I think it is a wise decision. We are getting all the publicity we need without greasing any palms.[20]

Welles and Naylor were so struck by the vibrancy of Brazilian popular culture that they both rebelled against what their employers wanted each of them to do. For Welles, whose insistence on photographing poor Brazilian blacks alienated not only the DIP but the OIAA and RKO Studios, *It's All True* marked the start of a career slide for him that ended in his ostracism from Hollywood in spite of his reputation as a genius. Naylor felt similarly, but she found ways to ignore what her bosses wanted without finding herself on the next ship back to the United States. Part of the reason for this may have been her unassuming personality and the fact that as a foreign woman venturing off the beaten path, she was always treated with courtesy by her hosts. She may also have benefited from her tendency of not seeking publicity and that she traveled without assistants, heavy equipment, or a press entourage trailing behind, as Welles did.

Naylor faced many obstacles as a woman photographer, not the least of which was the incapacity of most men to take her seriously. Brazilians of the upper class were always polite and formal, but they always mixed in an avuncular sense of paternalism. "She is an adorable American girl," eulogized composer Vinícius de Moraes, "elegant, with a youthful air, always with a feather in her cap, like Robin Hood. Nothing escapes her camera."[21] If she was affronted by such treatment, Naylor never let her feelings show, and in the end she was able to turn her femininity to her advantage; when she was in the field, the Brazilians showed deference to her, giving her more space than foreign male photographers might have received.

Not only did Genevieve wander beyond Rio's chic neighborhoods—where her superiors had expected her to

---

19   Letter, Genevieve Naylor to Cynthia Gillipsie, Rio de Janeiro, n.d.

20   Letter, Carolina Durieux to Olive Lyford, coordinator of American Art for South America at the Museum of Modern Art, Rio de Janeiro, courtesy of Peter Reznikoff.

21   Newspaper clipping, n.d., courtesy of Peter Reznikoff.

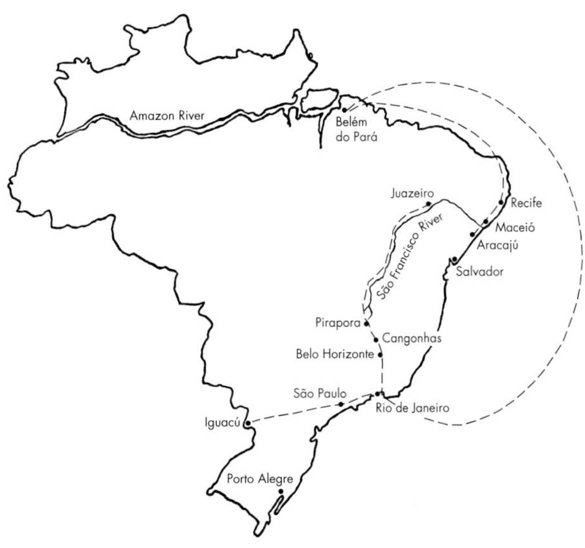

Naylor's photographic itinerary.

remain—but she and Misha took several extensive trips away from the Brazilian capital. They traveled south to São Paulo, the country's most industrialized city, in some ways more European in appearance than Brazilian. In a lengthy journey that started in February 1942, they traveled north from Rio to the gateway of the Amazon River in Belém do Pará. On their return they visited the capital cities of some of the northeast states, including Recife, Maceió, and Aracajú. If they went to Salvador, none of Genevieve's photographs or negatives from that visit survive. On another trip, they went from Rio de Janeiro to Belo Horizonte in Minas Gerais, then to the baroque town of Cangonhas, and then to Pirapora, where they boarded a paddle-wheel steamer that plied the San Fran-

cisco River. This region was populated by cowboys who dressed in suits of leather and who herded cattle in ways unchanged for generations. Naylor spent time in the dusty, anonymous towns along the river in the interior of the state of Bahia, photographing scenes that appeared worlds removed from the affluent neighborhoods and clubs of the coastal elite.

The São Francisco River winds from the mountainous region in Minas Gerais where gold was discovered in the 1690s, and later diamonds. Thousands of prospectors descended upon the Brazilian colony in search of their fortunes. The gold rush also brought to the region members of the Portuguese nobility and tens of thousands of African slaves. Ranches and farms were developed along the riverbanks to supply food for Minas's burgeoning population. These developments led to the growth of towns along the river, although as time went on they were bypassed, and they fell into a sleepy decline.

Genevieve and Misha's riverboat trip not only produced some of her best photographs of the Brazilian interior but, as evidenced by an undated letter written during the trip to friends, revealed a good deal about her personality. Few examples of Naylor's correspondence survive, but this letter is telling:

> This voyage is definitely not a trip from Pirapora [Minas Gerais] to Joazeiro; it's one from this sand bank to the next. The first time we got stuck (five minutes after embarking) it was *too* picturesque— those fine, strong, bronzed MEN, literally lifting us off those unique sand formations—*BUT* after spending a day knawing *[sic]* our nails, waiting for

the next sand bank (with a little engine trouble thrown in), we have finally given over to God and a lone bottle of genuine Gordon's gin and agua tonica (tonic water). The only trouble is there seems to be an unlimited supply of agua tonica and a bottle of gin that just seems to evaporate, God knows where.

Naylor, then, was not any wide-eyed tourist visiting exotic places with her camera. Her letter goes on to describe the difficulties of getting out of Rio de Janeiro:

> That last day in Rio was a Heller what with gathering last minute letters of introduction and Lourival's (I hear he is out on his bunda [ass], Graças a Deus [thank God]) card of permission to take photos and the squeezing of last minute elephants into match-box suit-cases, we finally got off in a terrific rush leaving last minute telephone calls, etc., undone, only to have a first class disaster smack us in the face half way to Bello Horizonte. Mish and I had the last beds in the last car of the train and were killing time and dirt having a drink in the restaurant car when we stopped with a boom in some small station. The xixi (pee) I had decided to take previously simply couldn't wait, so we wandered back to find the back end of our car folded up like an accordion and the rear engine (put on as an *aid*) puffing and steaming right in the middle of our beds. WELL, I lost ten kilos on the spot because we had previously stored all our baggage including my complete work (negatives) of a year and all of Mish's paintings in a small space in back of the beds and that engine steaming and (as I thought) melting my negatives to a grease spot and that f——da-p—— [son of a whore] conductor saying—"Well, we will leave the car here and you can get your things tomorrow," and another f——da-p—— calling us quinta columnas [traitors] (a year's work of negatives), so with a few tears on my part, and Mish's gestures on the other, we got the baggage out safe and OK. After that, B.H. [Belo Horizonte] was very tame, and Pirapora was a sleeping pill.[22]

Minas was the heart of traditional Roman Catholic religious expression brought by Portuguese settlers. Brazil's wealthiest colonial settlement after 1700, Minas Gerais saw the construction of dozens of handsome whitewashed churches. One of the most striking of the old baroque cities was Congonhas, a town perched high in the mountains filled with lovely Baroque churches decorated by the eighteenth-century statues of the mulatto Antônio Francisco Lisboa, known as Aleijadinho, the son of a slave. Crippled by leprosy, Aleijadinho worked with hammer and chisel strapped to the stumps of his arms. He sculpted dozens of magnificent statues of biblical figures at the church sites. By the early 1940s the gold had long given out but the striking architecture remained.

Naylor's Significance

We find in photographs what we look for. The mestizo Peruvian photographer Martín Chambí survived for decades at the pleasure of the Cuzco elites because they

---

22 Letter, Genevieve Naylor to "Dearest Amigos—Ruth & Caloca," probably on board ship on the São Francisco River, c. 1942, courtesy of Peter Reznikoff. "Lourival" was Vargas's DIP head, Lourival Fontes. "Bello" is the old way of spelling Belo, the capital of Minas Gerais. Pirapora is the river town where their steamer set off on its trip upriver heading northward to Juazeiro in the state of Bahia.

thought that the displays of luxury he showed (and the cringing, deferential poses of the Indians who served them) enhanced their prestige, while to us he clearly was mocking their cruelty and pretension. Naylor's goal was quite different: to depict what she found striking in Brazilian life and to convince Americans that Brazil was a stalwart wartime ally. She never mocked or knowingly distorted her subjects. Nor did she produce simple propaganda, although her employers might have been happy if she had—World War II–era Hollywood films on war-related subjects certainly did so. Naylor was too free spirited to produce pedestrian images, though that is what she had been hired to do in Brazil.

Genevieve Naylor's photographs satisfied the OIAA because most of the time she stuck to the subjects they had assigned to her, but at the same time they hold significant documentary importance for us, as she was determined to broaden her subject base as much as possible. Because of the DIP's powerful bureaucratic presence, few unofficial photographs of Brazil in the early 1940s are available to us. Because she traveled widely, to places where Brazilian photographers found little of interest, she documented scenes that otherwise would never have been recorded: massive religious processions, life on a São Francisco riverboat, butchering cattle for meat, remnants of Brazil's dwindling aboriginal population, scenes from everyday life in the cities. Just as Dorothea Lange eloquently photographed destitute farmworkers, Naylor photographed migrants on food lines on their route south to the slums of Brazil's industrial cities. More often than not, however, Naylor's images conveyed messages of small victories in daily life. She never emphasized futility or downright misery. Her photographs were, on the other hand, tied closely to not only an artistic but a moral function.[23] In this way her photographs went beyond DIP guidelines and therefore have a vibrancy that the official record never showed.[24]

In the end, by using her camera to emphasize Brazil's distinctive character, Naylor was fulfilling not only her assignment but Roosevelt's Good Neighbor Policy objective. Her depiction of the Brazilians as an industrious, reliable, educated, vibrant, racially harmonious people should have been reassuring images to an American public preparing for war. Her vision projected a nation the United States could confidently count on should fascist infiltration undermine the hemisphere's stability. Her task was made more difficult by having to walk a tightrope between the restrictions of the DIP—affirmed by the directives from her own agency—and her fascination with the Brazilian world usually hidden from foreign lenses. Her solution was an approach that was, in the words of Catherine Benamou, "at once prismatic and intimate."[25]

Naylor recoiled at photographing sanitized travelogues and picture postcards of idyllic landscapes, waterfalls, and famous corners. Instead, she and Misha traveled up and down the coast seeking to capture what Brazil was really like. In so doing, she elevated her reportage to something more evocative than the usual run-of-the-mill documentary photograph. What emerged was an intense photographic style that allowed the viewer to peer beneath the surface of mere picture taking to the human aspect of being Brazilian. Naylor's compositional skill was evidenced by her reluctance to manipulate emotionally. Without

---

23   See Sarah Boxer's excellent contrast of 1930-era documentary photography with that of the mid-1990s, where subjects pose defiantly, menacing the viewer (*New York Times*, April 30, 1995, 6).

24   On Lange, see Maren Stange, "The Record Itself," 3.

25   Catherine Benamou, review of the documentary *Brazilian Images*, H-LATAM network, posted July 22, 1996, 1.

sacrificing visual content, she enabled her American audience to identify with her subjects. With her lens, Naylor captured not just faces and places but the character of Brazilian society.

Vargas's drive to centralize Brazil under the semifascist Estado Novo 1937 Constitution created conditions that hindered the couple's travels. By the late 1930s, government paperwork had become even more bureaucratized than ever, but the arm of the national government in reality reached not much farther than the federal capital of Rio de Janeiro. As a result, persons travelling from place to place, as did Naylor and Reznikoff, had to deal with local officials knowledgeable about the rules issued in Rio de Janeiro but interpreting them in unpredictable ways. Some mayors demanded transit fees for passing through their towns—nothing more than a bribe—and others collected fees for local versions of visas, which were inserted into the travelers' passports. Naylor's camera and equipment were confiscated several times during her travels and she was held for interrogation, even though she carried with her a travel permit with her photograph signed by Lourival Fontes, Vargas's propaganda agency head and one of the most powerful members of the government.

Naylor's travels with her camera allowed her to explore places foreign even to the great majority of educated Brazilians. Above all, she captured ordinary people going through their daily lives with optimism. Few of her photographs capture despair, in stark contrast to the photojournalistic tradition of the United States out of which she emerged. In the FSA photographers produced depictions of the effects of anxiety and deprivation on the

faces of Depression-era Americas. In Brazil, Naylor's impoverished subjects more often than not show stoicism seemingly ameliorated by their acceptance of their condition. It may be that the Americans caught up in the Depression suffered so much because theirs was an experience of downward mobility, the painful experience of men and women whose standard of living had declined. Brazilians, never prosperous or expectant about the promise of their future, may have been more inured to their condition and therefore were more able to cope. Benamou explains Naylor's technique as follows:

> In place of the panoramic views one tends to obtain in more complacent, naturalist renderings (by foreigners and metropolitan Brazilians alike), Naylor invites us to experience the specific texture of [the country's] regions through human scenes shot at extremely close range. Keeping within the bounds of what would have been either politically or ethically transgressive, hers is a subtle, patient, yet penetrating gaze at a country in the throes of rapid change.[26]

After two years and nine months in Brazil, Naylor and Reznikoff sailed back to New York in late 1942. From January 27 to March 5, 1943, two months before her return from Brazil, New York's Museum of Modern Art (MOMA) exhibited her Brazilian work in a one-woman show, *Faces and Places in Brazil*, along with an exhibit of architectural photographs, *Brazil Builds*, by G. E. Kidder Smith, also an employee of Rockefeller's agency.[27] During 1943 and 1944, the dual exhibit toured the United States with stops in Boston, Rochester, Colorado Springs, Se-

---

26 Benamou, review, 2.

27 The only other female photographer to be invited to have a show at the MOMA was Helen Levitt, information courtesy of Peter Reznikoff.

attle, San Francisco, and up and down the West Coast. *Brazil Builds*, Smith's photographs of buildings, received a tepid reception—one newspaper called Smith's work "rather boring . . . cold, and detached." The same reviewer praised Naylor for capturing "the feeling, flavor, joy, pathos, of all the blending cultures, white and negro, of this fascinating nation. . . . Her love of the people is remarkably demonstrated through this excellent series of prints."[28] A show by a female photographer was a rarity for the time, and it was a success; Alfred Barr, the museum's curator and founding director, lauded her work as "remarkable" and "outstanding." He noted that she was only twenty-eight years old at the time of her show, and he declared that her photographs of Brazil seemed the work of "a native acquainted with the fine nuances of the culture and its people."[29]

The review of *Faces and Places* in the *Colorado Spring Daily* typifies the warm words Naylor received:

> [The exhibit] is a first rate photographic exhibition which should appeal to camera enthusiasts as well as those who have a yearning to see something of the Great Coffee Nation. . . . A little less of the education and a bit more of the everyday life of Brazilians, Miss Naylor's camera has recorded a few of the commonplace activities of everyday people brought into sharp focus through her discriminating eye.[30]

By the war's end Naylor's career as a fashion photographer was launched, primarily at *Harper's Bazaar*. There she came under the influence of Alexy Brodovitch, its renowned art director, who encouraged her to apply a documentary style to pure fashion layouts. Her associates at *Bazaar* included Toni Frissell, Lillian Bassman, Lisete Model, and Louise Dahl-Wolfe, the magazine's first female photographer. During her stay at *Bazaar* she worked alongside most of the famous photographers of the 1950s, including Richard Avedon, Robert Frank, Saul Leiter, and Diane Arbus.[31]

During the 1950s Reznikoff played an important role in the postwar expressionist vanguard, exhibiting his paintings in such New York City galleries as Leo Castelli's and Sidney Janis's.[32] Naylor, in addition to becoming Eleanor Roosevelt's personal photographer, did most of her work for Condé Nast's publications, and she made her mark as a high-fashion photographer and portraitist. Among the luminaries she photographed were John F. Kennedy, Henry Fonda, Frank Sinatra, Errol Flynn, Jackie Robinson, Natalie Wood, Richard M. Nixon, Jean-Paul Sartre, Simone de Beauvoir, John Huston, and Louis Armstrong, a friend of Reznikoff's.[33] She always felt more creative, however, when she was assigned to human interest stories for the magazines. She referred to some of her assignments as "commissioned hackwork," especially when as an older woman she was no longer given work she could do creatively. All throughout her career, though, she considered herself to be in the Cartier-Bresson camp, and was therefore more inclined to try and catch a spontaneous moment than a studied mood.

Misha and Genevieve settled in Dobbs Ferry, New York, where they raised their two boys, Peter and Michael. Sometimes the boys' parents would talk in Portuguese so they would not be understood. Genevieve used the Portuguese expressions *obrigada* (thank you)

---

28   *San Francisco Chronicle*, November 14, 1943, clipping courtesy of Peter Reznikoff.

29   Alfred Barr, *Museum of Modern Art Quarterly*, 1944, clipping courtesy of Peter Reznikoff.

30   *Colorado Springs Daily*, October 7, 1943.

31   See David Bailey, *Shots of Style: Great Fashion Photography* (New York: Rizzoli, 1985); Martin Harrison, *Appearances* (New York: John Cale, 1991); *125 Years of Harper's Bazaar* (New York: William Morrow, 1993); Rosenblum, *A History of Women Photographers*.

32   Mota, "A fotógrafa e o pintor," 9–13.

33   Also, Althea Gibson and the duchess of Windsor. Naylor's portrait of Eleanor Roosevelt is included in Rosenblum's *A History of Women Photographers*.

and *Deus me livre* (God forbid) continually, and she drank Brazilian tea all her life. In the early years of that decade, Misha and Genevieve became friends with a new generation of Brazilian musicians passing through New York City, including Luis Bonfã, João and Astrud Gilberto, and Antônio Carlos Jobim. She retained her knowledge of Portuguese through the end of her life. Misha died in 1971 at the age of sixty-six. Genevieve died nearly two decades later, in 1989, at the age of seventy-four.

Concluding Remarks

Many if not most of Genevieve Naylor's negatives from her Latin American years were lost or destroyed. We know, for example, that in mid-1942 she applied for and received a visa to travel in neighboring Paraguay, but no photographs from Paraguay survive. Naylor probably took more photographs in São Paulo than the handful we have, and she may have visited Salvador, but we have no evidence of such a trip. Virtually no photographs from her mid-1942 visit to Pernambuco, near the tip of Brazil's bulge into the Atlantic, remain. If she traveled across Guanabara Bay to the state of Rio de Janeiro, or to historic Goiás, or to the far South, no photographic record remains.

Although they were as subjective as any documentary photographs, Naylor's photographs held back from editorializing. Her training was in art, and her photographic style was more "painterly" than journalistic. Her attraction to subjects was based on her empathy for ordinary people and for the texture of life she witnessed.

Naylor frequently photographed subjects against backgrounds devoid of clues that would have dated them. Like the FSA's photographers, she loved to shoot groups of people, in close, with only enough props to convey a sense of what the persons were doing. She was especially skillful at photographing children, and she always captured them naturally. Even her photograph of a boy performing illegal child labor is neutral, not condemning. She loved to take pictures of large groups of people, as if to capture their remarkable diversity. Hundreds of her photographs depict conditions of poverty, but she captured even impoverished men and women in ways to highlight their dignity. Indeed, the ability of ordinary Brazilians to enjoy life with exuberance amidst conditions that to outsiders were harsh and unfair was a characteristic seized upon by Naylor, who relished the opportunity to photograph people in such circumstances. This was a subjective approach, but it was honest as well. Naylor's letters from Brazil and the comments of Brazilians who knew her there convey her sincerity and her lingering excitement about what she saw around her.

In the United States, the Farm Security Administration's Historical Section took upon itself an activist role because of the forceful personality of its chief, Roy Stryker, not because of government policy. The FSA differed from the WPA, whose historical section was run largely to give work to artists and photographers, just as the New Deal's Civilian Conservation Corps (CCC) had given shovels to young men mainly to get them out of the cities and into the fresh air. Stryker, however, rankled when it was suggested that he was hiring artists to support their work; he made them, in the words of Ansel Adams, work "not as photographers but a bunch of sociologists."[34] Not only was Naylor not a sociologist but the agency that hired her—the OIAA—was a wartime propaganda agency, and her photographs have to be understood in this context.

What Genevieve Naylor chose to photograph during her nearly three years' stay in Brazil is telling. She neither took the easy road, which would have been to photograph the city's hundreds of handsome, ornate mansions and stately neighborhoods; nor did she seek out pictures of urban misery, which would also have been easy to do but which would have gone counter to the spirit of her assignment, which, although unstated in so many words, was to assure the Americans who saw her photographs that Brazil was an energetic and progressive wartime ally. She concentrated on anything she found to be photogenic. When she photographed architectural subjects she tended to show them in repair or in abandonment. She avoided scenes of conflict, and she seemed not to be willing to photograph scenes of misery or deprivation.

A student of painting and the avant garde, Naylor employed a variety of techniques in her work. More than anything, she likely was influenced by the work of the photographers in New York's Photo League, who collectively came to form what became known as the New York school (1936–1963).[35] There is a complementarity, for example, between Naylor's Brazilian work and the New York City photographs of Helen Levitt. Both photographers looked at the world through humanistic eyes, and they loved to photograph children. Both had the knack of extracting from even grim subjects pictures that preserved the subjects' dignity. Yet Levitt's subjects show urban stress on their faces and in their body movements;

Naylor's do not. Levitt's photographs teem with life and latent violence. Naylor's capture moments of reflection and respite. Neither Levitt nor Naylor emphasized dismal conditions, although as urban photographers during difficult times this would have been easy enough to accomplish, but Levitt's photographs more often than not capture the city's grimness in the background.[36]

Even if she was influenced by the New York school and by the work of the WPA and FSA photographers of the 1930s, Naylor's photographs are far less grim. In many of the WPA photographs, women are photographed with their hands on their faces, as if awaiting blows. Men stand hopelessly, knowing that there will be no work for them. Agency photojournalists framed people against spare lines that seemed to indicate the spareness of their lives. By contrast, Naylor's subjects were caught at moments of contentment or hopefulness. Never does she show despair.

Through her selection of camera angle, the details of a scene became both a record of daily life and an abstract grouping of multiornamental figures framed against an environmental canvas. Even her interior and exterior shots of churches and stately mansions with their own phantasmagoric lighting display a sense of grandeur that escapes our everyday perception. This is all the more remarkable because her working conditions were primitive at best. She had no assistants, no fast film, no strobes. All she used was a Rolliflex, a 4 x 5 Speed Graphic camera, and natural light.

Genevieve Naylor's hallmark in Brazil was the way she portrayed the vibrancy of ordinary life. Her images convey what Vicki Goldberg terms the "quiet humility of ob-

---

34 Ansel Adams, quoted by Mary Hawthorne, "Light and Shadow," *New Yorker* (August 14, 1995), 80.

35 See Margarett Loke, "Inside Photography," *New York Times*, February 14, 1997, B37.

36 See Helen Levitt, *A Way of Seeing* (Durham, N.C.: Duke University Press, 1989).

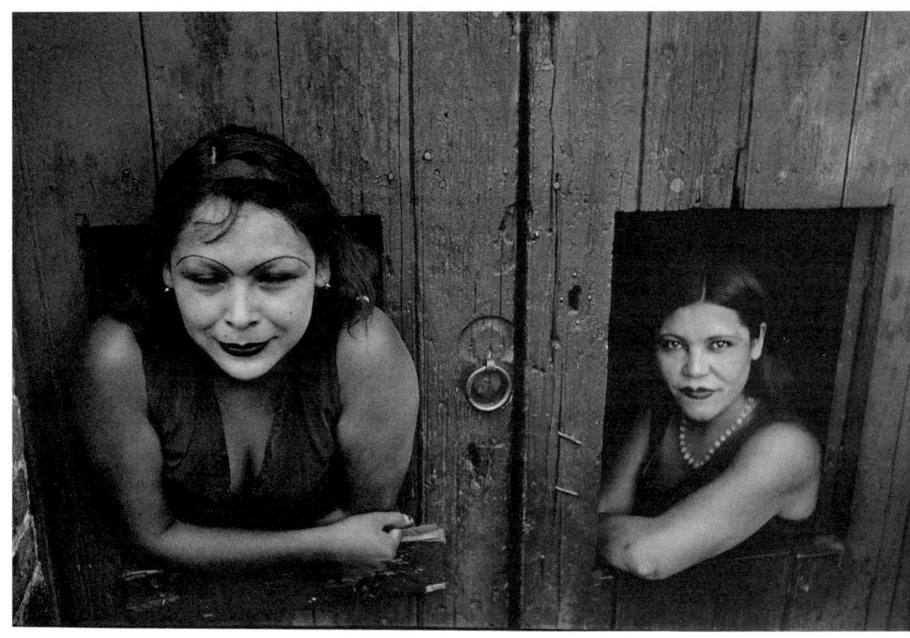

Calle Cuahtemoctzin,
Mexico City, 1934.
Photo by Henri Cartier-
Bresson. Courtesy of
Magnum Photos.

servation and a basic trust in the worth of ordinary people."[37] Never, however, did she show the raggedness in which some 70 percent of the Brazilian population, rural and urban, lived. Had she sought to capture squalor or social injustice she would have been sent packing immediately. Nor was this her style. She chose not to single out blacks or the very poor, as some did. One photographer notable for this was Pierre Verger, the French photographer who began during the 1930s to portray working people in Brazil, Africa, and Spanish South America, who focused his camera on straining muscles, exhaustion, and sinewy poverty. He so closely identified with Brazilian blacks during his four-year stay (1946–1950) in Salvador da Bahia, he took the African name Fatumbi, even though he was a white from the same social background as Naylor's.[38]

Like Verger, Naylor felt as naturally at home with the poorest Brazilians as with upper-class intellectuals and their peers. She photographed subjects similar to those of Verger, but waited until they relaxed, capturing them at rest, in moments of contemplation or playful humor. In some ways, her photographs resemble the work of the African American photographer Roy de Carava. Although he used a 35-millimeter camera and Naylor her large format Speed Graphic, both of them paid painstaking attention to detail, and both applied aesthetic rules to their documentary vision, keeping in mind all the while the intimacy of their compositions. Both capture on black-and-white film quiet moments of poetry, shadows, and people at peace with themselves. This is not to say that Naylor

37   Vicki Goldberg, *New York Times*, April 9, 1995, sec. 2, p. 39.
38   See Jean Loup Pivin and Pascal Martin Saint Léon, *Pierre Verger: Le Messager: Photographies 1932–1962* (Paris: Editions Revue, 1993).

avoided scenes of travail: especially after she left Rio de Janeiro and toured the Northeast, and, to cap her long journey, up the São Francisco River from Minas Gerais to Juazeiro in the drought polygon of the Northeast, she photographed hungry people; her portrait of migrants waiting for food (photo 82) rivals anything by Dorothea Lange. But taken as a whole her Brazilian work was not very photojournalistic in approach; it comprises, rather, a collection of individual portraits, affectionately crafted and seeking to bring out the human and sympathetic character of her subjects.

Unlike Lange, Cartier-Bresson, and other masters of the 35-millimeter camera, she worked with the larger format Speed Graphic. This meant that she needed much more time between clicks of the shutter, but it also permitted her to compose her subjects more carefully. Her Brazilian photographs in some ways strikingly resemble Cartier-Bresson's work, but his images sought to capture the surprising conjunctions of everyday life—its lurid side—whereas Naylor captured life's normal texture.[39]

For this and other reasons Naylor's Brazilian work differs meaningfully from the dramatic documentary portraits of Sebastião Salgado, which show human anguish. Salgado's brilliant photographs are so stark and so shocking that critics have felt the need to apologize for him. "Salgado's camera moves about the violent darkness," writes Eduardo Galeano. "It shows us that concealed within the pain of living and the tragedy of dying there is a potent magic, a luminous mystery that redeems the human adventure in the world."[40] This may be so, although it has become a cliché to rationalize the subject choices of photographers (Salgado, Diane Arbus, and many others)

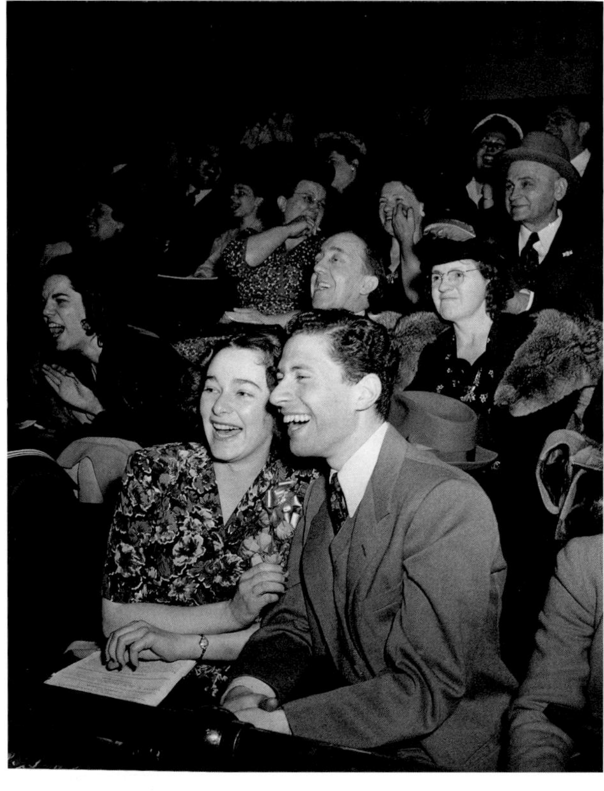

Laughing audience by Weegee (Arthur Fellig). © 1994, International Center of Photography, New York. Bequest of Wilma Wilcox.

who specialize in portraying the depths of the human experience as "not violating but penetrating the human spirit in order to reveal it."[41] In any case, Naylor did not see the need to photograph her subjects in this way. She never compromised the dignity of her subjects, nor left interpretation to be puzzled over by the viewer.

The images she framed in her viewfinder were influenced by the neorealistic, lyrical cinematography of the 1930s. She was aware of the work of the Russians Sergei

---

39   For a comparison with the Mexican photographer Manuel Alvarez Bravo, see Vicki Goldberg, "Photographing Mexico Where a Silence Reigned," *New York Times*, March 23, 1997, sec. 2, pp. 39–40.

40   Eduardo Galeano, *An Uncertain Grace: Photographs by Sebastião Salgado* (New York: Aperture, 1990), 7.

41   Ibid.

Eisenstein (1898–1948) and Pudovkin, of Jean Renoir, Rene Clair, and Robert Flaherty. Her hammocks (photo 95) are reminiscent of Eisenstein's *Battleship Potemkin*; her low-angle shots and subjects framed against the sky (photos 4, 11, 20, and 26, for example) seem right out of John Ford and D. W. Griffith. Naylor's print of men conducting passengers in a small boat (photo 93) and of a laborer carrying a heavy pile of skins on his head (photo 98) bear a striking resemblance to Flaherty's luminous

Black man at a procession.

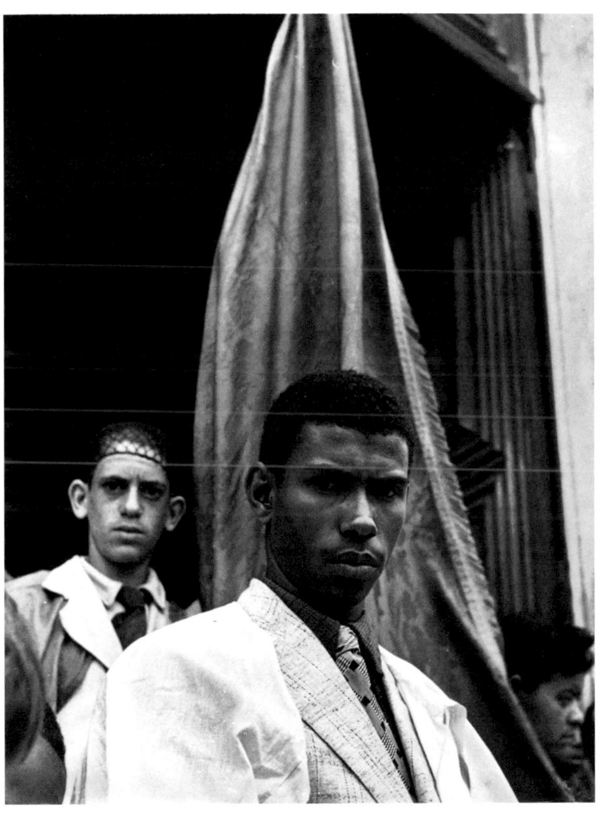

documentaries of common people going about their lives, especially *Man of Aran*, filmed in Ireland. Her photographs of groups (photo 46), and of couples, are very reminiscent of the photographs of her friend, the New York City photographer Arthur Fellig (1899–1968), known as Weegee.[42]

Naylor found photography a heightening experience more akin to music and art than reportage. Photography was for her a way to express wonder at the world around her. The freshness of her photographs of Brazil comes from the fact that she was seeing her subjects for the first time. In contrast to the DIP photographs of Brazil, which, like all propaganda photographs, were too theatrical, her photographs revealed the commonplace to be extraordinary.[43] She found Brazilians to be simple and open, easy to befriend, less pliant than trusting. For an intruder with a large camera, with strange clothes, and lacking the ability to communicate verbally to be able to do this among people for whom the larger world was largely unknown was a special achievement. Naylor's subjects either accept her presence without letting it affect what they are doing or they figuratively wink at the lens, knowing somehow that her presence is a friendly one. Not a few professional photographers have shied away from attempting to work with people from a different society or social class.

Naylor's photographs offer detailed evidence of how people looked and in what settings they lived and worked. More than anything else, Naylor elected to celebrate the strengths of her subjects, not to emphasize their plight or their quality—to outsiders—of being quaint or exotic. She shared her outlook with only a handful of documentary photographers of her day, many

---

42   See Weegee's *Naked City* (New York: Da Capo, 1945) and *The Village* (New York: Da Capo, 1989) as well as *Weegee* (Millerton, N.Y.: Aperture, 1978). For John Ford's films, see the Turner Broadcasting Corporation Web page: www.turner.com/tcm/pressroom/ jford.htm. For Sergei Eisenstein, see *Beyond the Stars*, trans. William Powell (London: BFI Publishing, 1995); Richard Taylor and Ian Christie, eds., *Eisenstein Rediscovered* (London: Routledge, 1993).

43   See Ruth Bernhard statement in *Women of Photography: An Historical Survey* (San Francisco Museum of Art, 1975).

of them women. Like Imogen Cunningham, Naylor was more concerned with the ordinary qualities of her subjects, not their heroic traits. Both Cunningham and Naylor shared respect for differences among people that resisted letting impressions become stereotypes and both rejected compositions that made their subjects seem larger than life. Both tried to penetrate masks, to touch people. Both photographers applied a touch of theater to their compositions—consider Naylor's photographs of religious life of Minas Gerais, for example—but not so much as to detract from the centrality of the people in her range finder.[44]

Like Dorothea Lange, whose work among California migrants a decade earlier brought her acclaim as a documentary photographer and, like Naylor, whose craft was learned in a photo studio, both photographers understood the importance of posing people in their own world, against the backdrop of their livelihoods, and without any attempt to conceal their cameras. Their subjects seemingly became unaware of the photographer's presence. Lange, however, working for Roy Stryker's FSA, logged 17,000 miles photographing victims—of drought, soil erosion, the Depression.

Naylor did not bring back harrowing images from Brazil, because she had been hired explicitly to produce images that would assure American audiences that Brazil was making great strides toward social and economic development. On any given day she could have captured dozens of scenes of pathos, substandard housing, beggars, the close juxtaposition of affluence and poverty that characterized all of Brazil. Instead, she was attracted to compositions that showed men and women and children

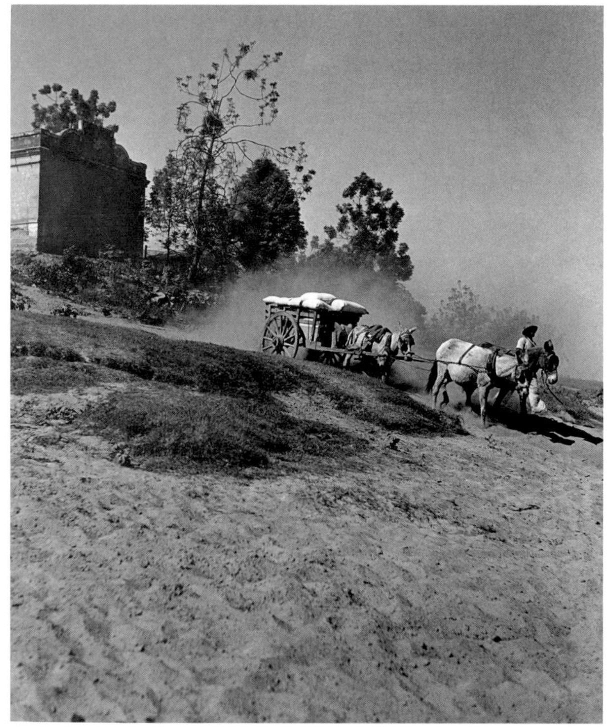

Mule-driven cart.

at ease with their circumstances. A tourist in the best sense of the word, she was able to visit new locations and frame in her viewfinder scenes reflecting her fresh sense of surprise and delight at what she saw. Yet unlike many photographers working far from home, she did not choose subjects for their exoticism; she took photographs to bring out the best in the scenes she photographed. For this reason her compositions reanimate 1940s Brazil. What gives her photographs an even greater appeal is their aesthetics balance. Her photographic compositions were so handsome that they took her beyond the virtuosity of most photojournalists.[45]

---

44 Margaretta Mitchell, introduction to Imogen Cunningham, *After Ninety* (Seattle: University of Washington Press, 1977), 13.

45 See Tadeu Chiarelli, "Casal usa arte para a diplomacia," *Folha de São Paulo*, caderno 2 (November 5, 1994), 4.

If any common thread runs through Naylor's photographs of Brazil, it is her seeming preoccupation with innocence, as James Agee puts it, "not as the word has come to be misunderstood and debased, but in its full, original wildness, fierceness, and instinct for grace and form."[46] This tendency reflects her fascination for children, for Carnival celebrants, for simple people going on with their lives. Sometimes less innocent, her keen eye also brought back depictions of people coping with life. She visited places as bleak as the ones Lange photographed in, but she chose to dwell on images that conveyed a much lower degree of tension, a sense of communion with life. In some ways, though, their careers shared elements in common. Both learned their craft in the United States but photographed abroad. Lange went to Asia in 1958 and four years later to Egypt. Both times Lange experienced feared at entering unknown lands, but, like Naylor, she overcame her reluctance and produced eloquent photographs that captured . . .

Naylor's reaction of sheer delight she expressed when first arriving in Brazil never diminished. Her travels with Reznikoff through the interior stimulated anew her feelings of excitement, which are carried into her photographs. Her photographs document a world entirely unknown to Naylor before she visited it. Like those of Lange, they evoke the feeling, in John Szarkowski's words, that her subjects "are people of exceptional value, proud and independent and competent, who are unlikely to ask for help."[47] As such, they serve for us today as "historical markers of place." It is the natural way Naylor conveyed Brazilian life and the detail she captured in her lens that make her photographic work so important as records of mostly vanished places a half century in the past.

---

46   James Agee, preface to Levitt, *A Way of Seeing*, xiii.

47   Szarkowski was writing about Lange, but the description is apt for Naylor as well. See his *Photography Until Now* (1989), cited in Sarah Boxer, "How the Other Half Defines Its Image," *New York Times*, April 30, 1995, E6.

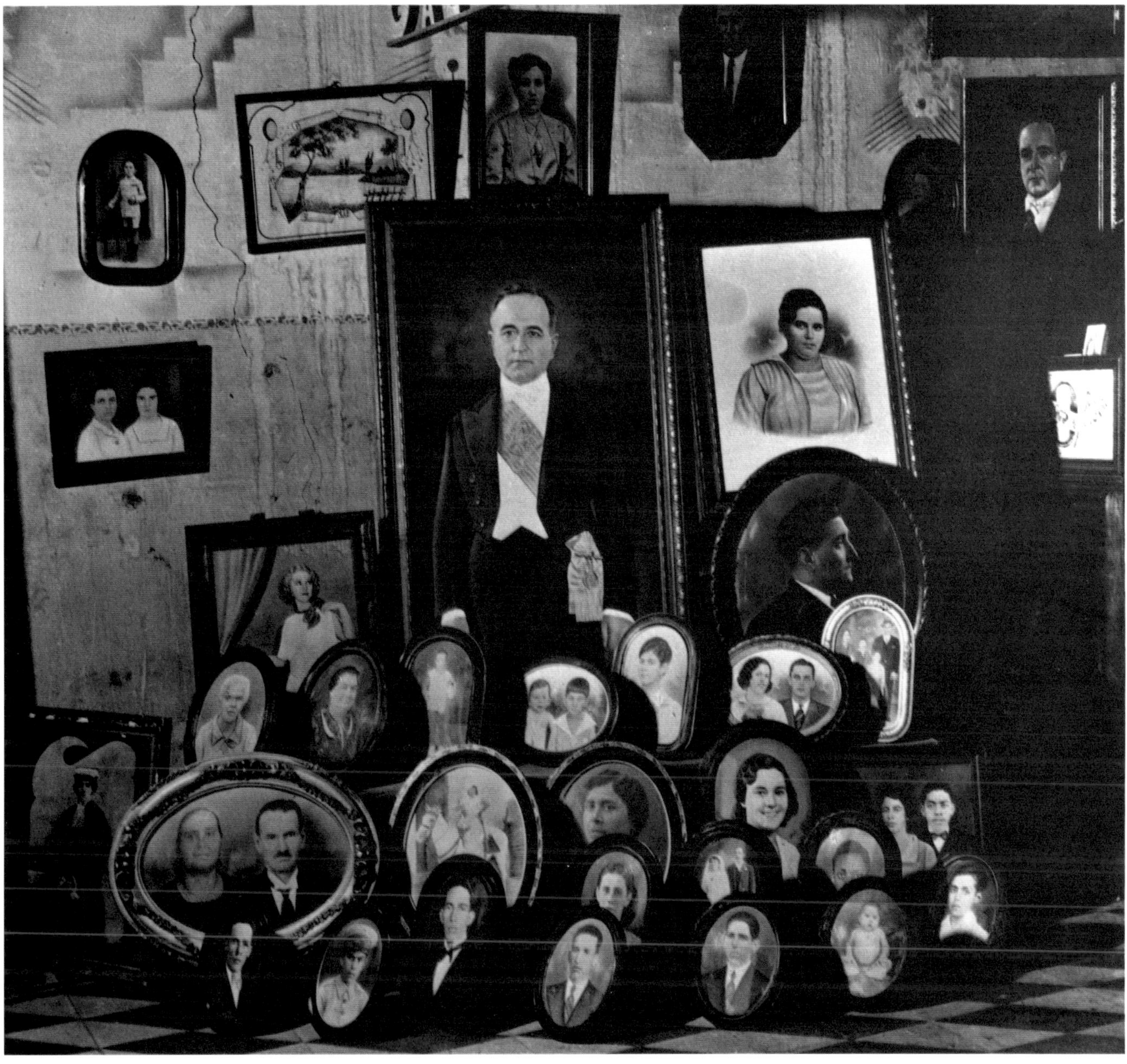

I PORTRAITS

The framed official presidential portrait of Getúlio Vargas sits surrounded by smaller family photographs in a studio display. There is a second Vargas photograph on the wall, suggesting that the studio was not only honoring Vargas but selling his images. One or more of the smaller photographs may also be of Getúlio when he was young. In her composition, Naylor captures the way that the Estado Novo pervaded people's lives during the early 1940s—not in the aggressive manner of Mussolini or Hitler, but in a manner that integrated Vargas's presence paternalistically into the fabric of normal life.

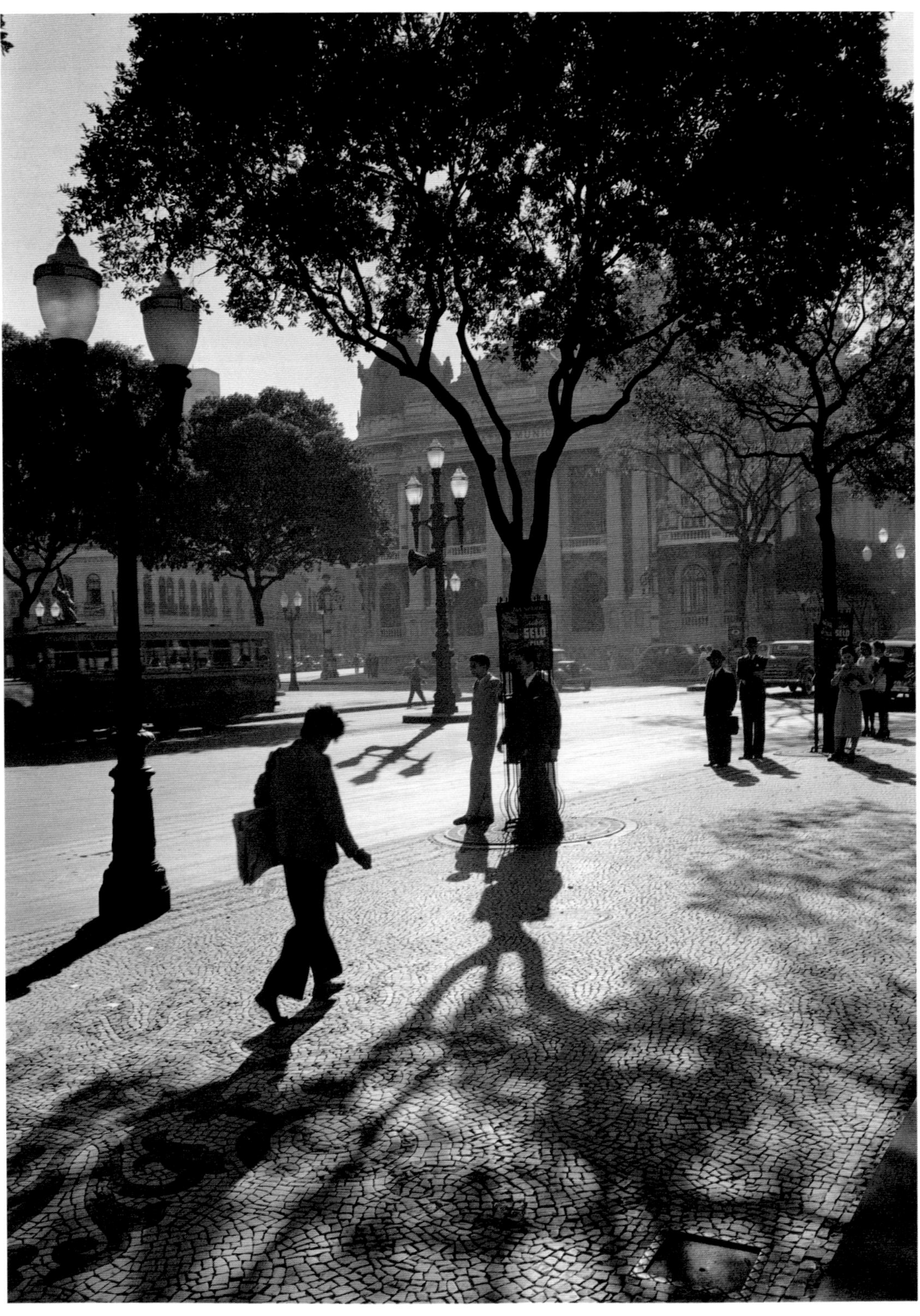

2 STREET SCENE

In this lovely view of downtown Rio de Janeiro late in the day facing the Teatro Municipal (Opera House) and taken from in front of the National Library, Naylor contrasts the tired and barefoot newspaper vendor selling a late edition of one of Rio's many afternoon dailies, with the well-dressed pedestrians waiting for public transportation or taxis. There is also a trolley in the scene, one of the many *bondes*, so called because their purchase was financed by municipal "bonds." The long afternoon shadows highlight not only the mood but accentuate the elegant mosaic patterns of the pavement, a masonry technique brought from Portugal.

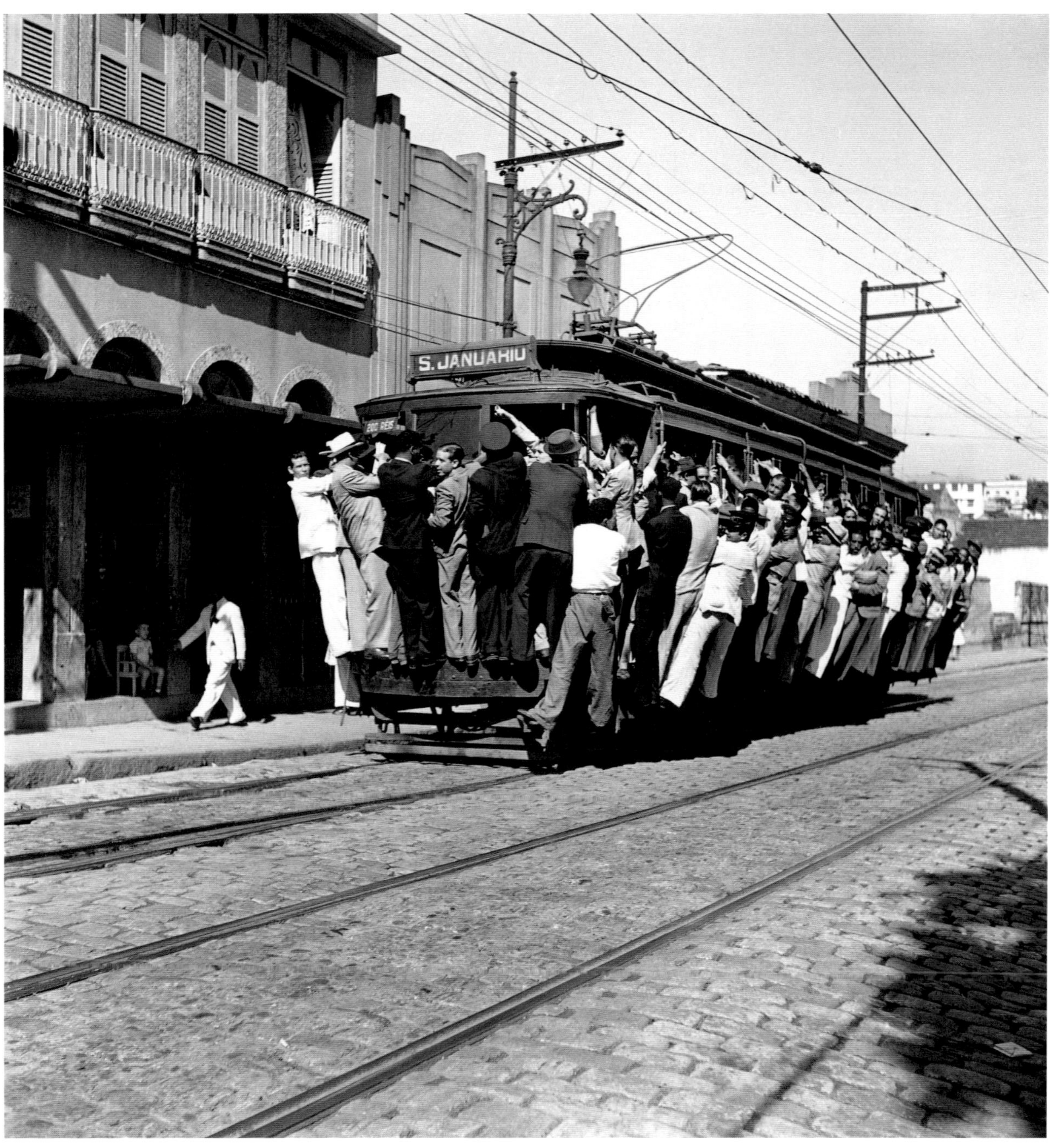

3 SÃO JANUÁRIO TROLLEY

Passengers riding the bondes risked their lives by holding on in
this manner, but the conveyance was inexpensive and missing
one meant a long wait.

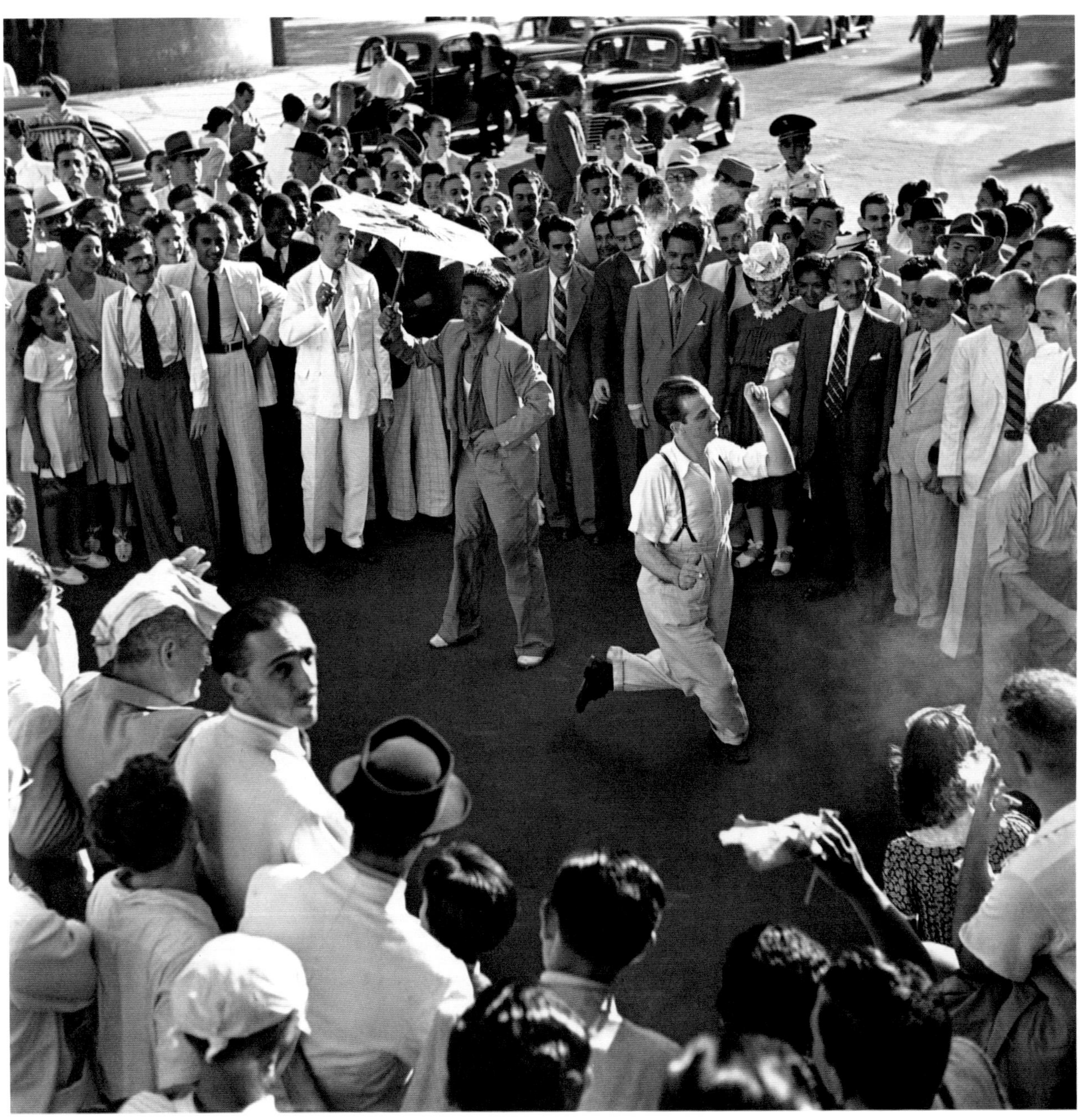

Many people had to make a living in the informal, or underground, economy. Every public square was filled with magicians, escape artists, poets who dueled with improvised verses, and dancers. Naylor captured the scene at a relaxed point in the performance. These dancers are performing the *frevo*, an intricate dance native to the Northeast during which dancers carry umbrellas.

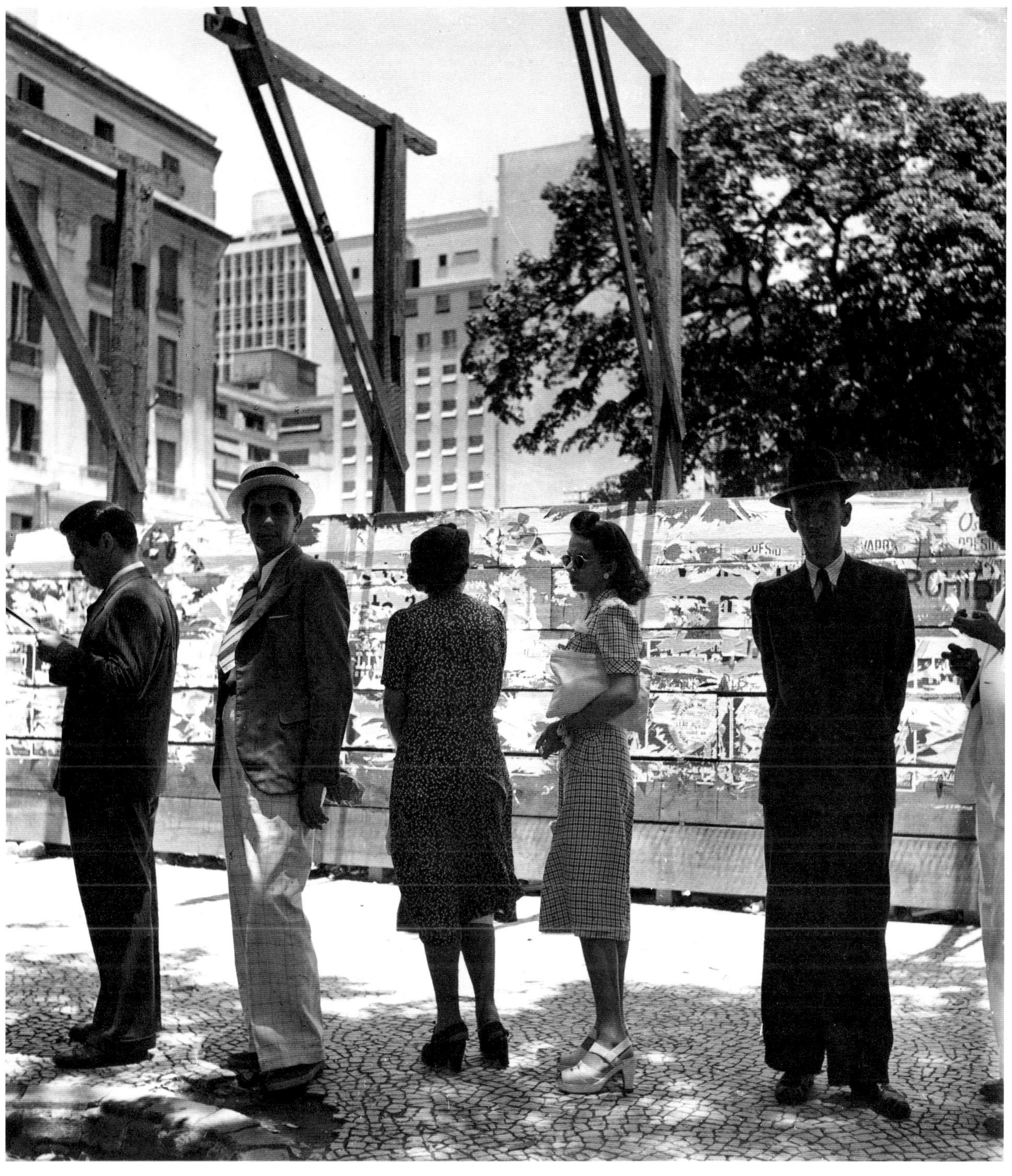

5 IN LINE

The camera captures some well-dressed pedestrians waiting for
a bus or a trolley.

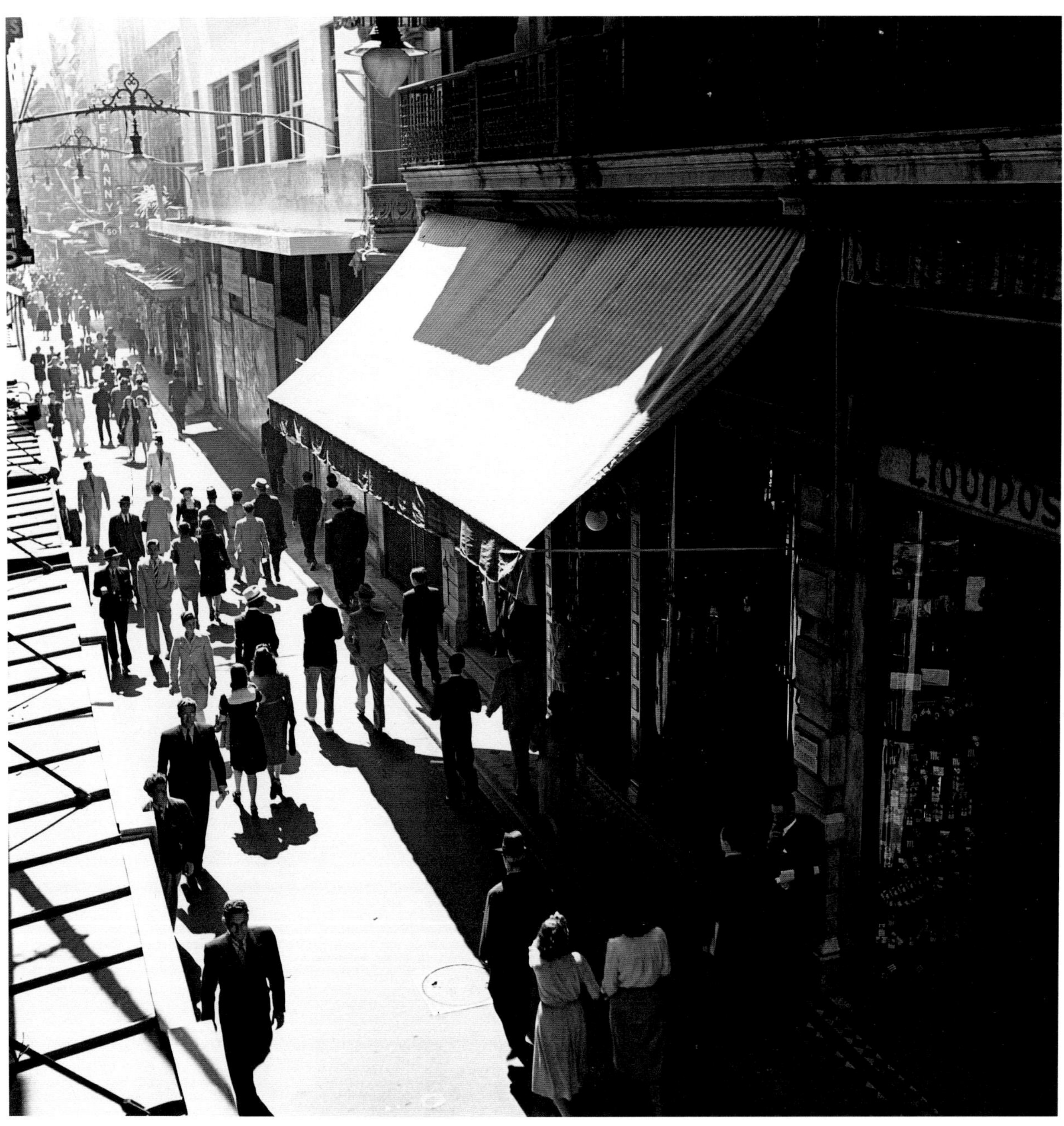

6 PEDESTRIANS

Some of the streets winding from the port through the commercial district were so narrow that they became in effect pedestrian malls, although at different times of day they would be thronged with hand-pulled delivery carts and wagons. Most of the city's elegant stores were in this district—women's clothing boutiques, where seated customers were served tea and shown modeled outfits; jewelers; mens' haberdashery. There were also shops that sold ranch equipment (saddles, knives, riding boots) and others that sold guns and rifles.

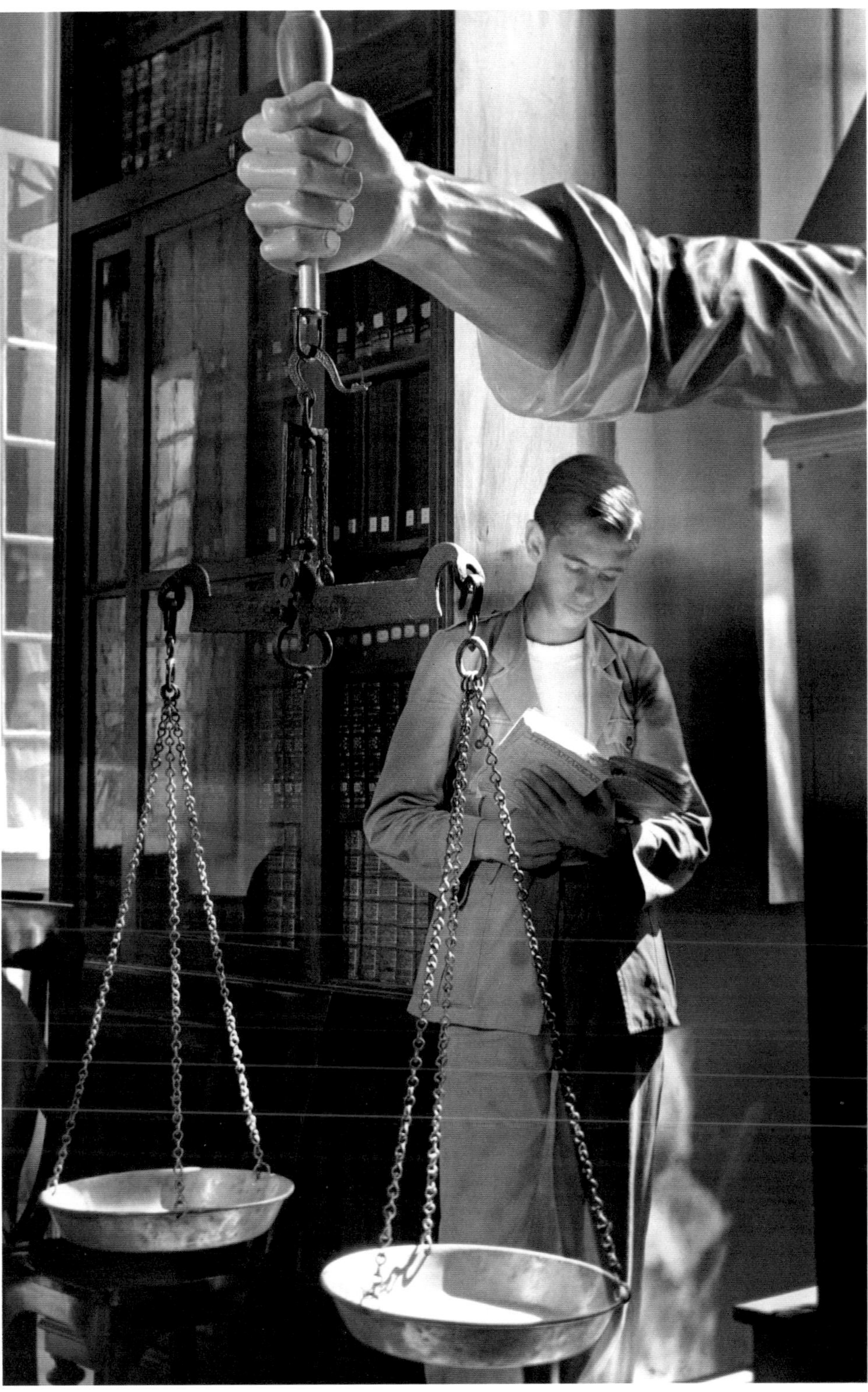

Rio de Janeiro's downtown commercial district was filled not only with shops but law and notarial offices where people could get documents authenticated or registered. This is probably either a law office or a room in the Justice Ministry. The wall cabinet is lined with tall leather-bound books. The boy reads a magazine, adding a human dimension to the otherwise contrived composition. This photograph is more obviously posed than most of Naylor's, and it presents the kind of composition that her OIAA and DIP supervisors preferred.

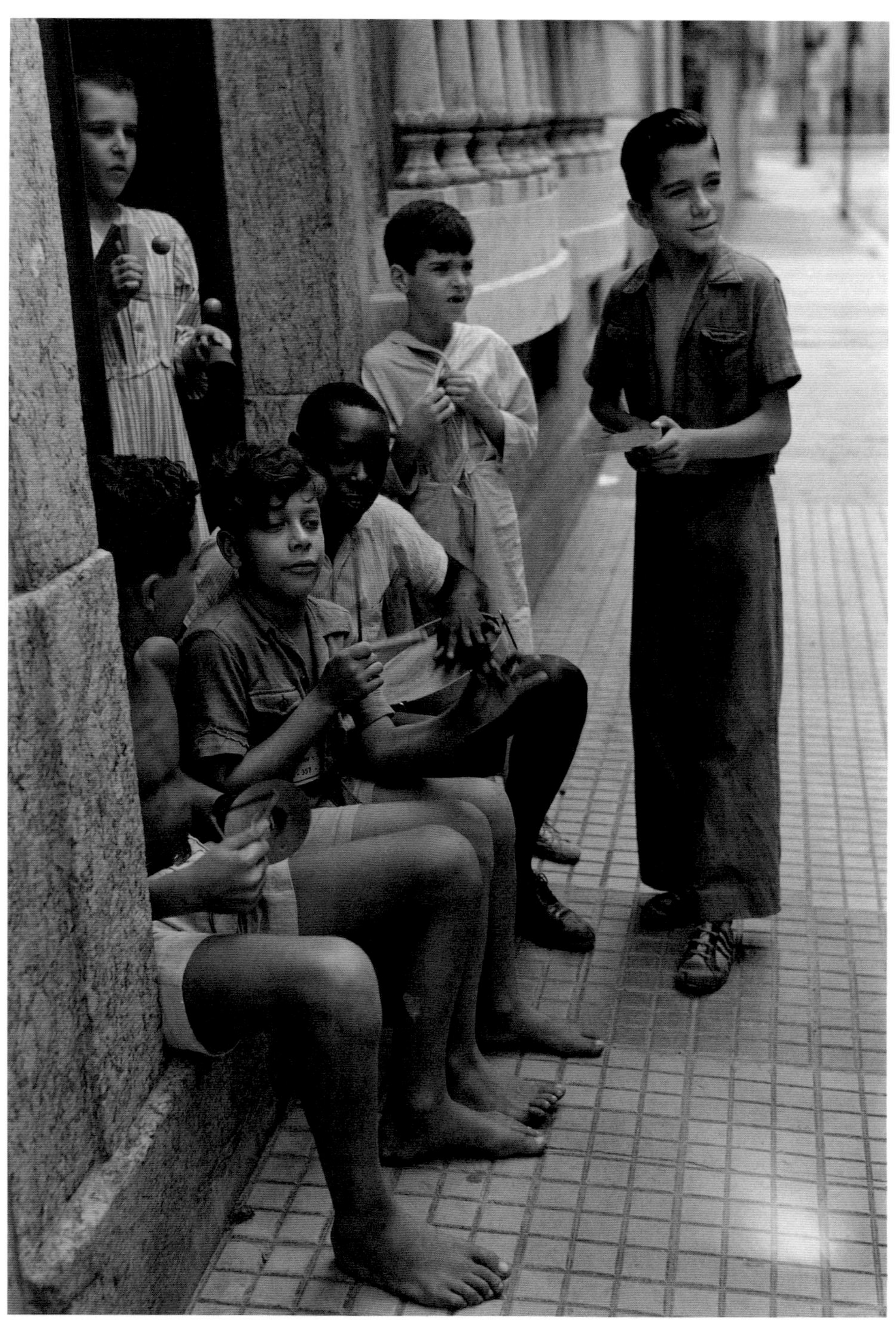

8 BOYS ON SIDEWALK

Naylor's camera invariably captured ordinary people with warmth. One boy (who is wearing wing-tip shoes) is black, another is mulatto, and the rest are white. They hold homemade percussion instruments; it is likely Carnival time. The scene is possibly taken in Botafogo, a residential neighborhood filled with apartment houses facing the famous Sugar Loaf across the bay, or in Catete, the district adjacent to Vargas's presidential palace. The photograph affirms the saying that Brazil was a racial democracy—at least for preadolescent children. In urban districts white children played without affectedness with the children of maids, although when they became teenagers class (and racial) lines suddenly deepened.

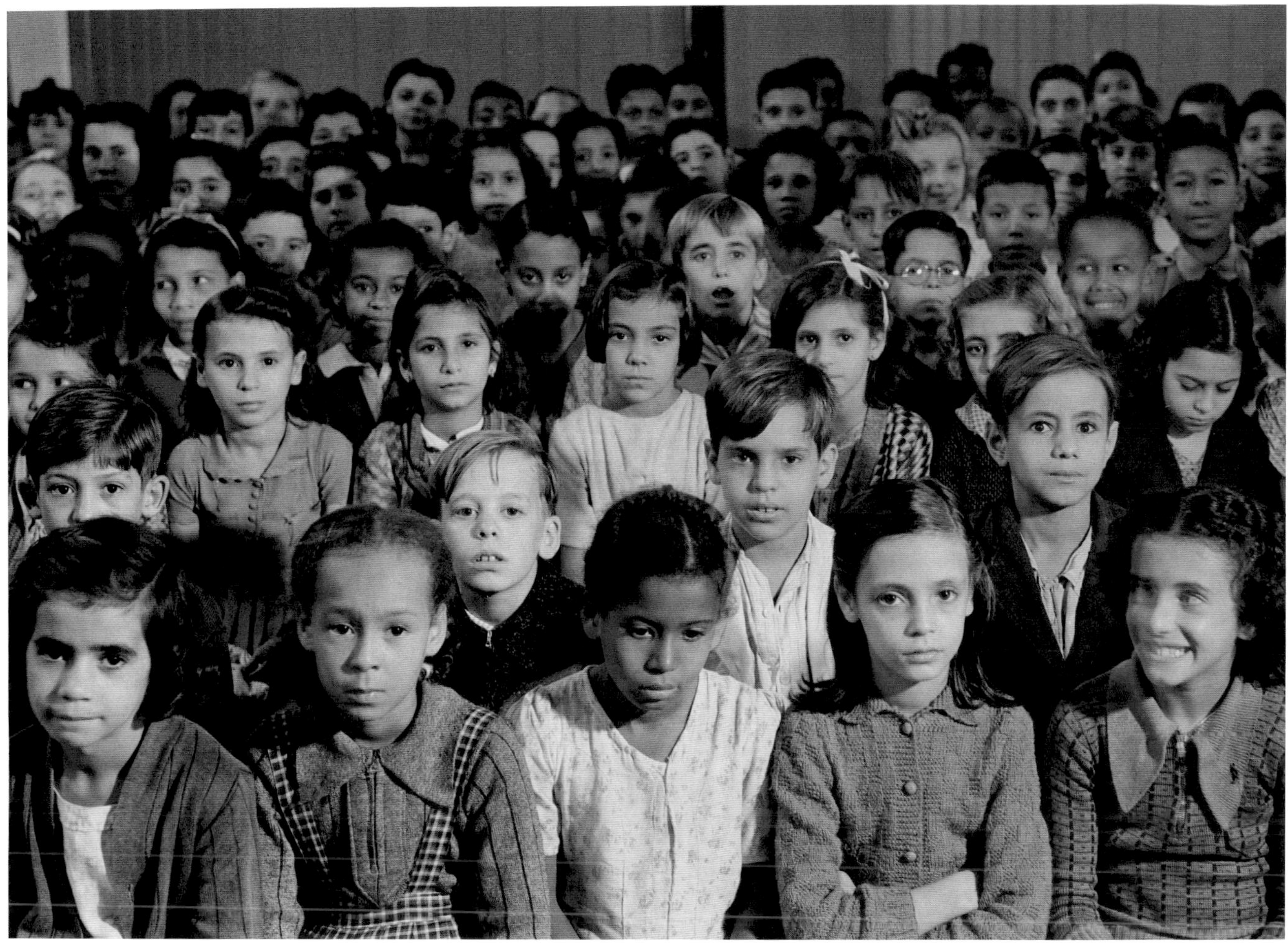

9 CHILDREN

This photograph of a large group encompasses a broad spectrum of race and ethnicity from dark-complexioned youths to a boy with straight blond hair.

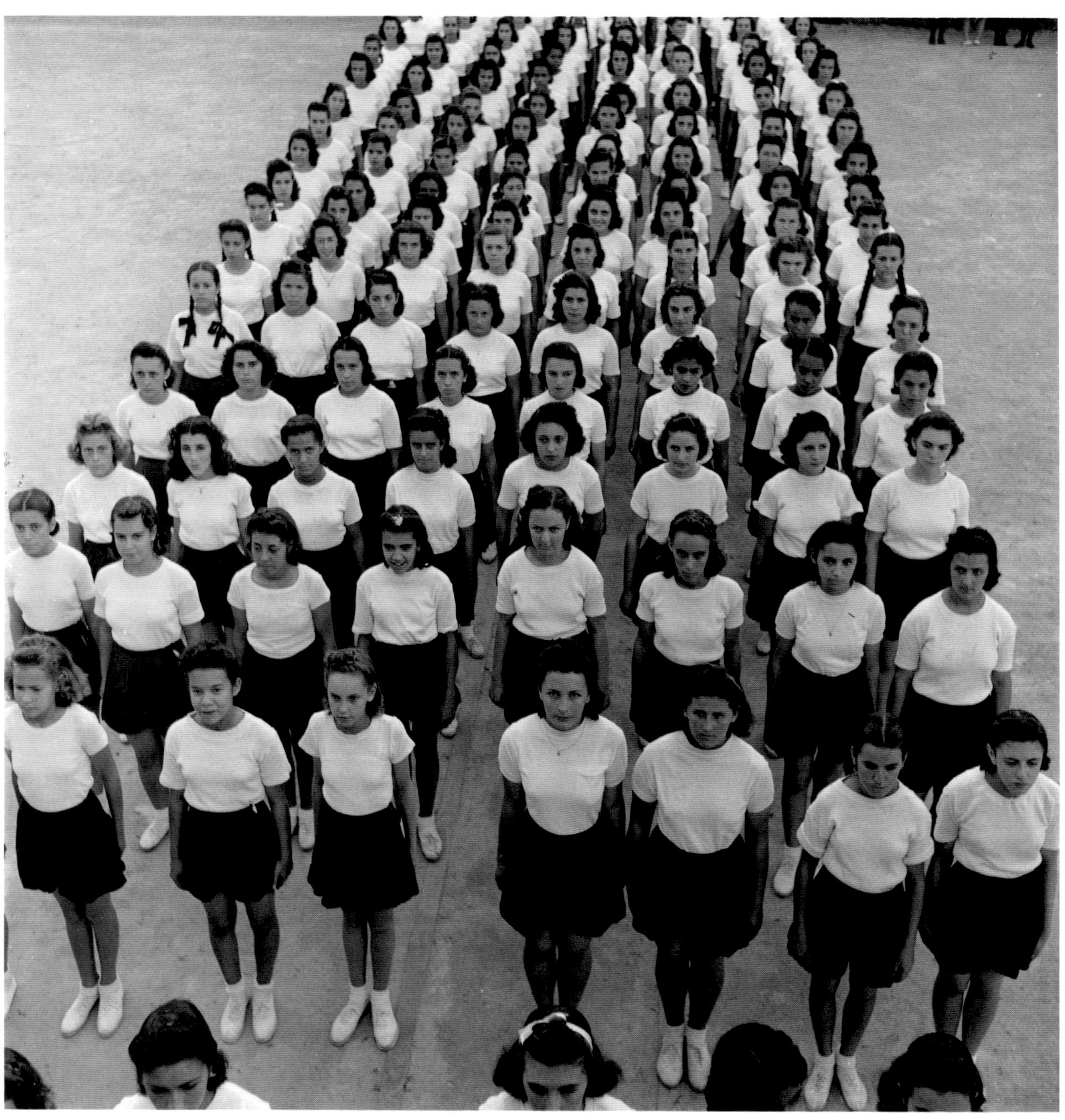

10 OUTDOOR PAGEANTRY

Naylor captures the militarylike regimentation that Vargas and his generals attempted to instill during the Estado Novo, an influence reminiscent of Portuguese or Spanish fascism. Schoolgirls gather in formation, probably during one of the frequent outdoor pageants held to celebrate civic occasions, perhaps Independence Day. A close look at the girls, however, shows that most are relaxed. Some are smiling; a few have their eyes on the camera. There was little of Mussolini's Italy or Hitler's Germany in Vargas's Brazil.

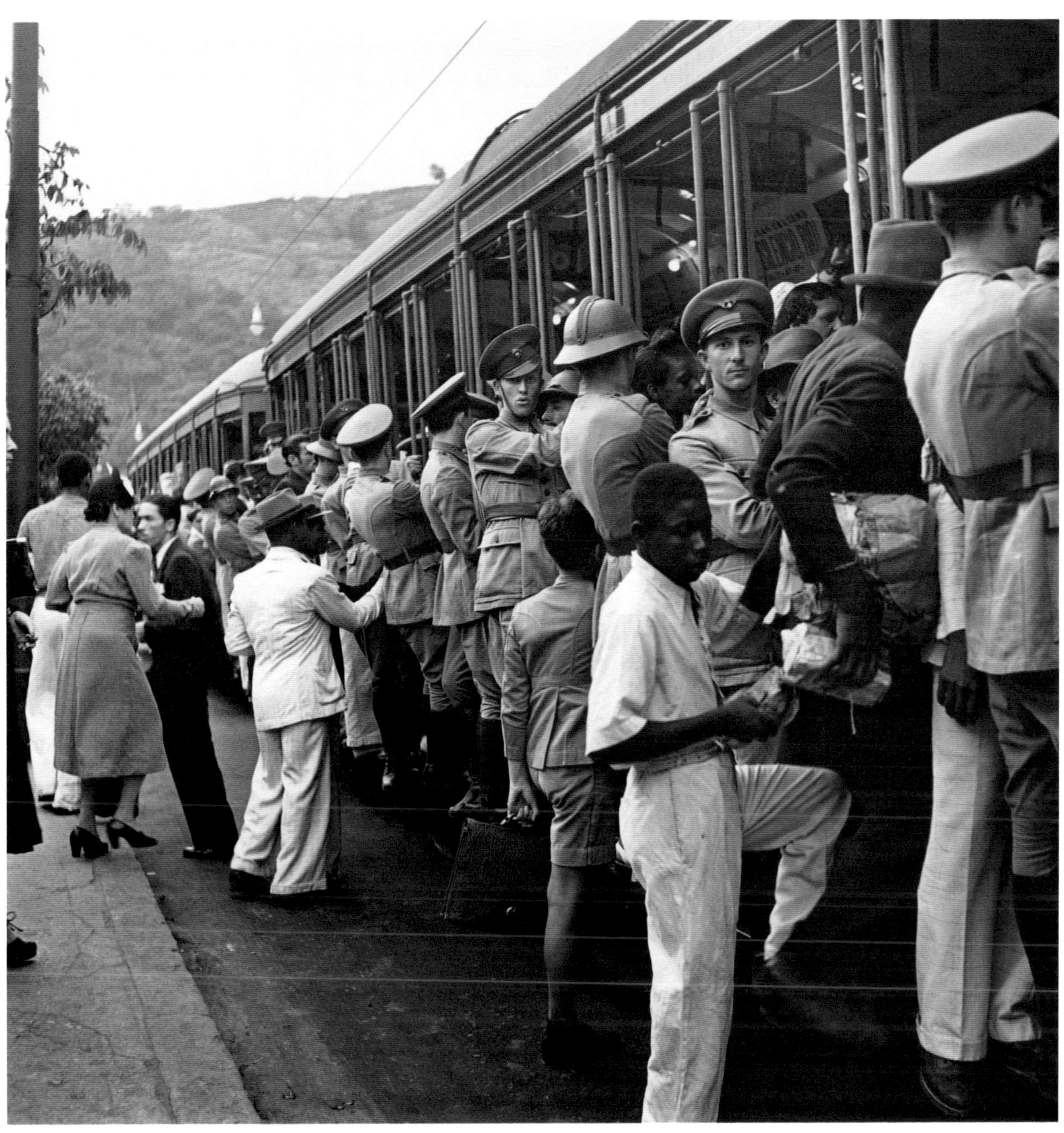

11 SOLDIERS BOARDING TRAIN

Soldiers in uniform appear to have been given first crack at the right to hold on to the sides of the two-car train. Other interesting people are found in the scene as well: a young boy wearing a militarylike suit (is he a cadet?); a black youth in ragged trousers who seems not to have found a place; a civilian man in suit and hat holding paper-wrapped packages who seems to be boarding the train as if to go inside. The photograph captures the racial mix of the population and the ease with which civilians mingled with soldiers.

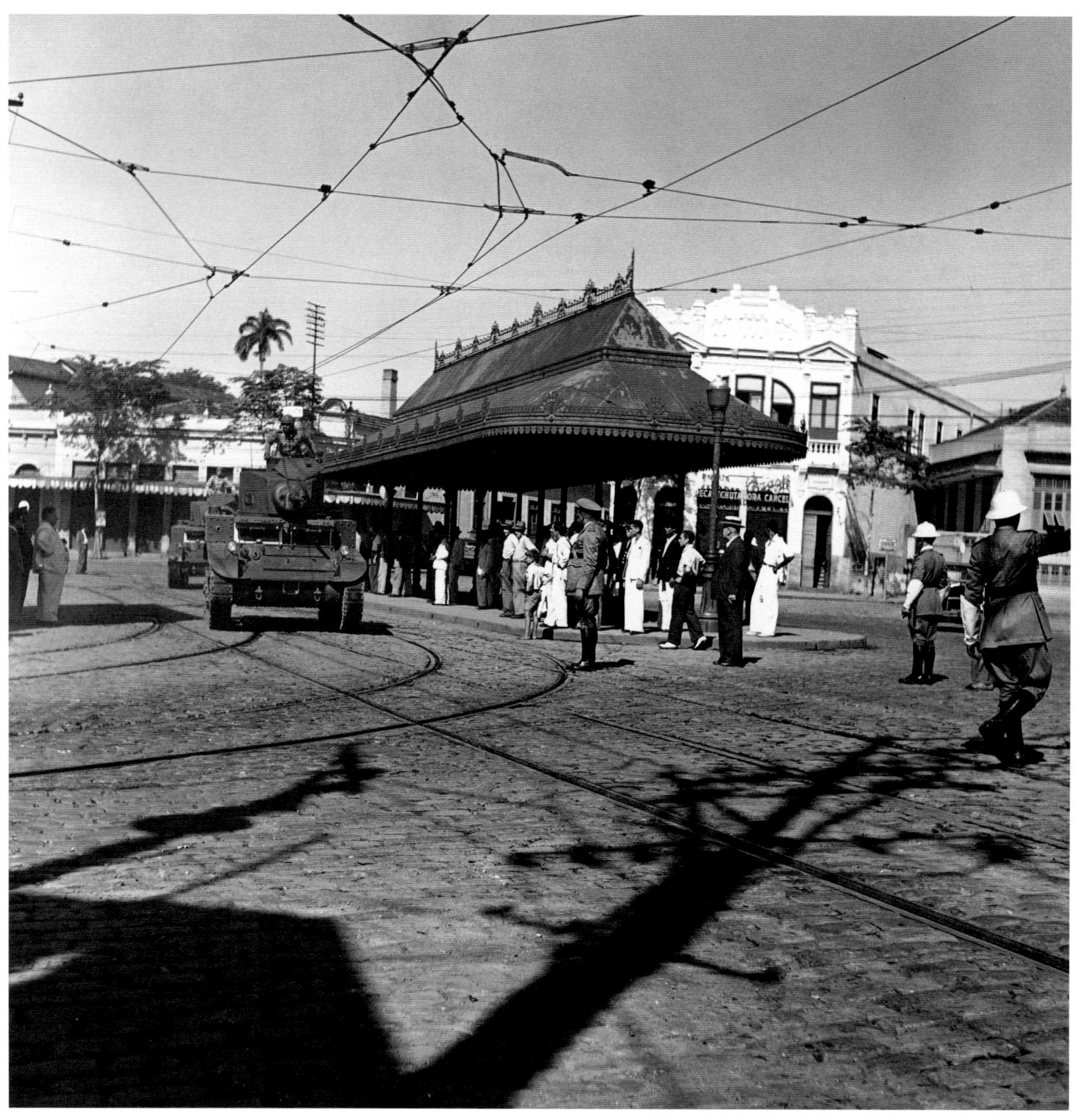

12 TANKS IN THE CITY

The presence of the armed forces was constant during the Estado Novo, although Vargas did not enjoy military parades, which are usually a hallmark of dictatorships. Here, armored vehicles follow the trolley tracks as they travel through the city.

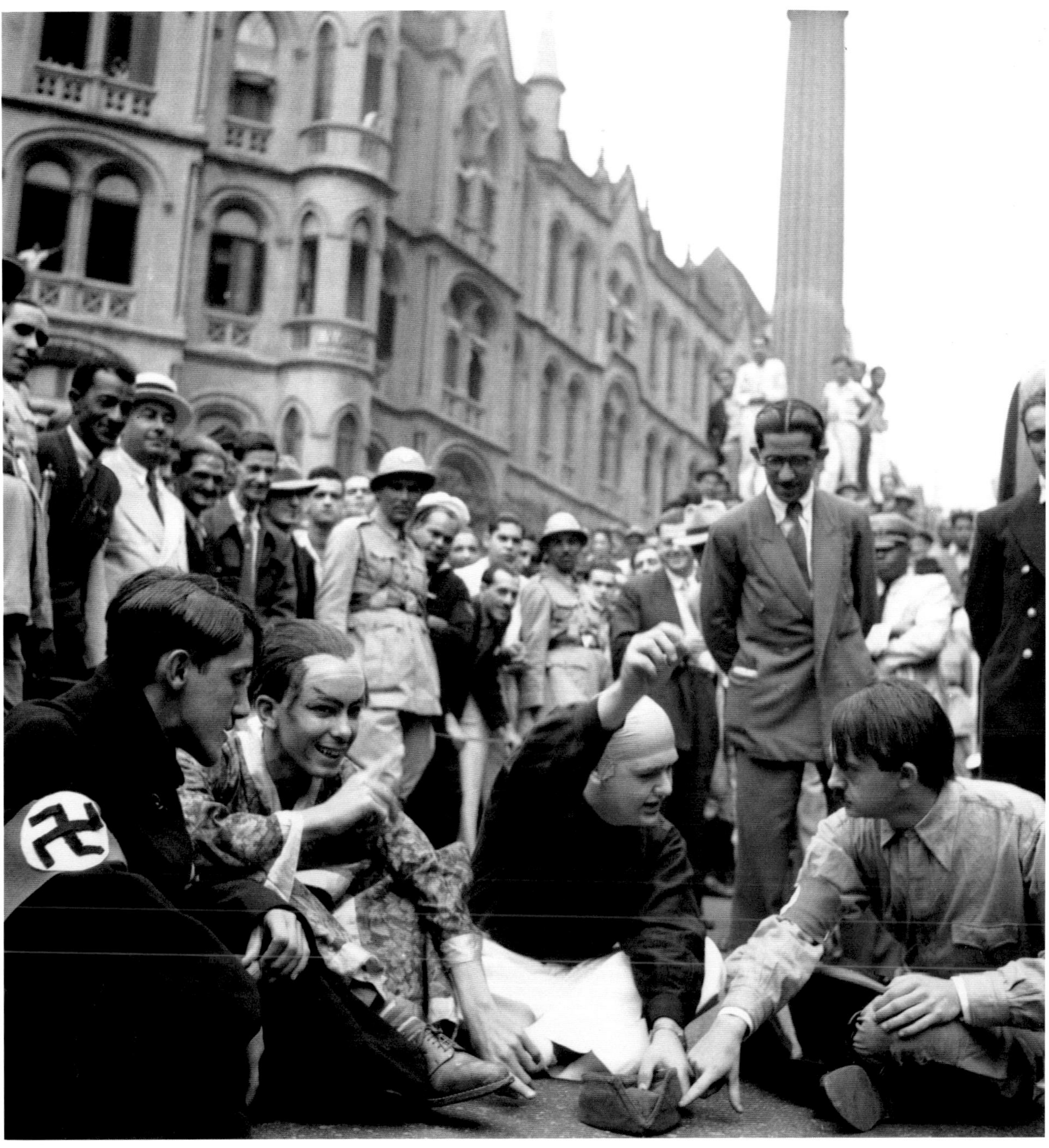

Youths dress up as Hitler, Mussolini, and the Japanese emperor in a spoof of the Axis powers. A crowd of well-dressed passersby watch, as do two uniformed policemen. Had this group at-tempted to stage such a performance before Brazil declared war on the Axis, the youths would have faced arrest and the crowd would not have been as docile.

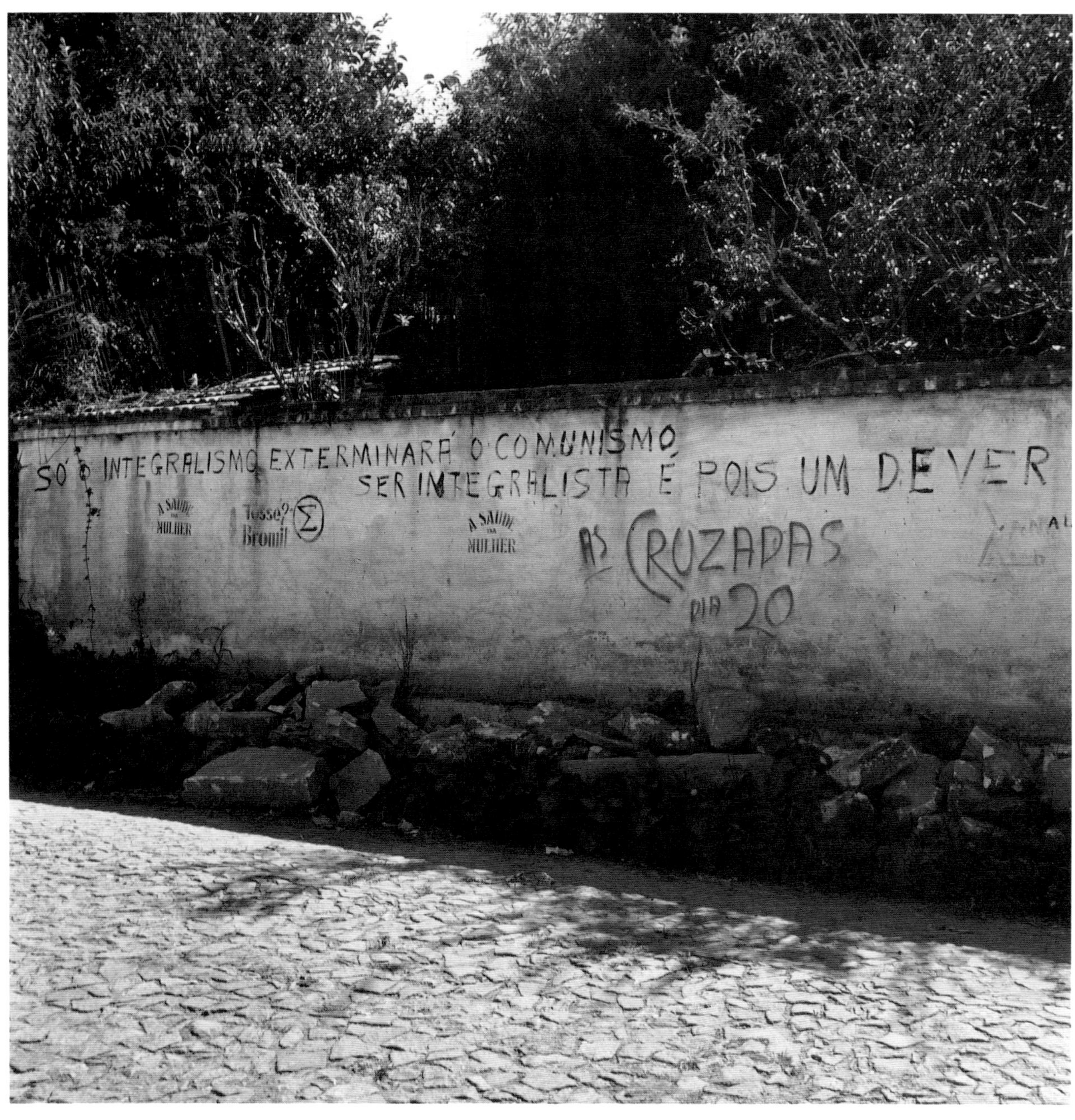

14 PRO-FASCIST GRAFFITI

Despite Vargas's ban on political organizations in 1938, members of the fascist Integralist movement came out at night to paint slogans on walls, as did the communists. The saying reads, "Integralism will exterminate communism, / To be an Integralist is an obligation." The Greek letter Σ was the Integralist symbol. The wall also holds stenciled messages advertising Bromil, a remedy sold to women.

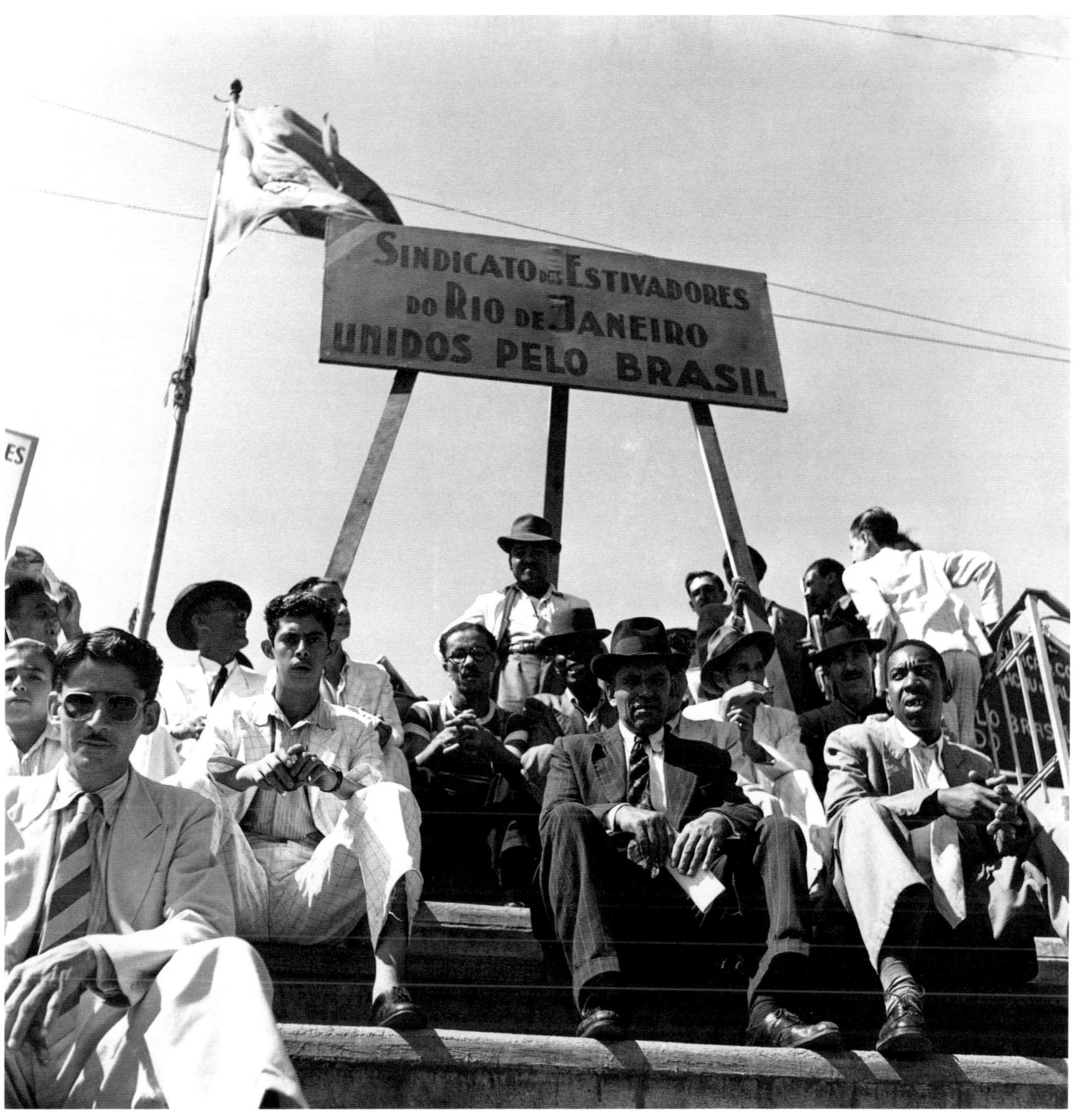

15 LABOR RALLY

These seated men are *pelegos*, labor officials on the government payroll for the purpose of mobilizing workers in support of the regime. Their sign identifies them as representing the Stevedores' Union. The men are too well dressed to be dockworkers, most of whom wore clothing made from burlap sacks and who worked under extremely arduous conditions. Some of the pelegos are black, a characteristic of Vargas's inclusive policies.

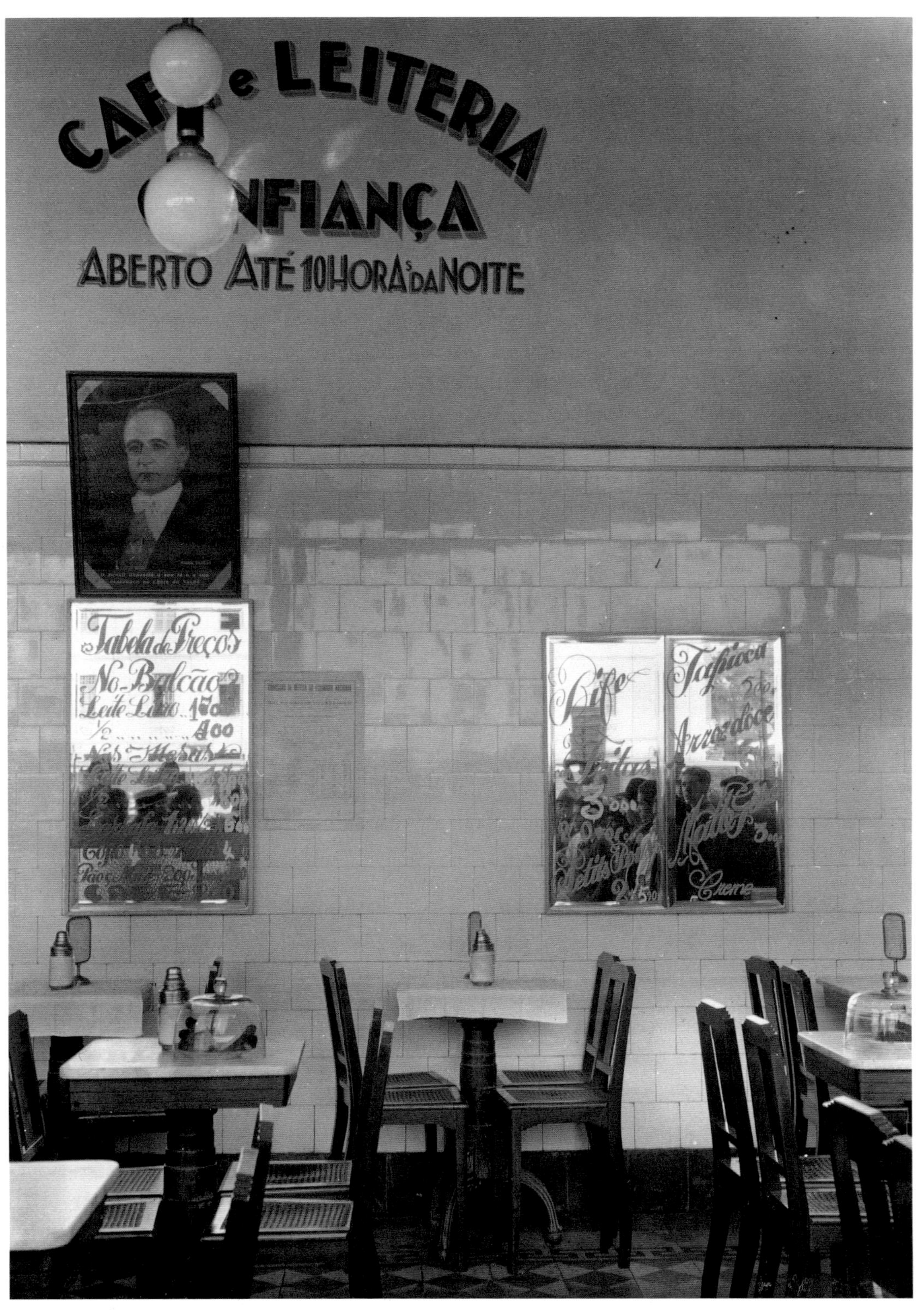

16 INTERIOR OF RESTAURANT

Some of the buildings in the commercial district housed *leiterias* (Minas-style restaurants), whose menus offered traditional *mineiro* dishes—rice and beans with greens and beef, fish prepared from recipes originally from Portugal, omelets with rice, desserts of goat cheese and jellied guava paste. All restaurants had to post their prices. A steak with fried potatoes costs $3000 milréis, worth about $1.50 today; tapioca pudding costs $500, or

$.25. Patrons who chose to eat standing up at a ledge outside the restaurant paid lower prices for the same food; some of them may be seen reflected in the wall mirrors on which the menu was written. The ubiquitous portrait of Vargas hangs above one of the mirrors. By photographing the interior without patrons or restaurant employees, Naylor accentuates the rich if sparse detail of the scene.

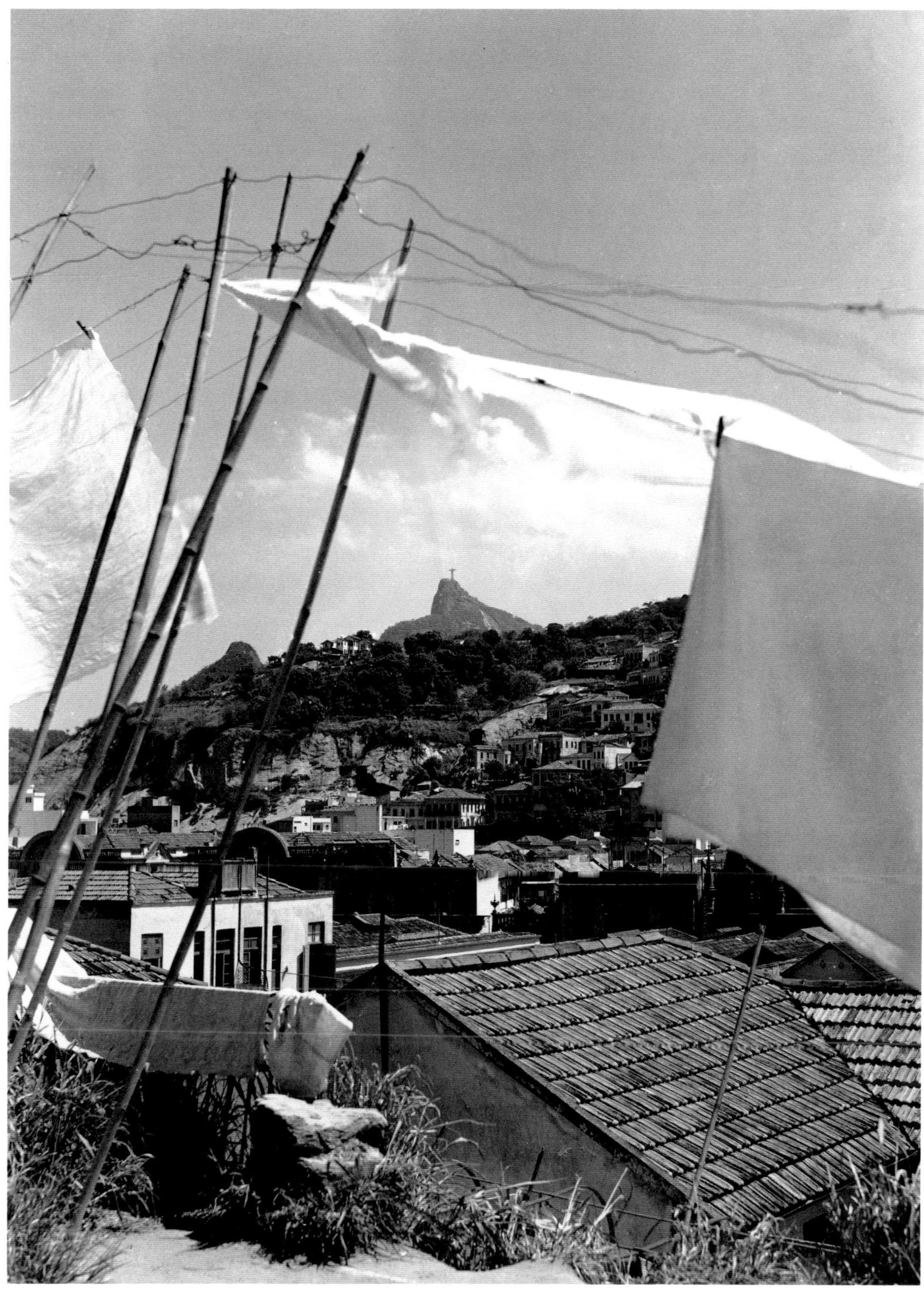

Rio's statue of Christ the Redeemer, inaugurated less than a decade before Naylor's arrival in Brazil, centers this composition framed by drying bed clothing hanging from wires. The houses are solidly constructed—these are not slums—with tiled roofs and stuccoed cinder-block construction. No people seem to be present, although the washed clothes testify to their presence. She may have photographed this from a shack or a favela to the rear of the scene, but it would have been out of character for her to have shot farther back (and therefore contrast poverty with the more solidly built houses in front of her). Knowingly or not, by photographing clothing hanging to dry, Naylor paid homage to a nostalgic element in popular culture, whereby songwriters and others romanticized domestic life by referring often to clothes drying in the breeze.

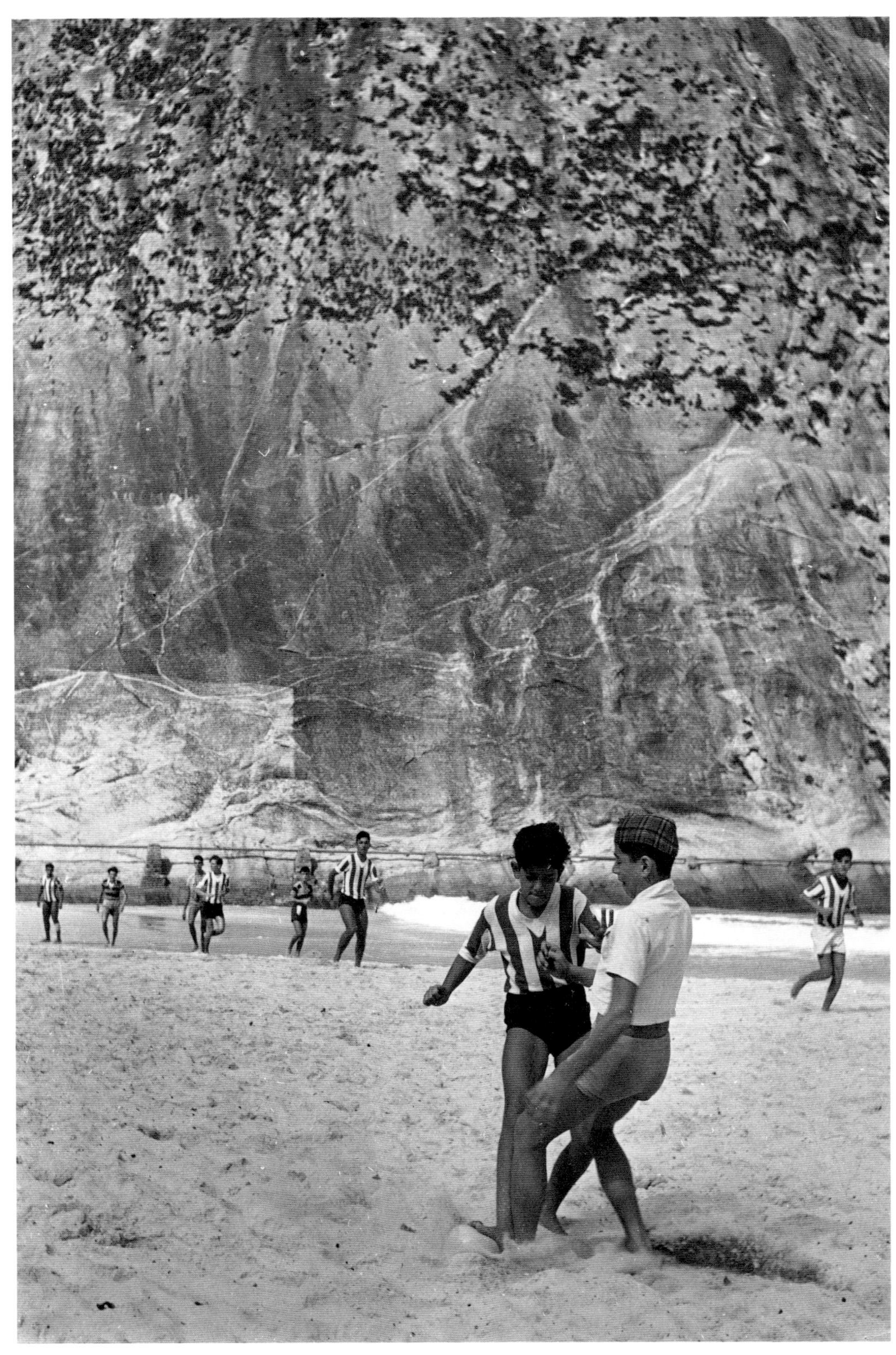

 SOCCER PLAYERS AT URCA BEACH

The towering cliffs of Sugar Loaf Mountain dwarf the soccer-
playing youths, most of them wearing club uniforms, possibly
provided by a team sponsor. Soccer was a way of life for Brazilian youths, and it was played constantly.

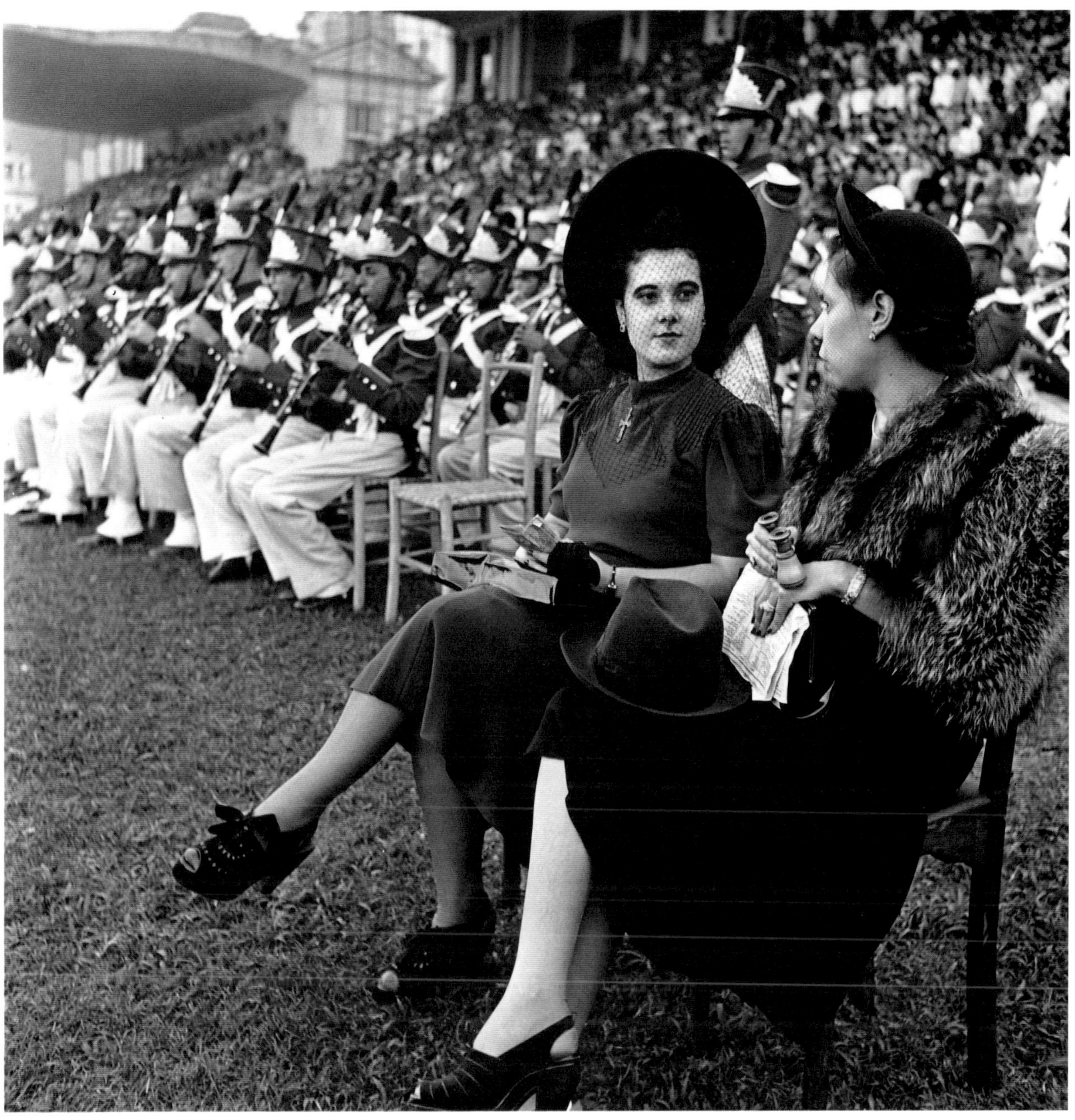

19 JOCKEY CLUB

Two elegantly clad society women sit alongside a band of musicians. Their privileged status is revealed not only by their dress (who else would wear a fur coat in Rio de Janeiro?) but by the location of their seats.

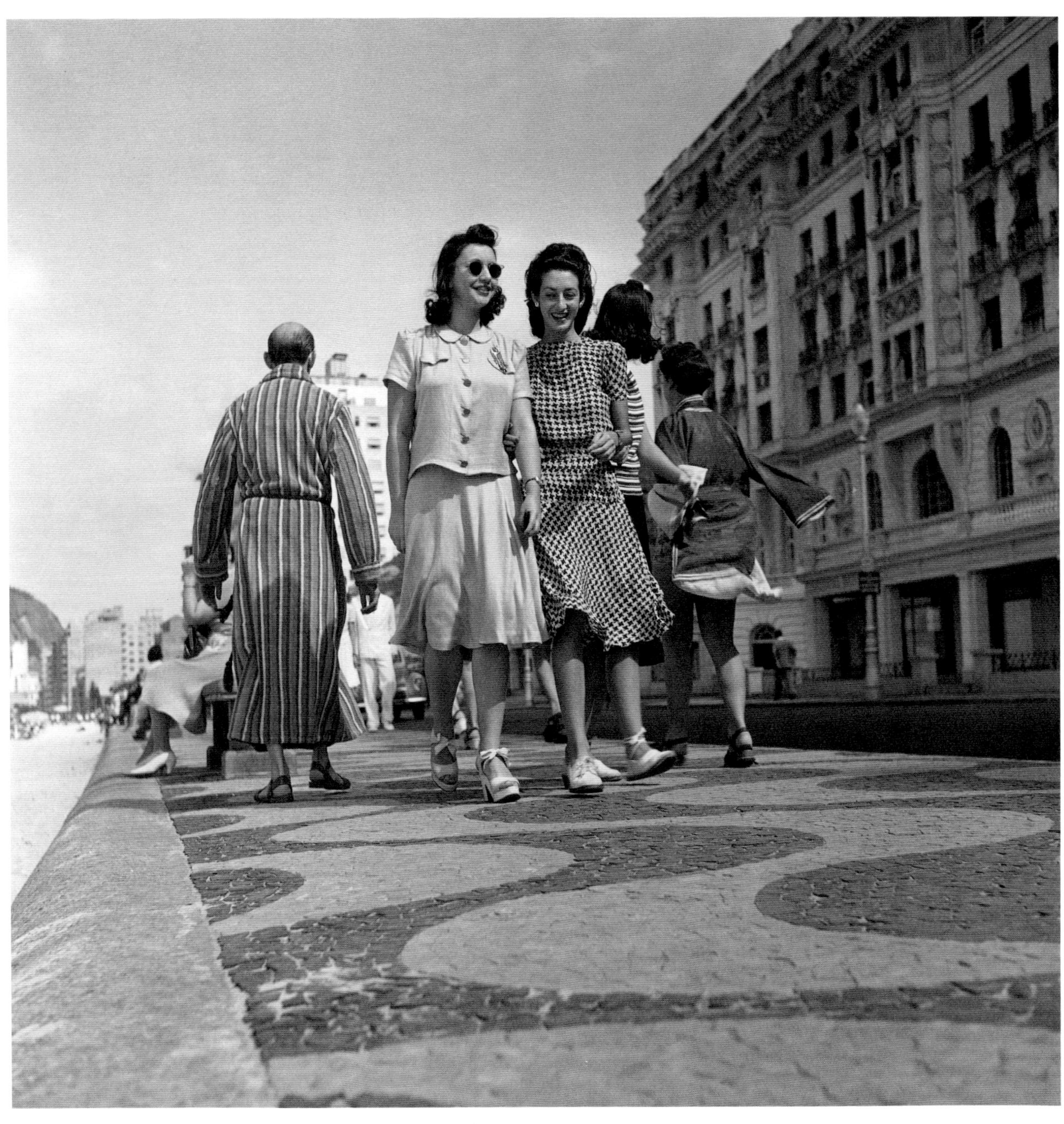

Fashionably dressed women walk in one direction while a man in his bathrobe and sandals walks in the other. They are walking in front of the Copacabana Palace Hotel. In rural areas and small cities it long had been the custom for men to sit outside their homes wearing their pajamas, but Copacabana by the early 1940s had attained an aura of glamour, so such attire was becoming less commonplace.

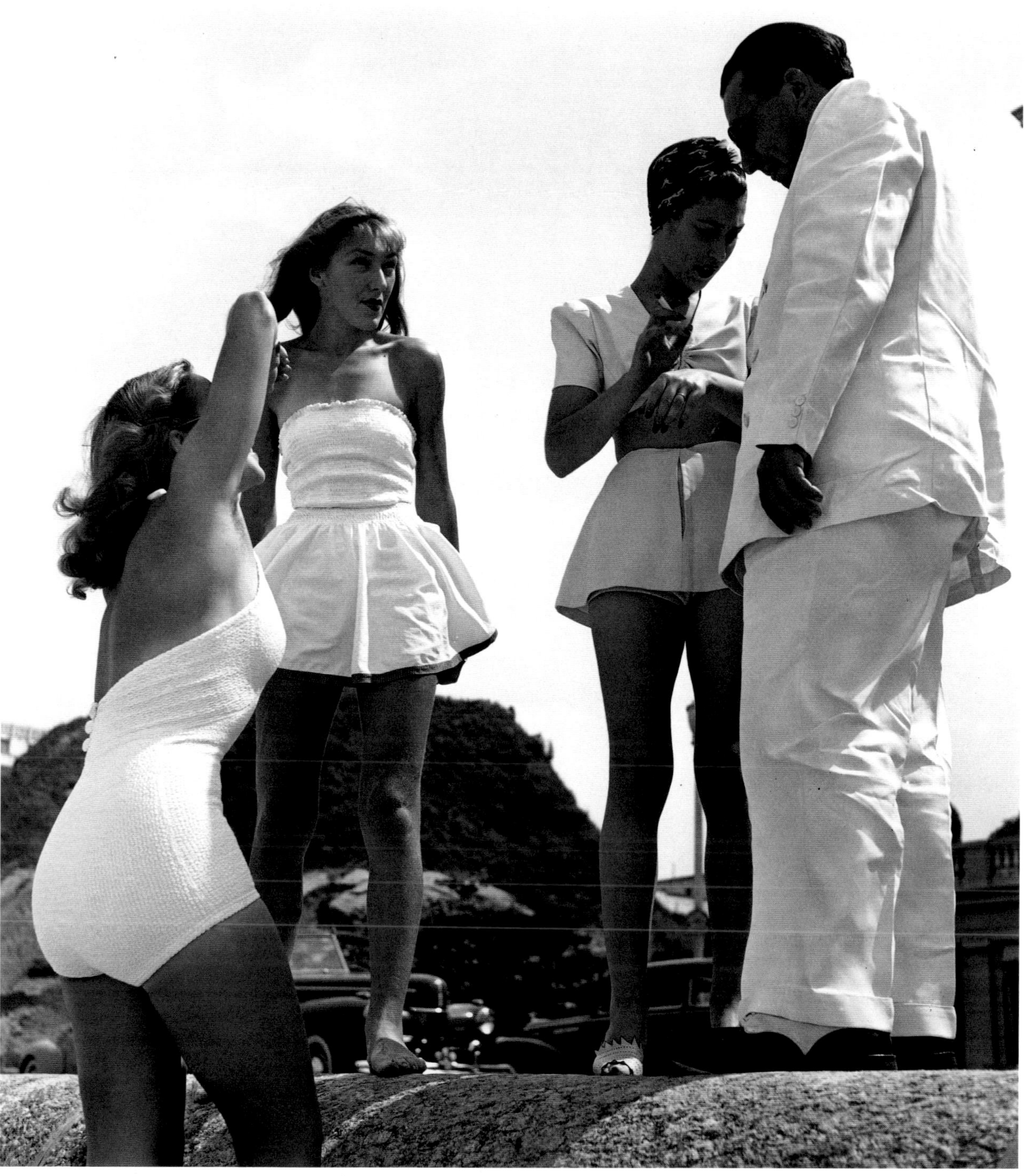

21 BATHING COSTUMES

Three young women stand on the edge of Copacabana in a portion of the beachfront zone where high-rise houses have not yet taken root.

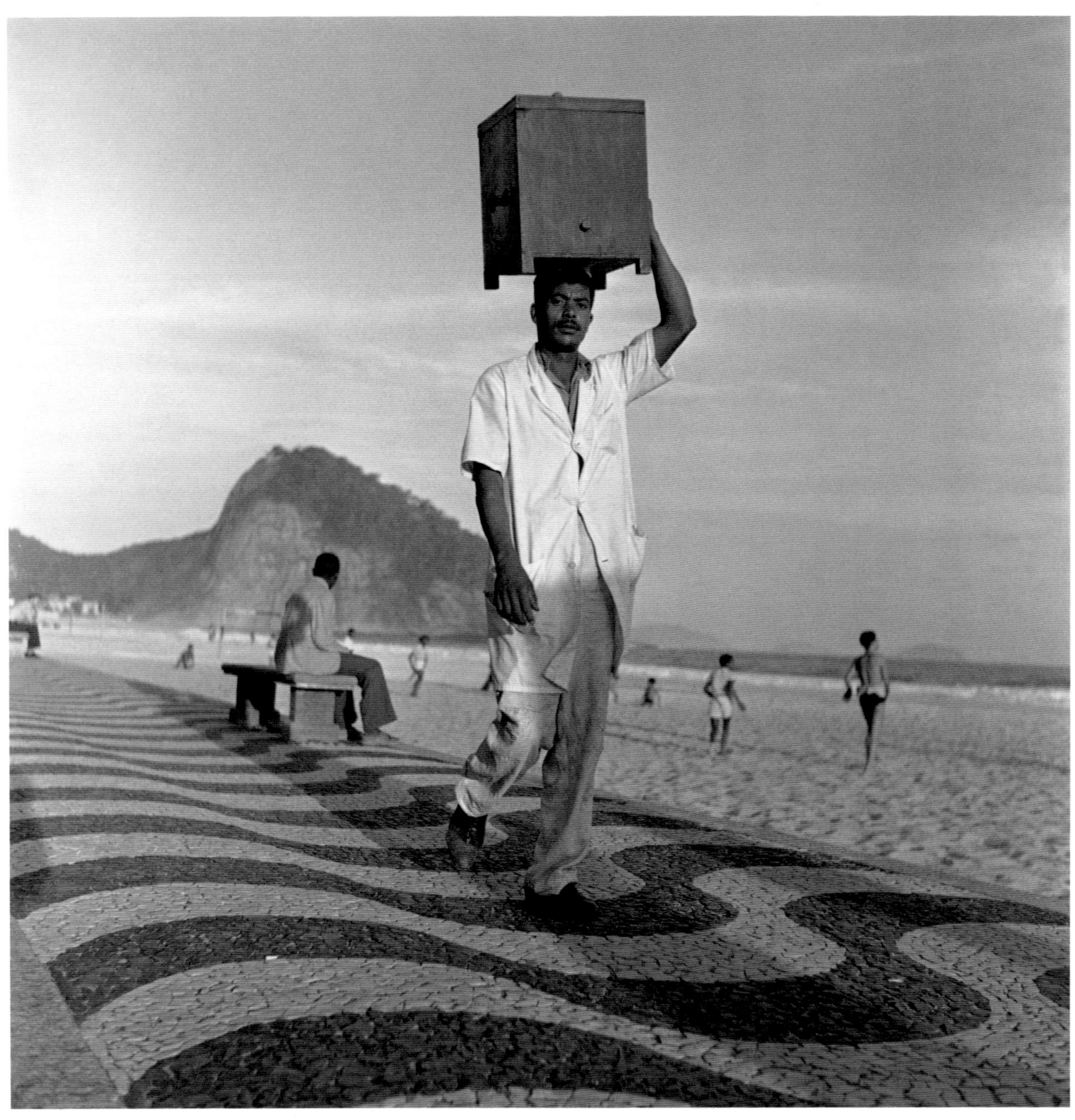

22 ALONG THE BEACH

A man walks along the beachfront. Here Naylor captures the
wild setting of Copacabana: tree-lined Sugar Loaf beyond Urca,
and the hills in Niteroi across Guanabara Bay.

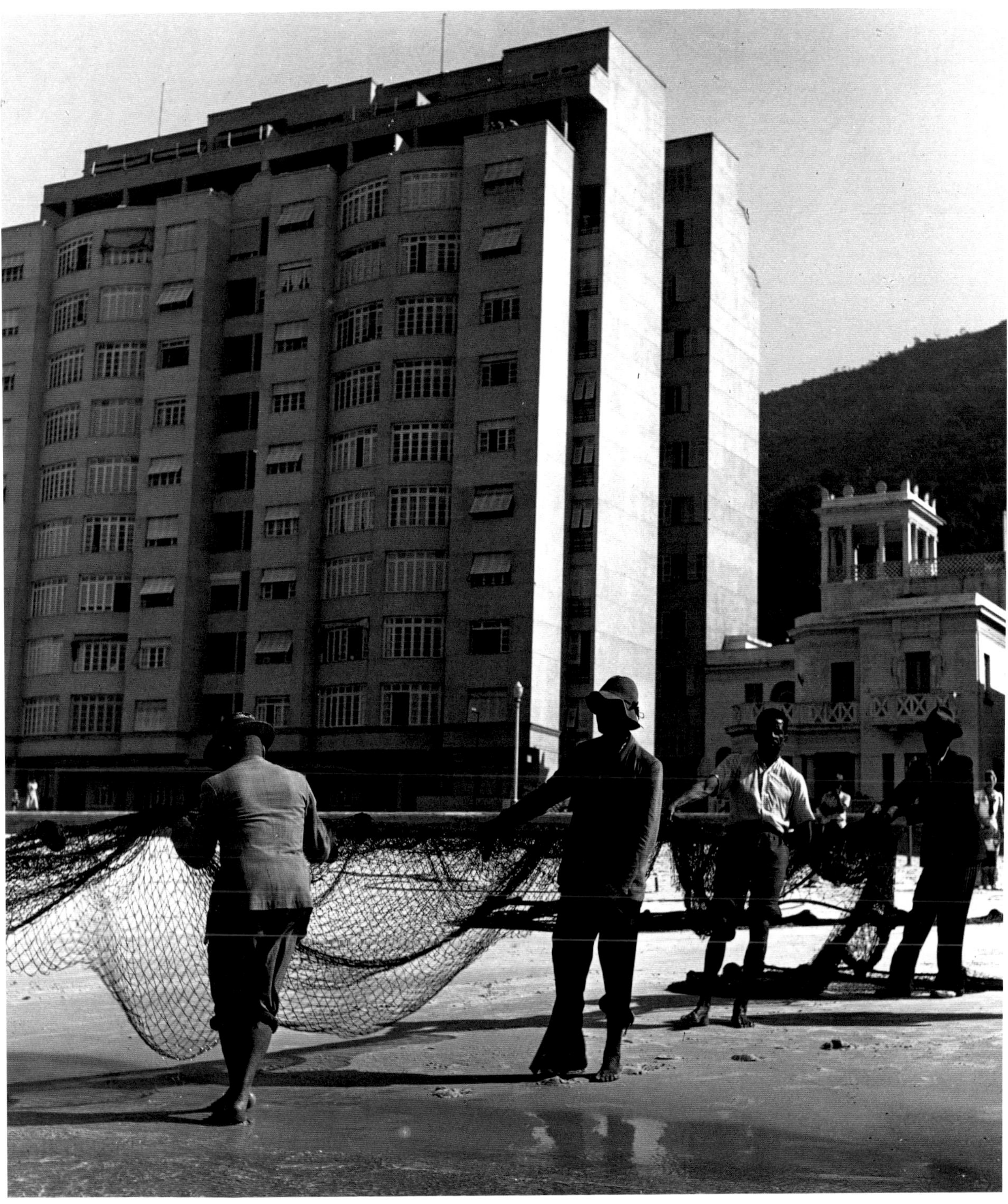

23 COPACABANA FISHERMEN

Naylor's photographs of the beach emphasized contrast: the fishermen in their work clothes hauling in their nets with a few well-dressed local residents watching. The high-rise apartment building is flanked by one of the many chaletlike single-family mansions that lined the avenue. By the early 1940s several of these had been razed to clear room to construct hotels and apartment buildings. Within a generation the private homes would mostly be torn down.

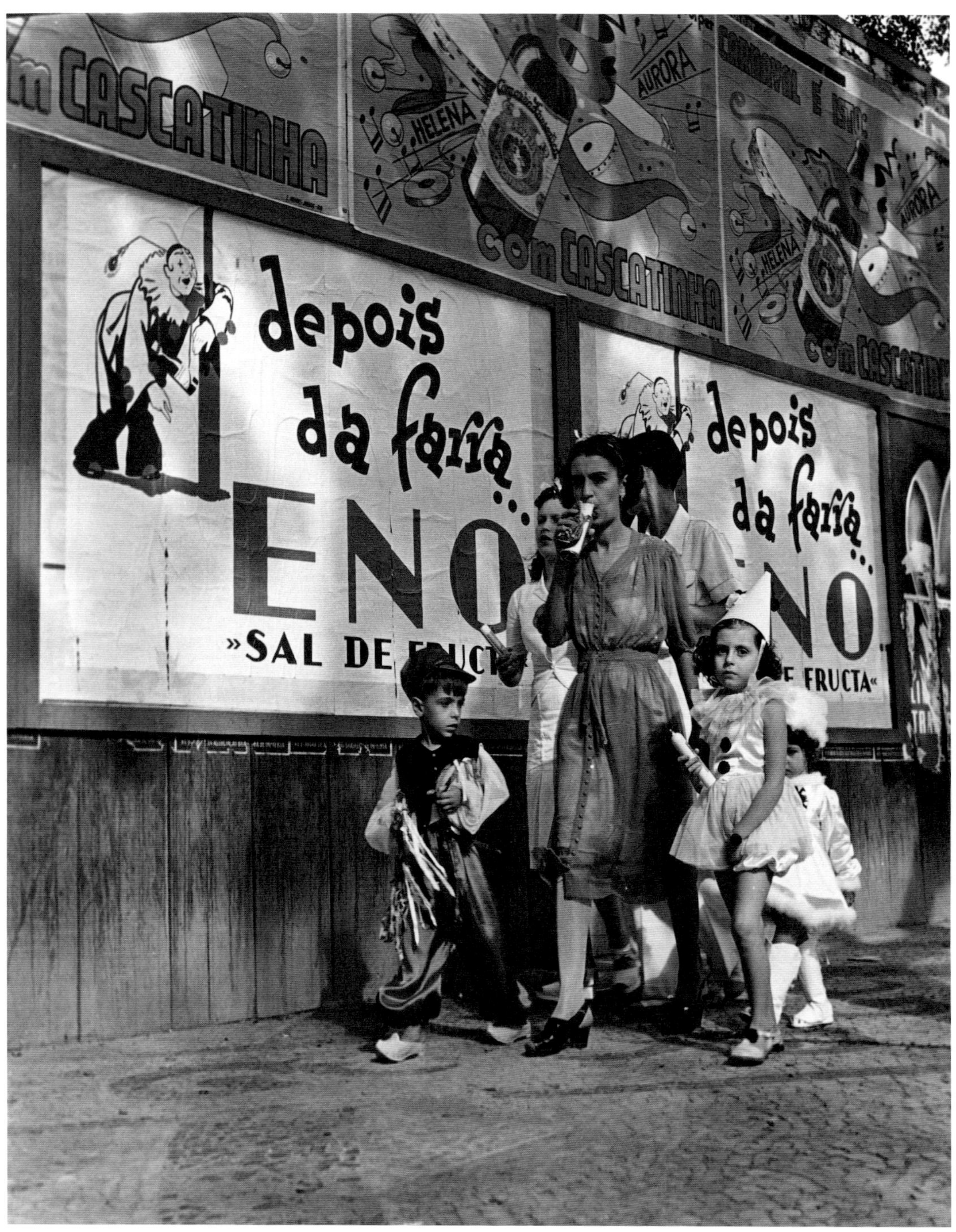

24 CARNIVAL

A mother walks with her costumed children in front of an advertising poster for Eno Salts, a version of Alka-Seltzer. By the 1940s Carnival had become both commercialized and institutionalized. What formerly had been a madcap frenzy stretching out over several days and entirely spontaneous by now had given way to children's parties in the elegant social clubs of the affluent. Note the uniformed nursemaid walking behind the mother. The girl in the front seems to be carrying a spray (*lança perfume*) canister, presumably emptied and filled with water or confetti. Long a fixture in Carnival revelry, these canisters, containing a mildly toxic substance similar to laughing gas, were banned in the 1950s.

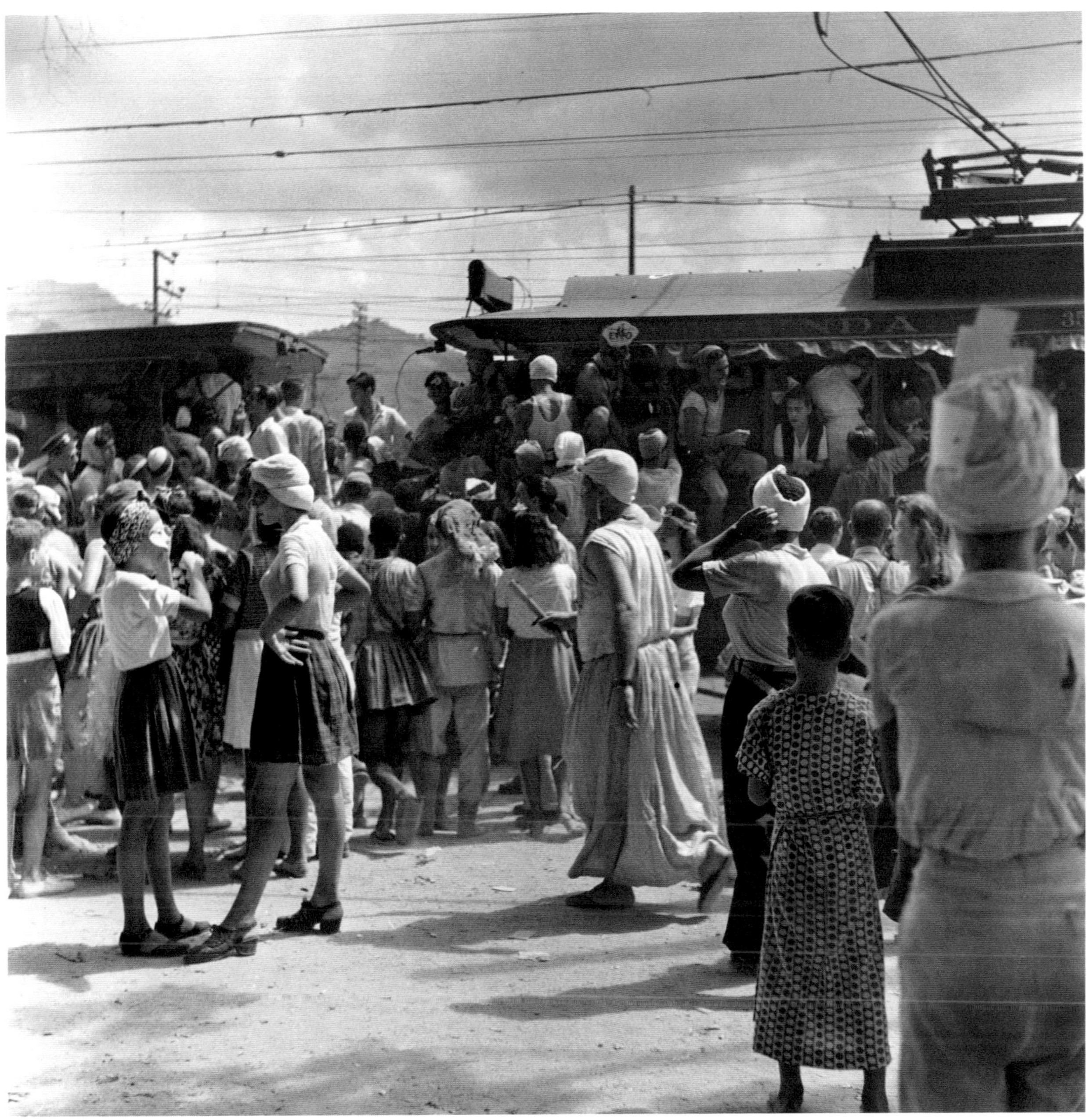

Unlike in the United States, where the suburbs were places for the newly arrived middle and upper-middle classes, in Brazil only working-class people commuted to jobs in cities. Some of the women on the platform are masked, evidence that this picture was taken during Carnival. Their dresses were also shorter than they would wear during normal workdays.

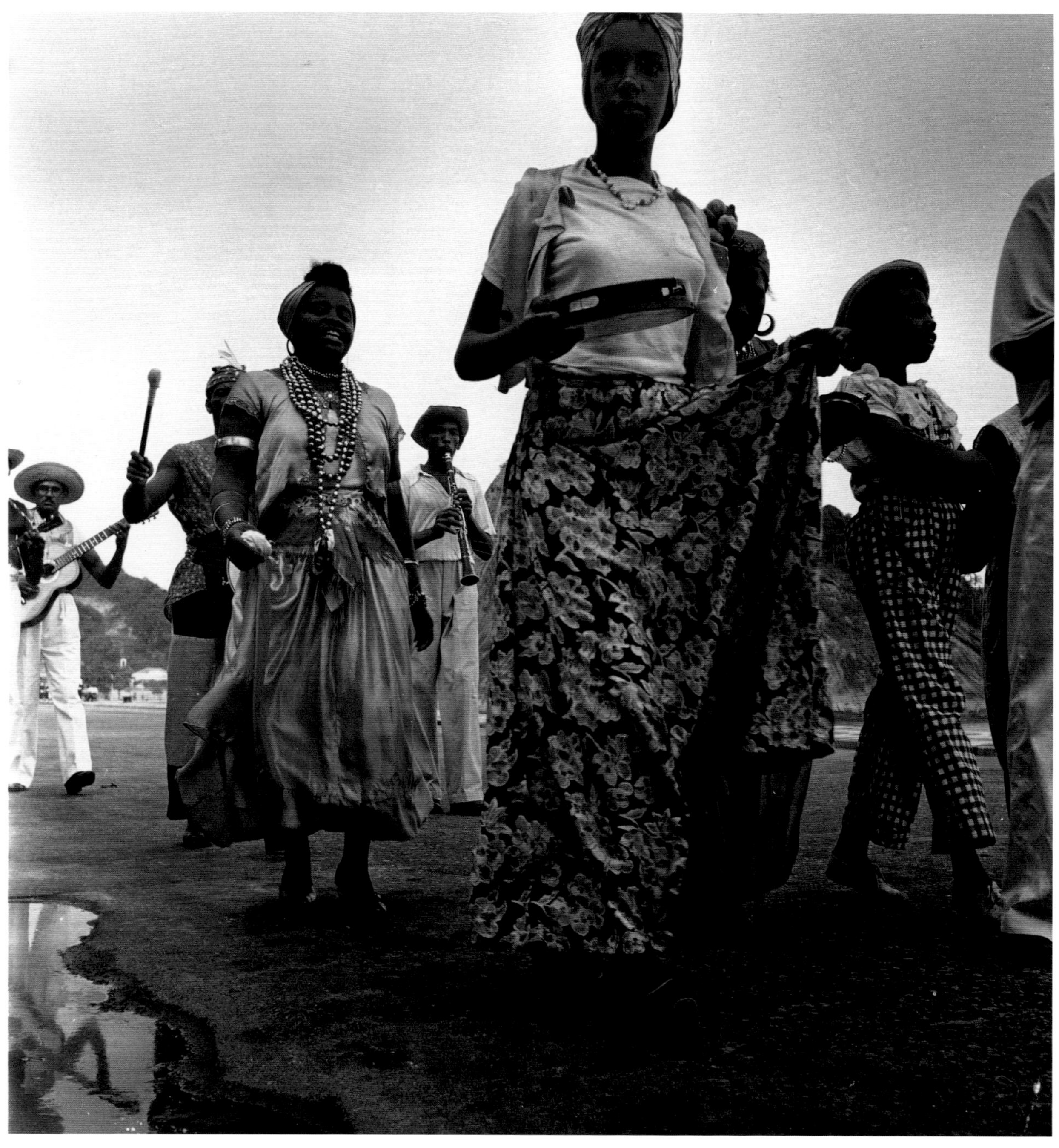

26 STREET MUSICIANS

Members of this Carnival band seem to be playing whatever instruments they have—from a string guitar to a clarinet to the tambourine carried by a woman and a bass drum being struck by another woman to the rear.

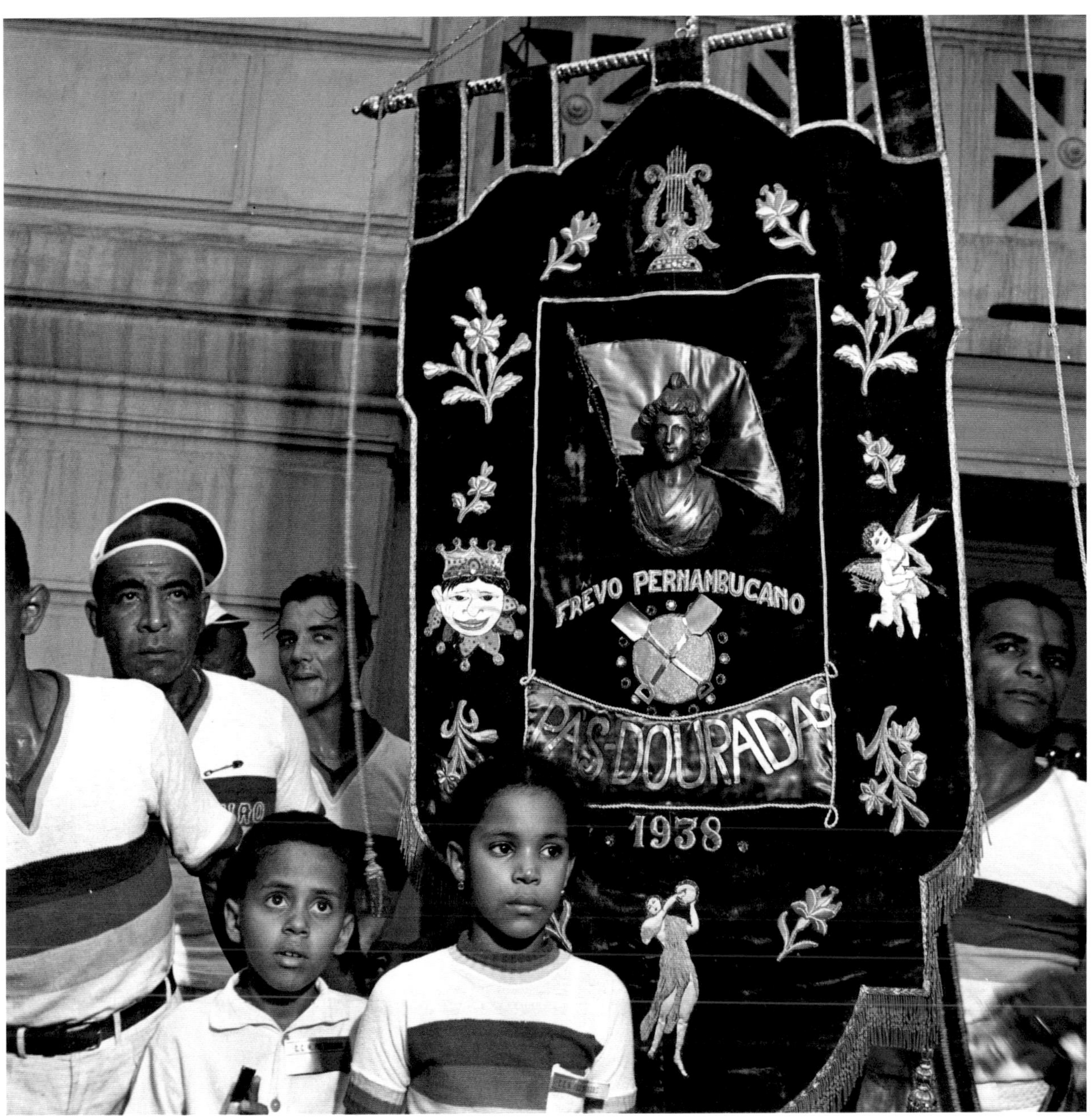

27 FREVO, C. 1941

Members of this Carnival association hold a banner originally displayed in Recife three years earlier. The photograph was likely taken in Rio de Janeiro, which provides evidence that migrants who trekked from the Northeast to the Center-South attempted to preserve their original cultural identities. The word *Peace (Paz)* is misspelled as *Pas*.

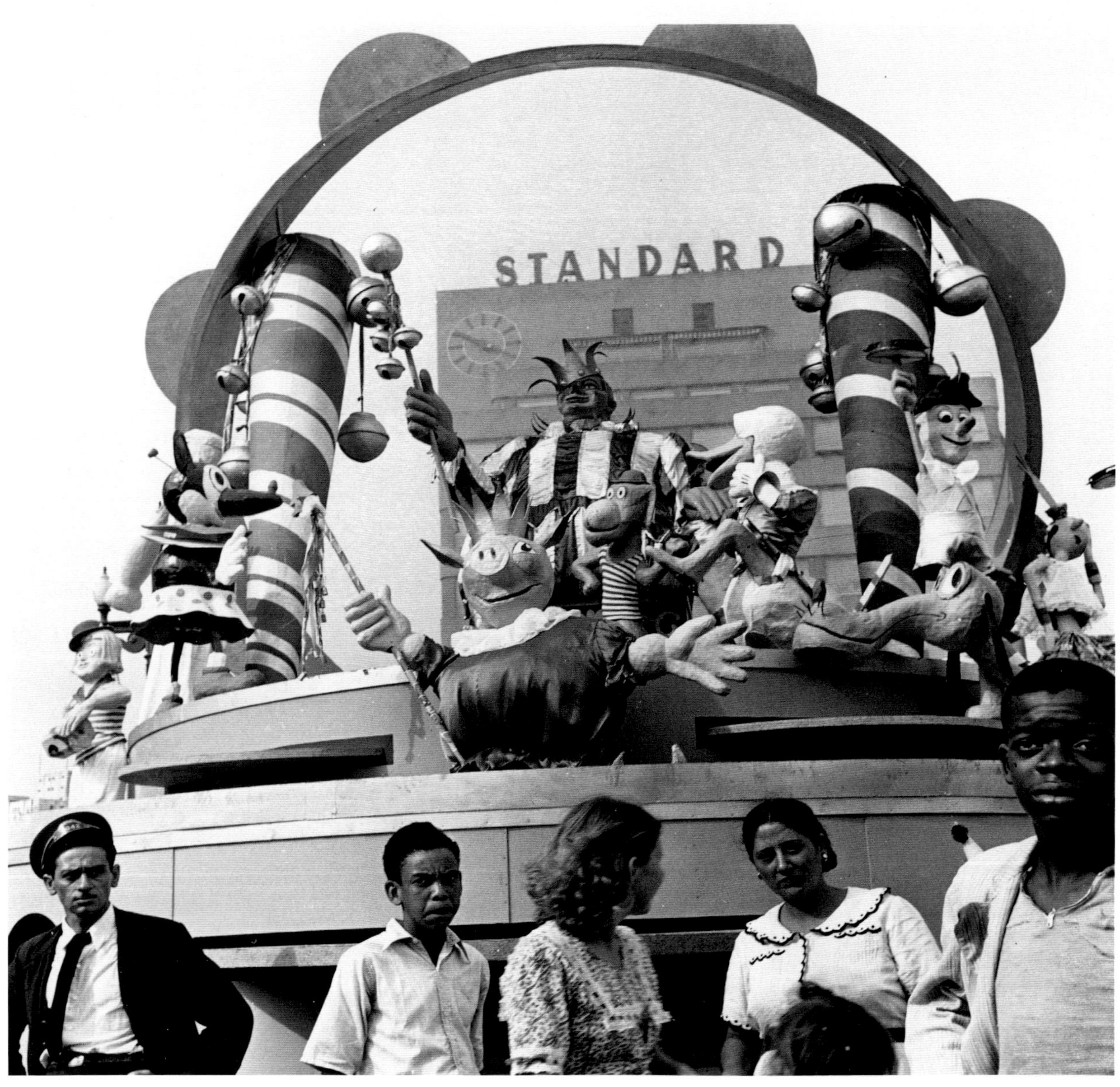

28 CARNIVAL FLOAT, C. 1941

The people standing in front of this Carnival depiction of the traditional Rei Momo—the king of the revelry—and a supporting cast including Pinocchio seem, unlike Naylor's usual subjects, tense and distracted.

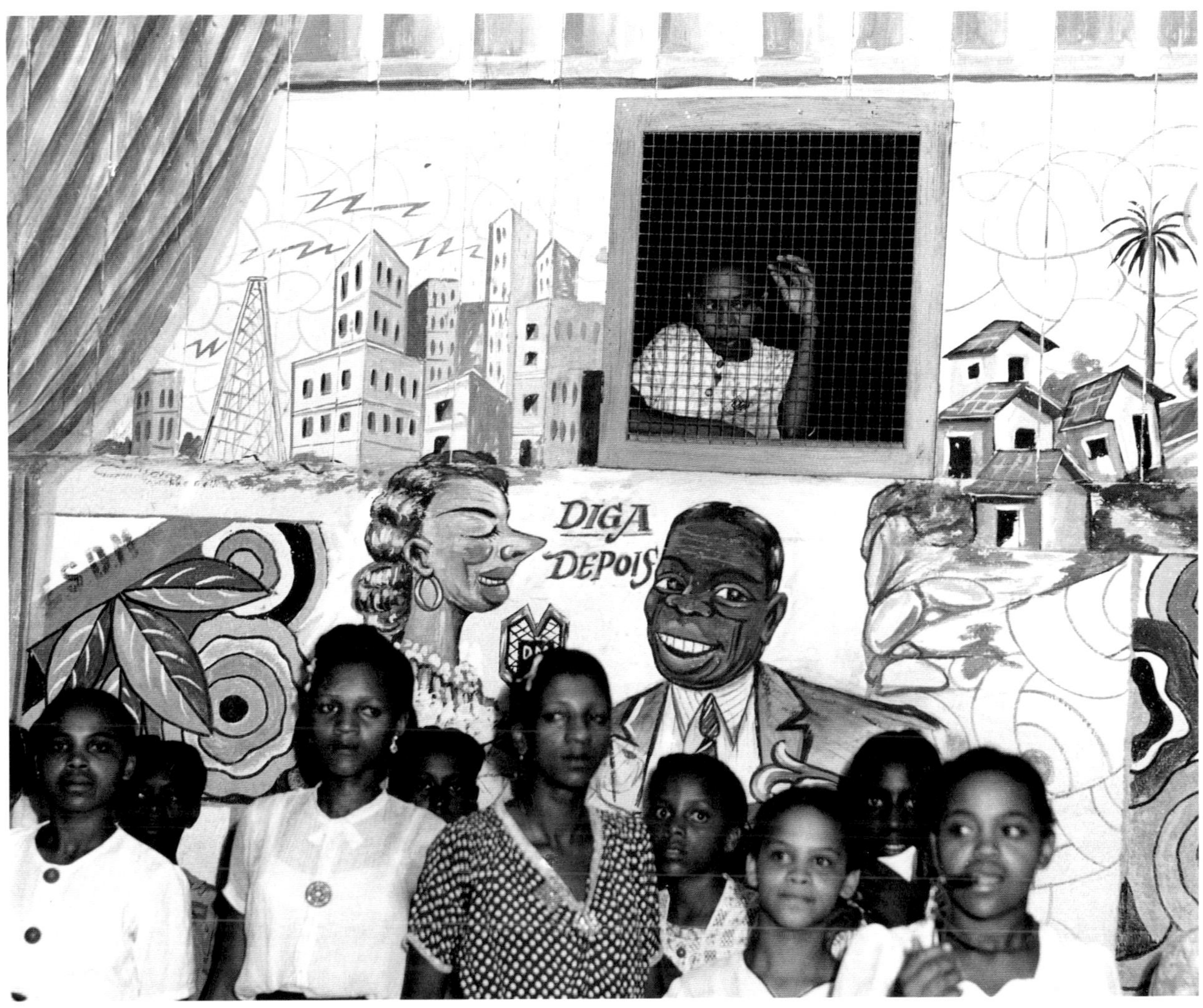

29 SAMBA SCHOOL

Escolas de samba were favela recreational clubs that prepared for the annual Carnival competition and functioned during the remainder of the year as social clubs. Naylor posed attendees against the backdrop of a wall design that included a romanti-cized image of a favela on one side and a depiction of the city (with radio tower) on the other. The woman singing into the microphone was a well-known entertainer.

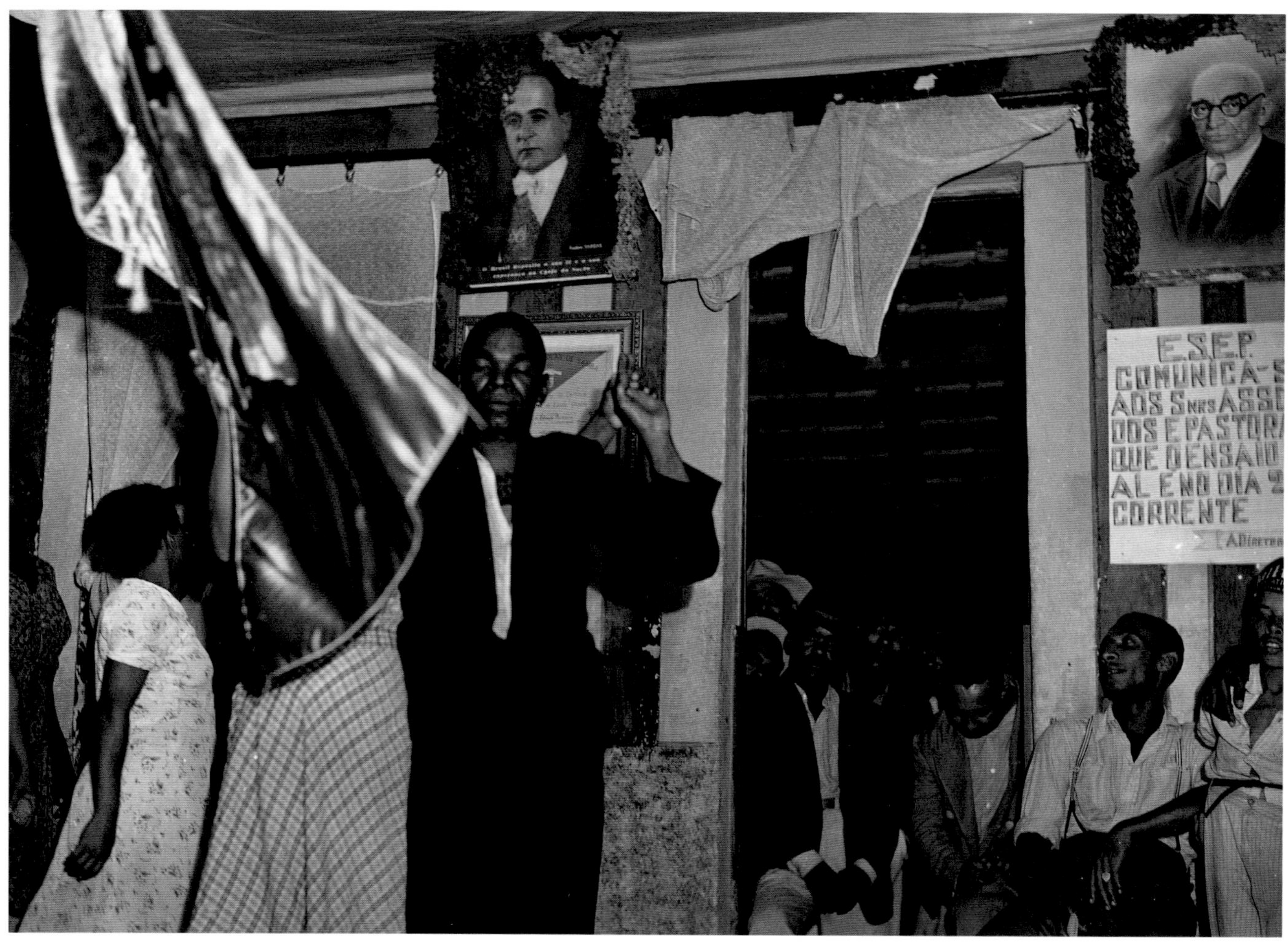

30 SAMBA SCHOOL

This is the Escola de Samba E.P., the Portella School. Vargas's portrait shares the wall with a photograph of the school's founder. The inscription reminds members that Carnival rehearsals are held on the twentieth of each month.

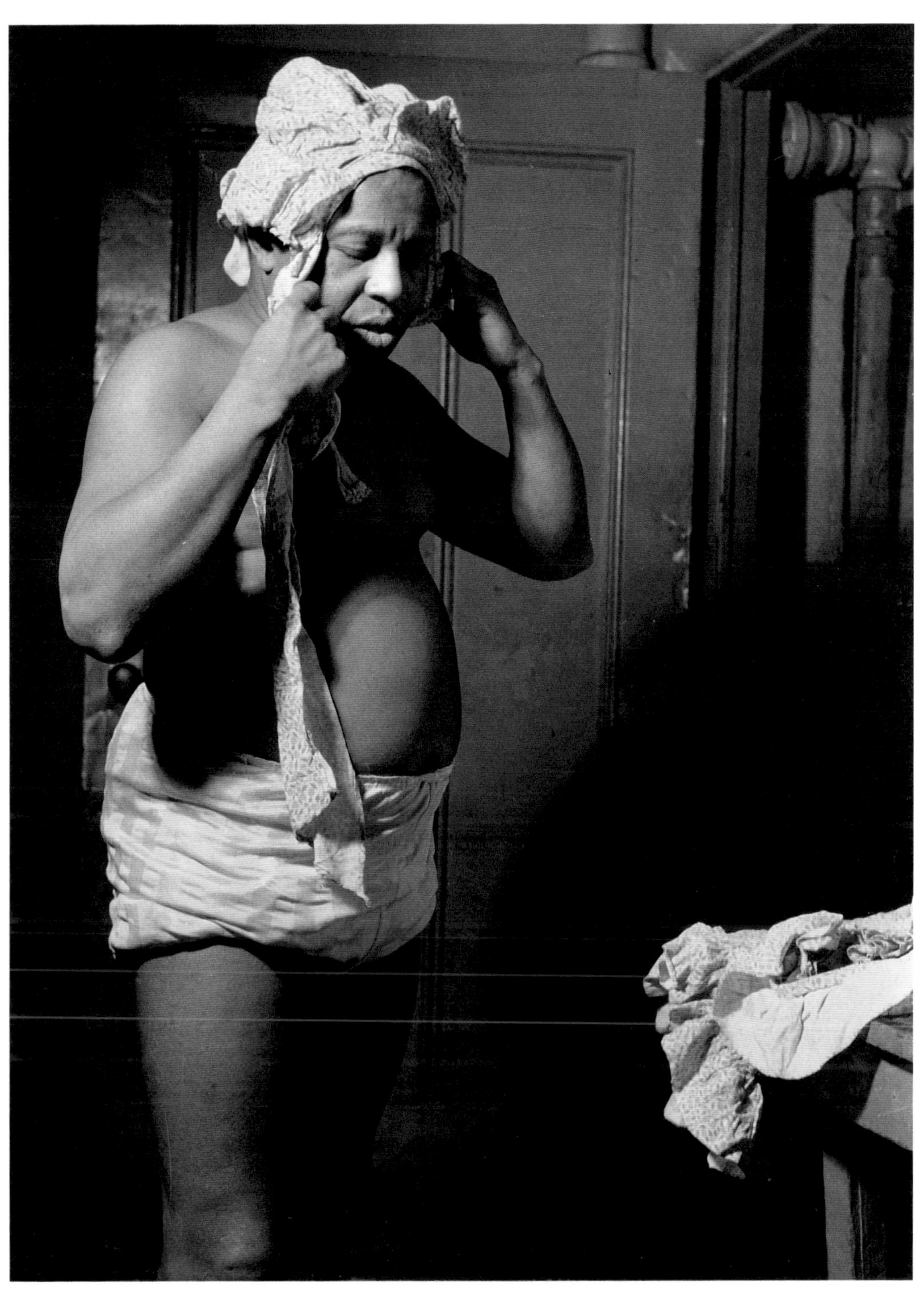

3 1 GETTING READY

A man readies himself for Carnival.

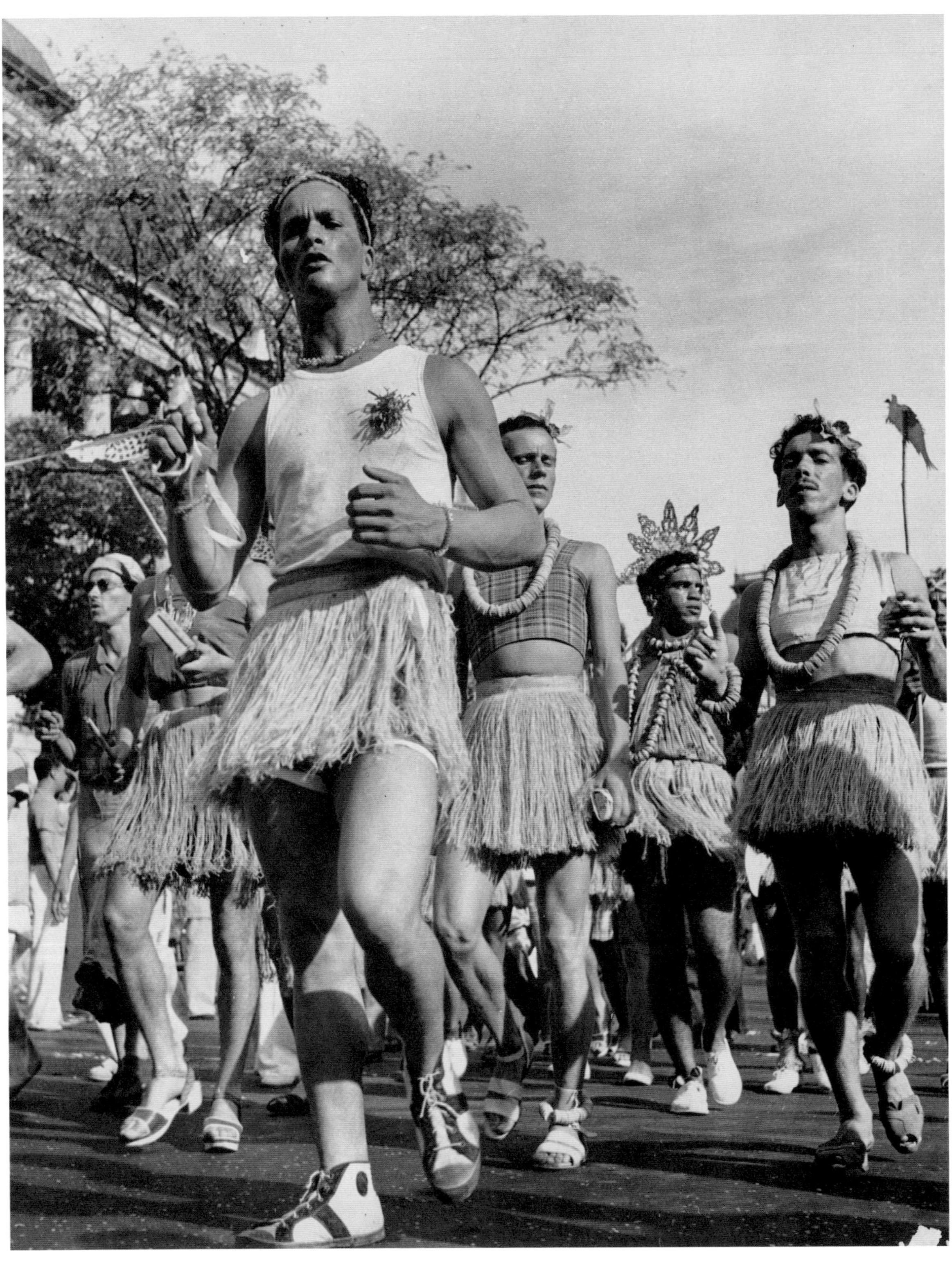

32 MEN DRESSED AS WOMEN

Across Brazil, on one of the early days of Carnival, men dressed as women and paraded through the streets. Until the 1940s this practice was universal, although after that time it survived mainly in small towns. These men wear grass skirts as if they were Indians—a popular Carnival theme, especially outside Rio de Janeiro.

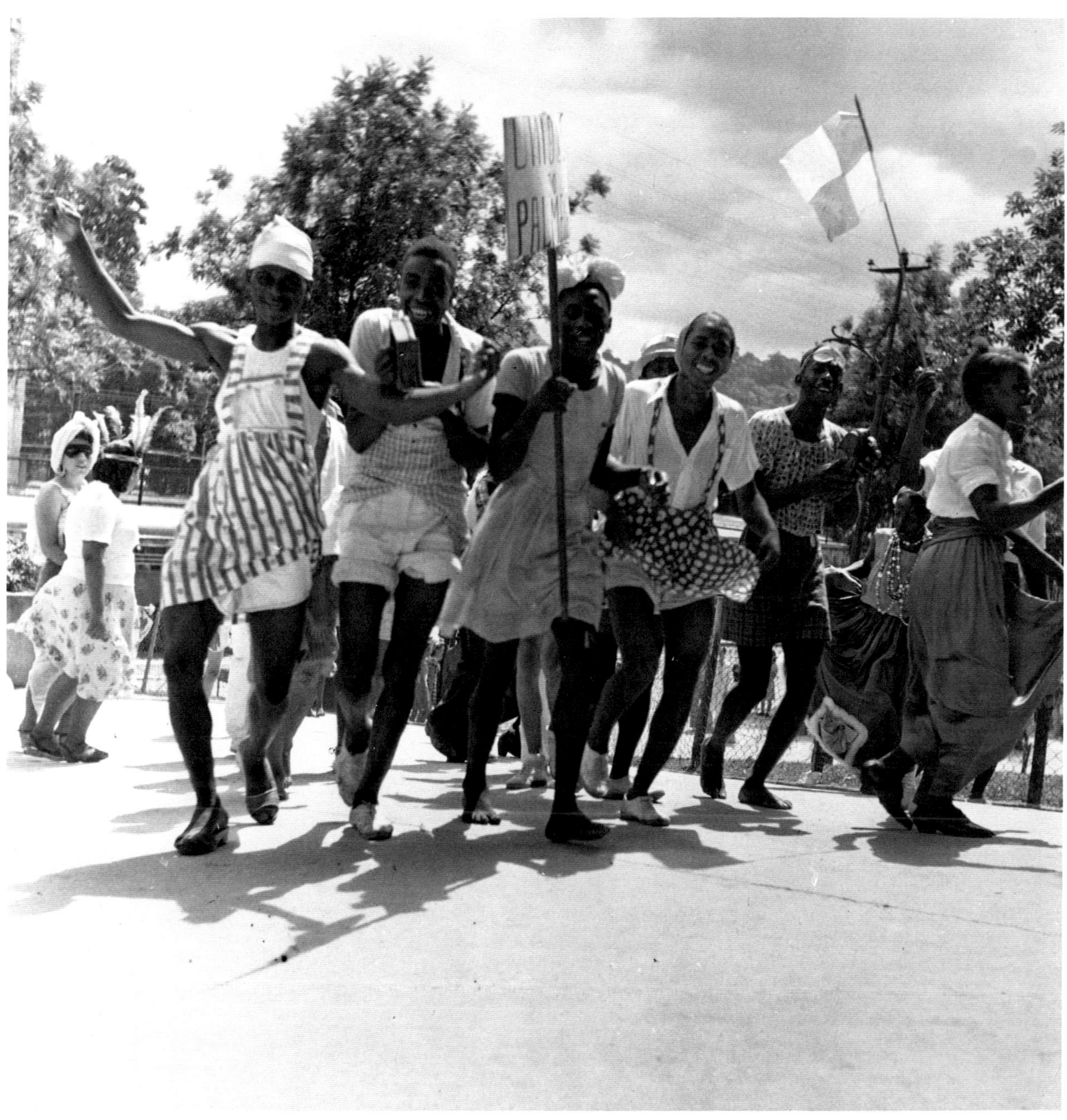

33 CARNIVAL CELEBRANTS

While the upper classes attended masked balls in formal dress or lavish costumes, Brazilians of the lower classes celebrated enthusiastically in the streets. Daytime merrymaking was benign (although people doused one another with unpleasant liquid) but after nightfall the revelry could be marred by drunkenness and violence.

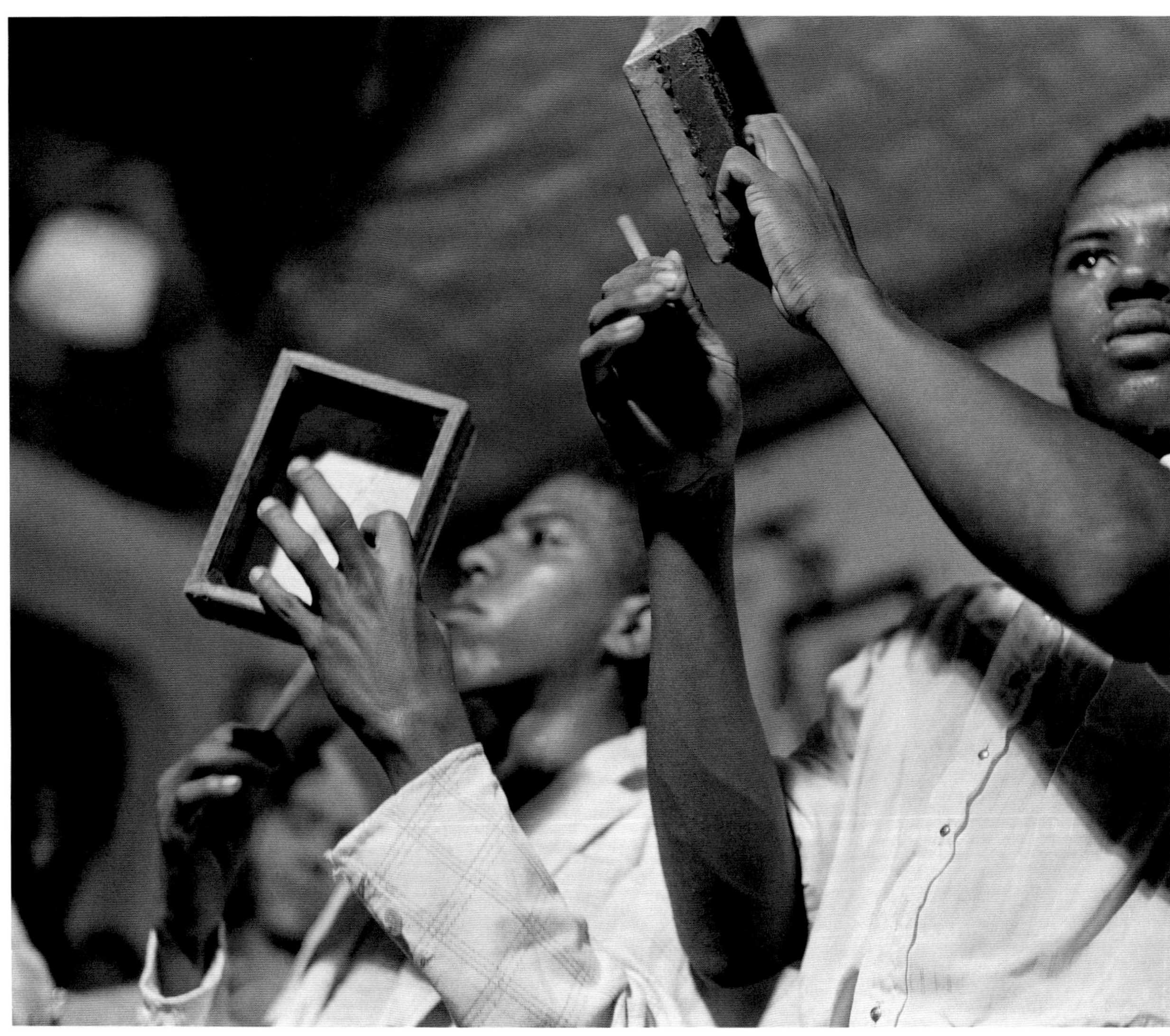

Affluent whites attended Carnival balls in their exclusive clubs, but on the street (probably Rio's Praça Onze) black musicians played their percussion instruments hour after hour, filling the samba schools, favelas, and poor districts with a heady, pulsating rhythm. The boxlike instruments are *reco-recos*.

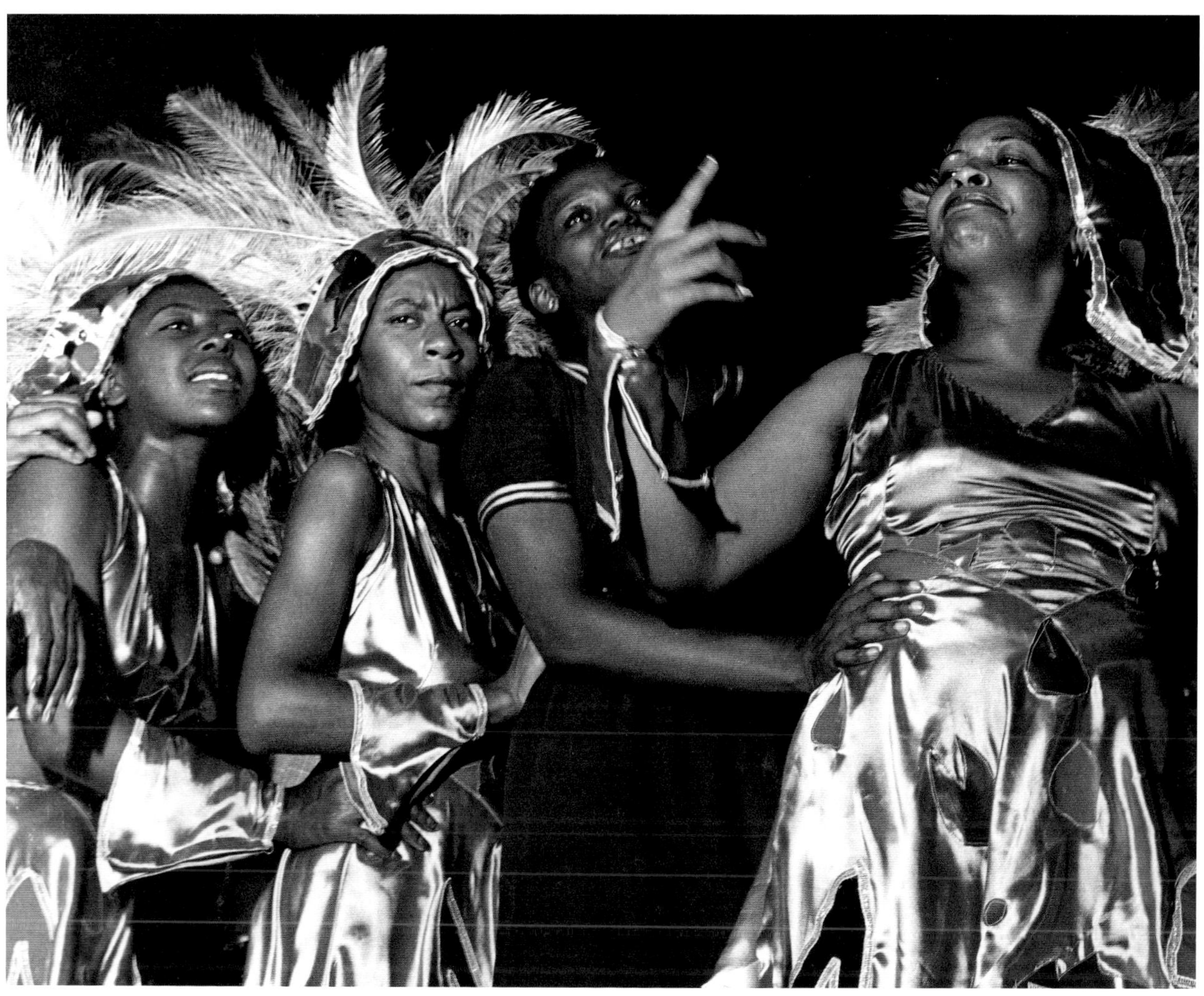

35 CARNIVAL DANCERS

A group of Afro-Brazilian women wear matching costumes of shiny fabric and headpieces based on an Indian motif, popular among samba school choreographers. Brazilian culture roman-ticized Indian life, although it did not do the same for African culture.

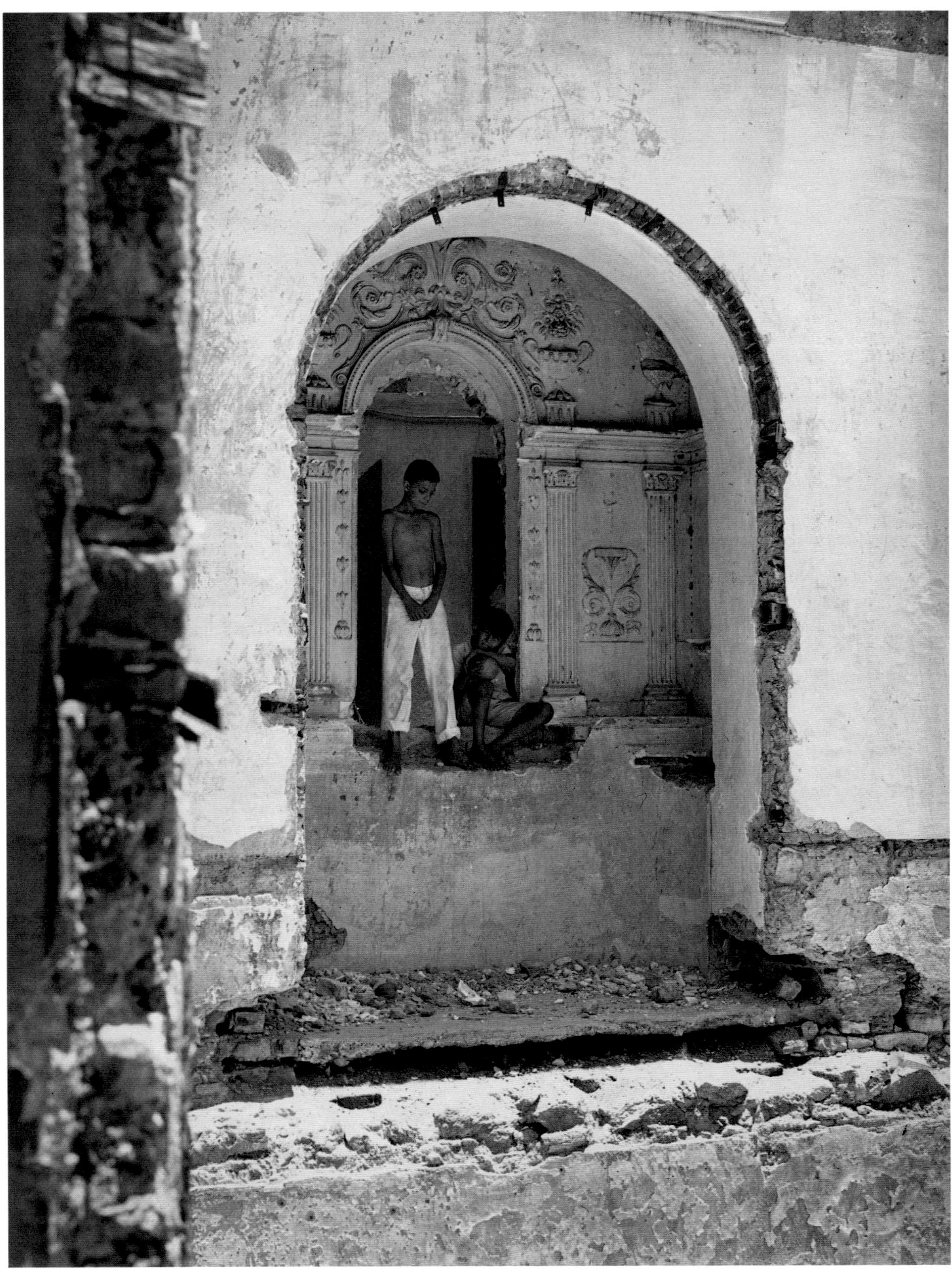

Naylor poses the youths in the portal of a church that may be in the process of being torn down to make way for a new building. The scene was characteristic of Brazil in the 1940s and later — thousands of colonial-era buildings lay abandoned, sometimes in the midst of flimsy modern-style buildings going up around them. In rural areas, parishioners sometimes tended the decaying churches, but the Roman Catholic Church had precious few resources for restoration or repairs.

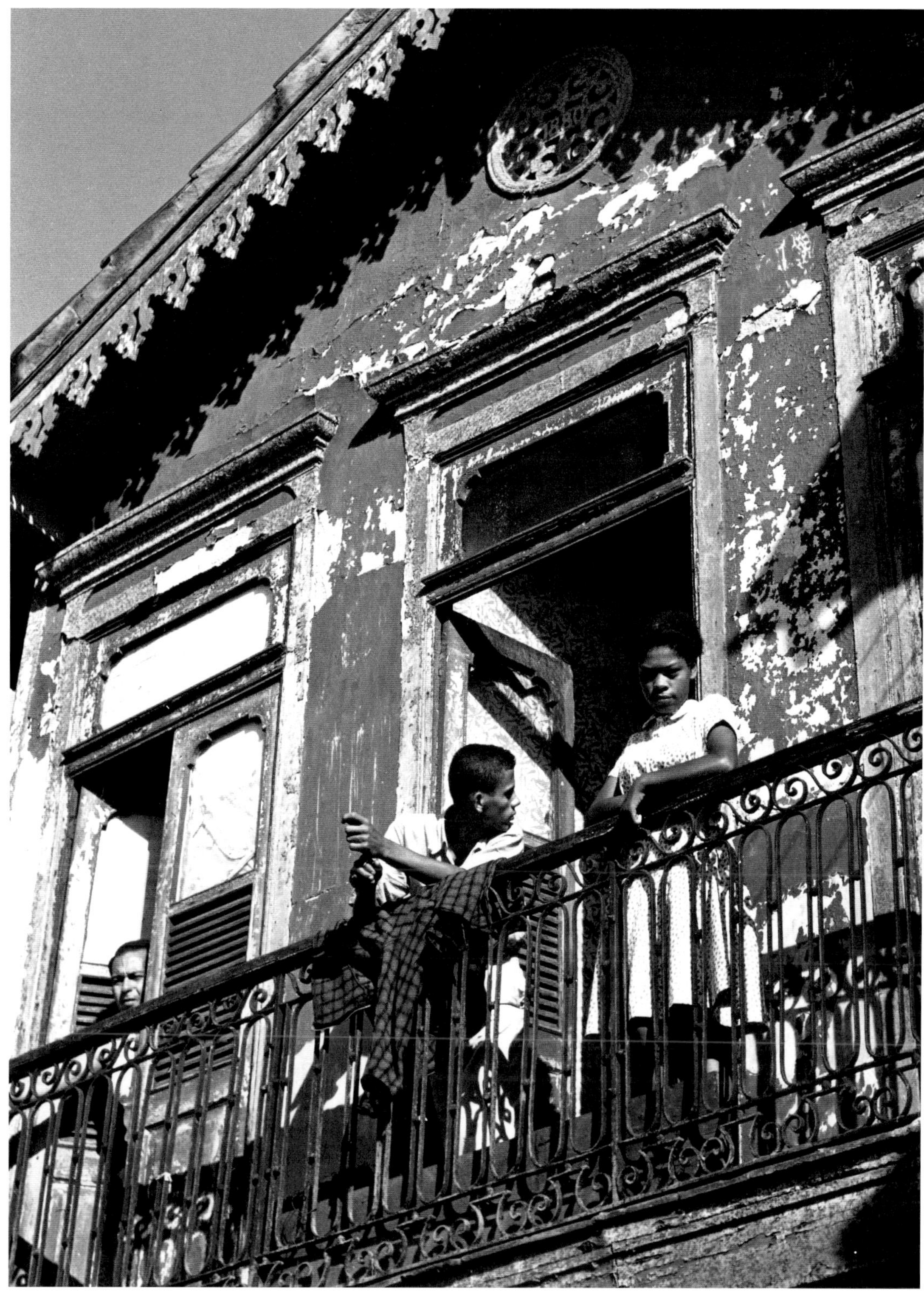

37 TENEMENT

Many old houses in crumbling industrial or commercial neighborhoods were divided into tenements, sometimes called *cabeça-de-porco* (literally, "pig's heads"). They were made available to families otherwise poor but well-off enough to pay rent.

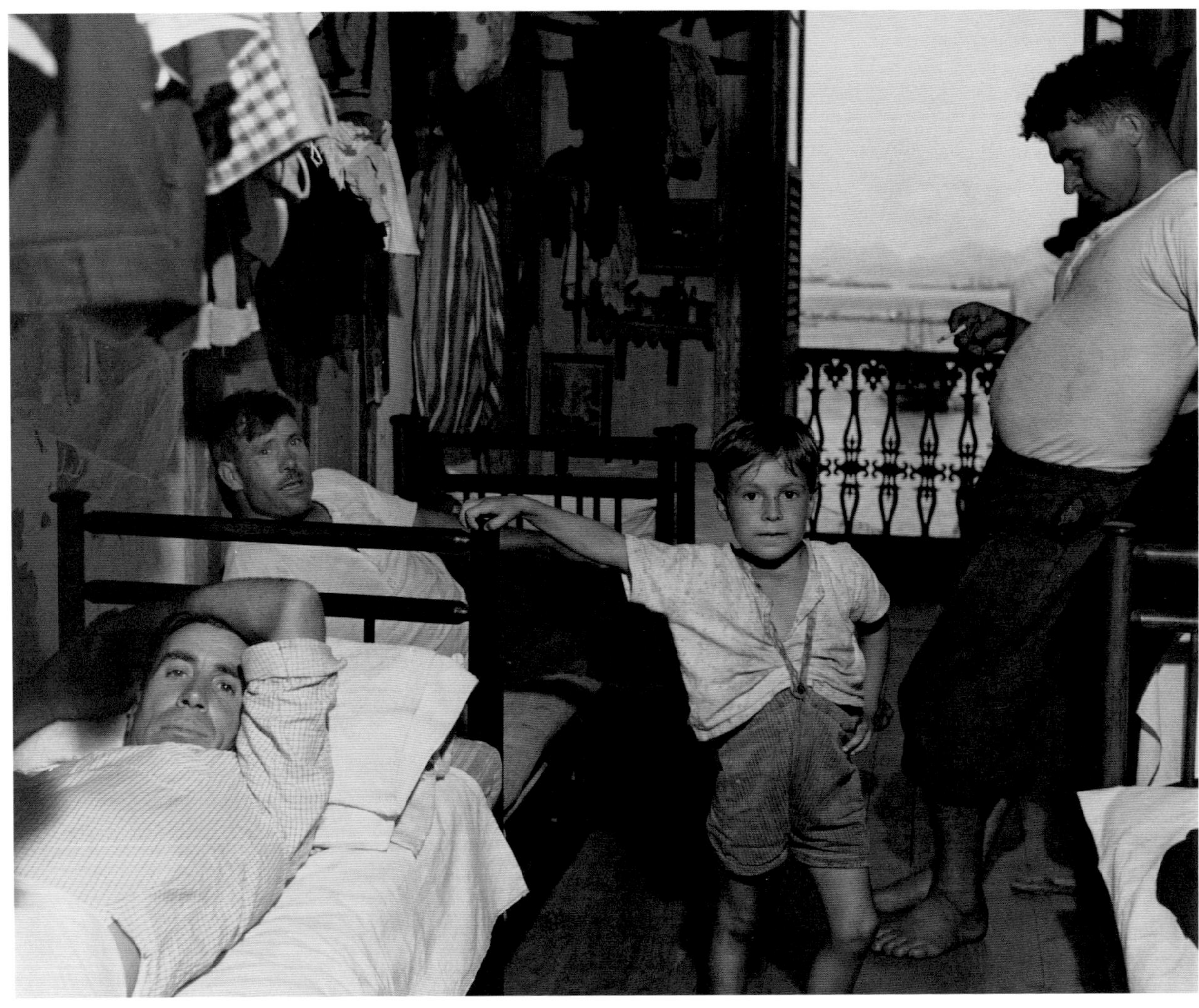

Men and a boy rest in a crowded cabeça-de-porco room on a Sunday or holiday. They may be immigrants; they do not seem related to one another. The standing man is smoking a hand-rolled cigarette. However hot and crowded it may have been, living conditions here were much better than in the shantytowns occupied by recently arrived migrants and by the urban underclass. Most of the residents of such buildings were male. Immigrants left their wives behind in Europe and only sent for them when they had accumulated sufficient capital.

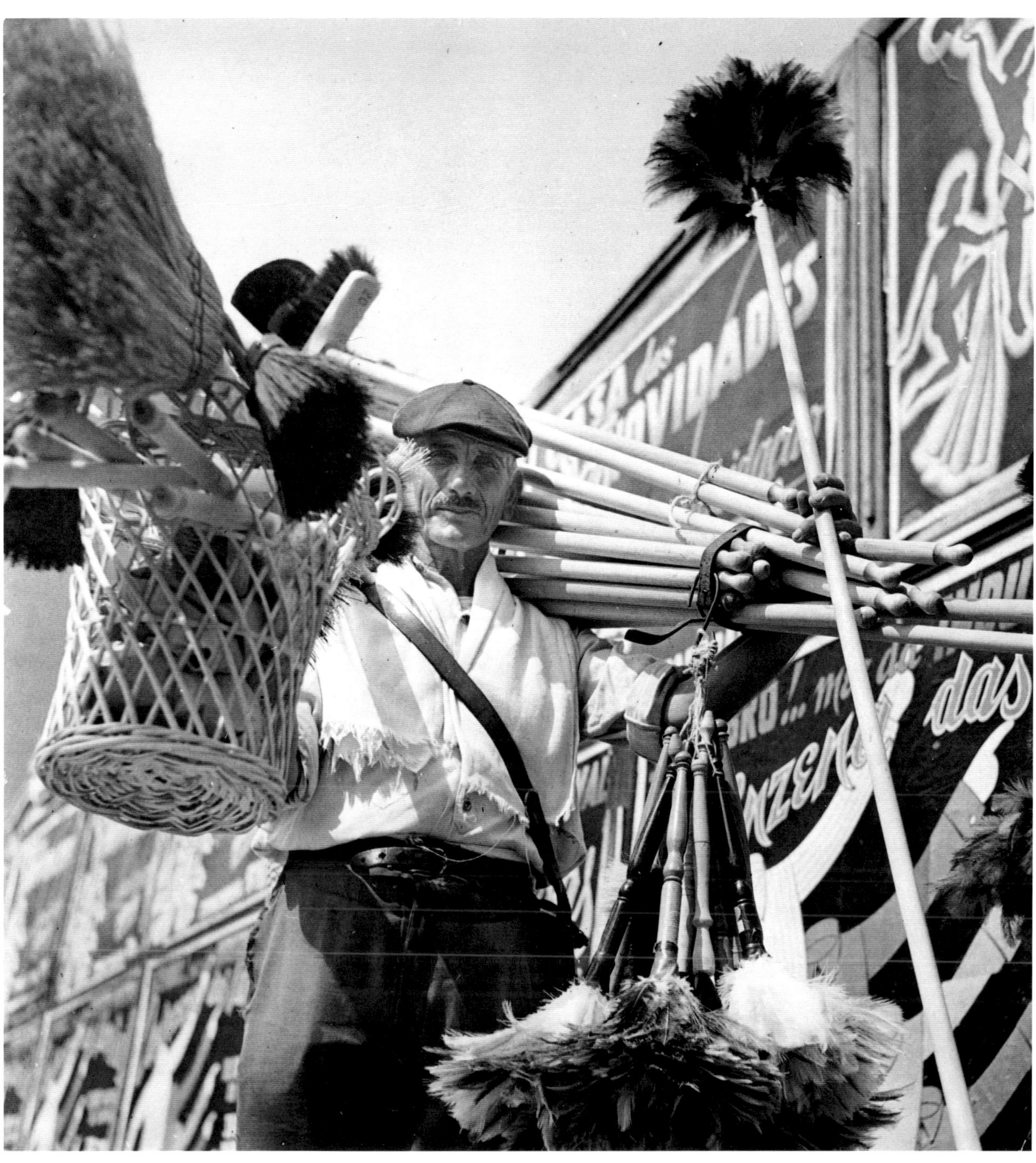

39 BROOM VENDOR

All of these brooms are locally produced, as are the feather dust-
ers. Peddlers carried their entire stock-in-trade on poles hoisted
on their shoulders.

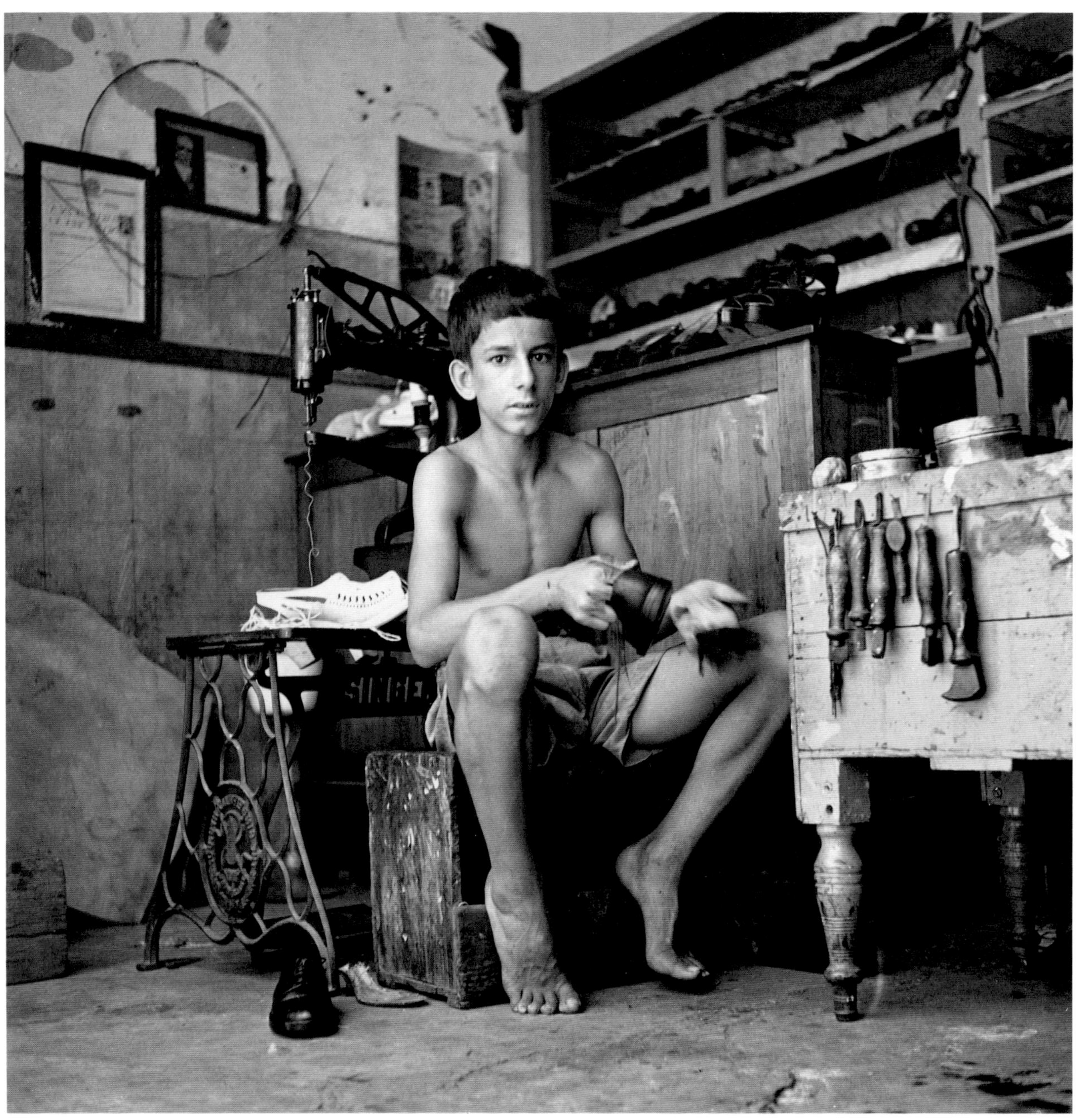

This barefoot adolescent boy sits at his cobbler's bench at work. Thousands of children performed such labor in spite of elaborate decree legislation forbidding it. Most affluent Brazilians did not buy manufactured shoes but rather went to shops like these to have shoes made to order. Ironically, given the regime's labor legislation, there is a small portrait of Vargas on the wall to the left.

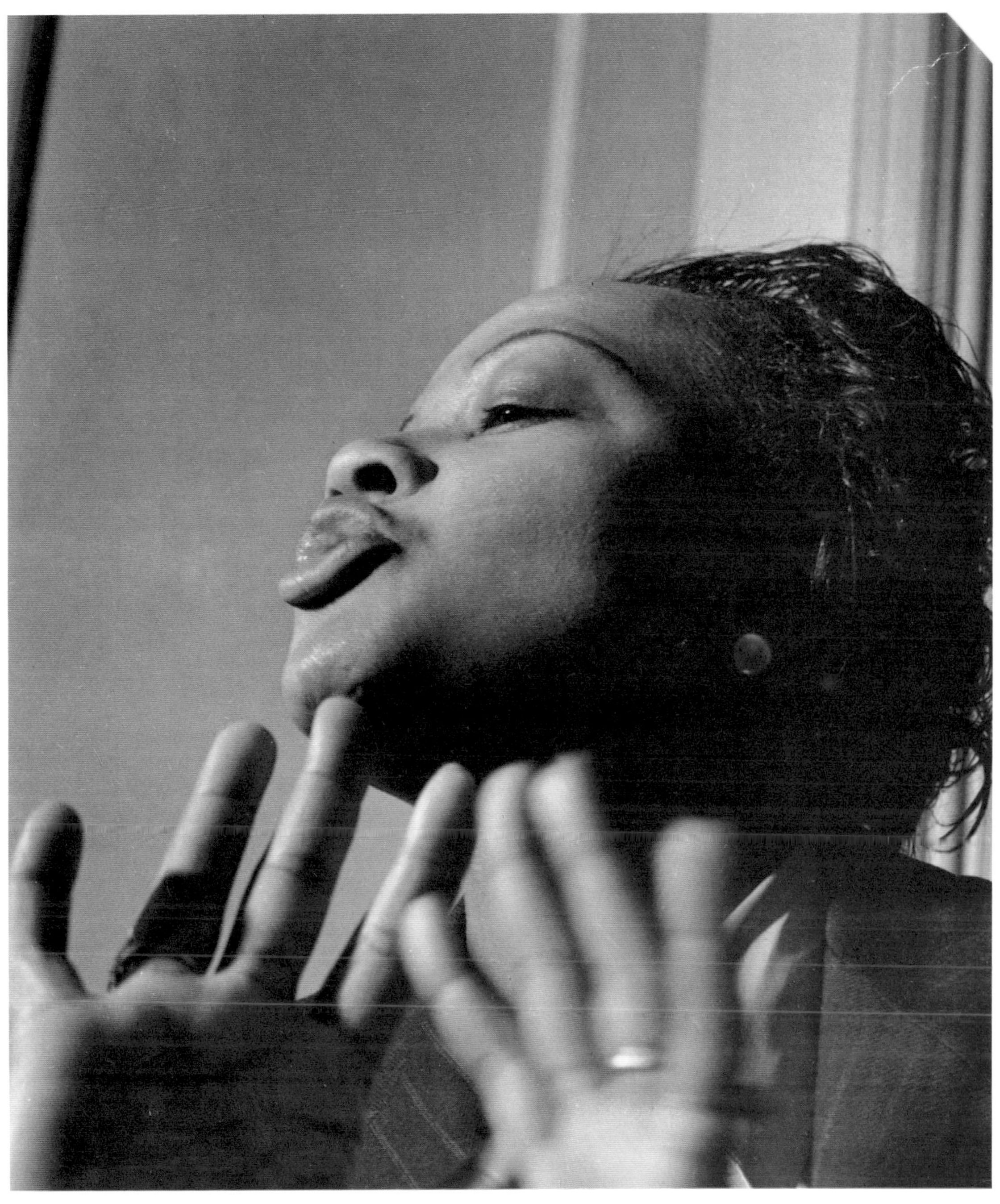

41 WOMAN

Perhaps she is performing, or she may be participating in a religious ceremony.

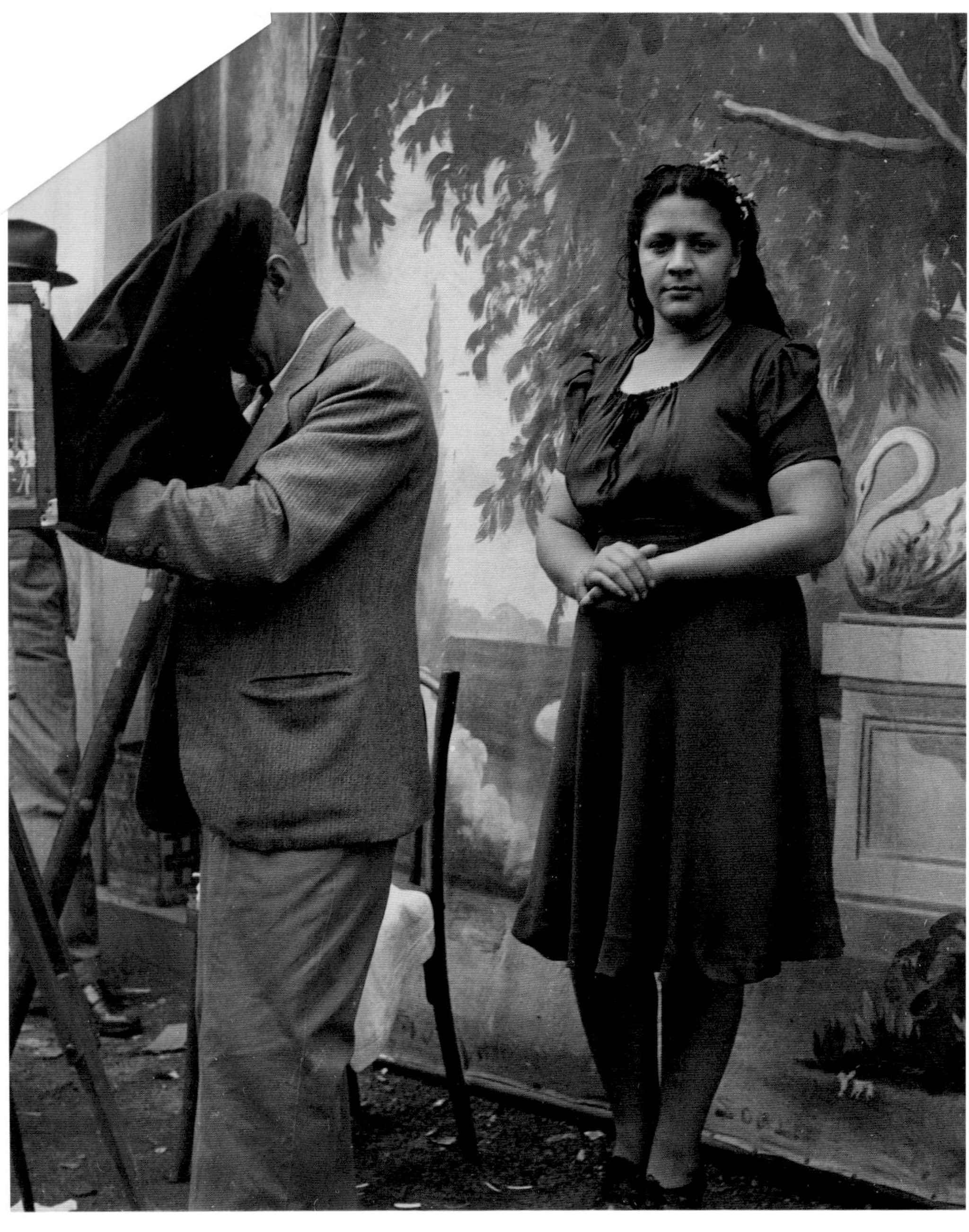

Men and women from the middle and even the lower classes valued photographs, which they gave to those close to them. The photographers used *lambe-lambes* (old studio cameras) and handsomely painted backdrops to convey a mood of success and comfort. Sometimes they provided clothing for their customers to wear. Most Brazilians paid to have their picture taken at least once a year, ordering copies to send to family members abroad or in the interior, or for use on official documents.

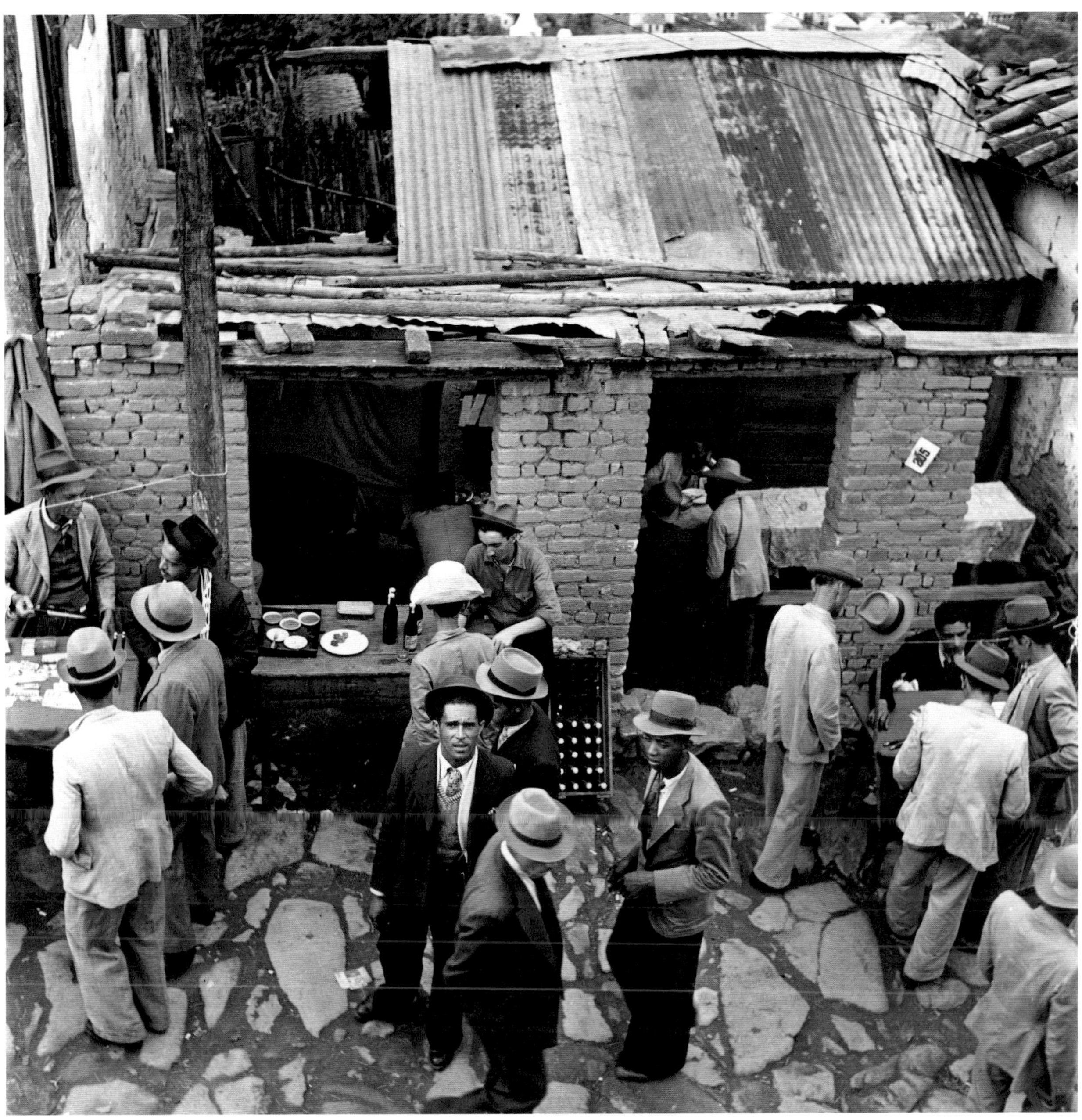

43 WORKING-CLASS RESTAURANT

Naylor has captured in striking detail an example of a scene un-known to upper-class Brazilians (and to foreigners). In a rude brick shack covered only partially by tin sheeting, a restaurant and bar operates. Its patrons are black and mulatto men. Their suits are well worn but proper; one man even wears a vest. Two men sit at a table, possibly doing business; one of them has a case on his shoulder. Papers are spread on the table at the left. A seated man at a table at the right has taken off his hat, as if he will stay for a while.

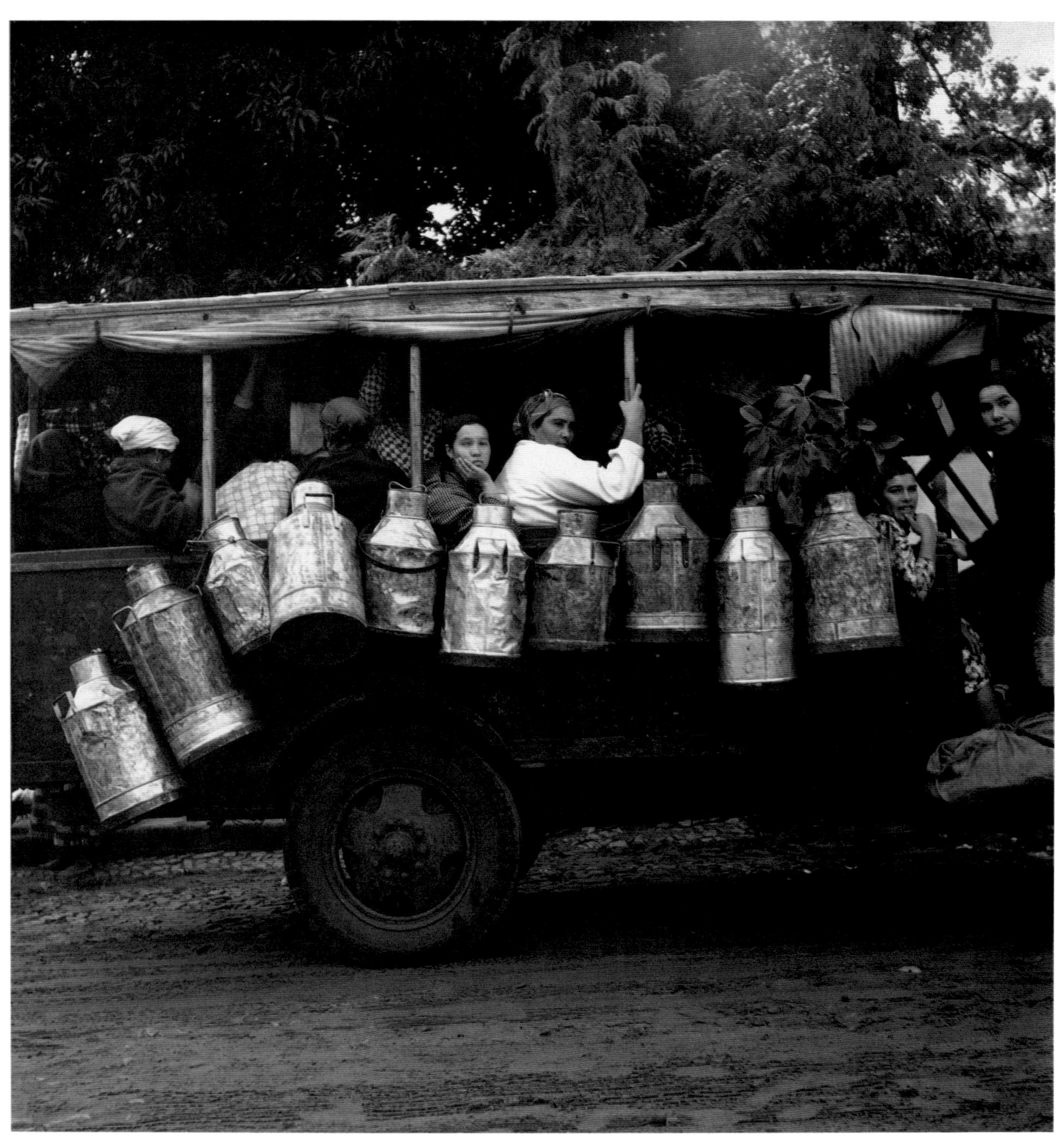

Girls and women ride a crowded delivery truck stacked with
tambos (milk cans). Very few homes had refrigerators in the
1940s, so fresh foods had to be purchased daily.

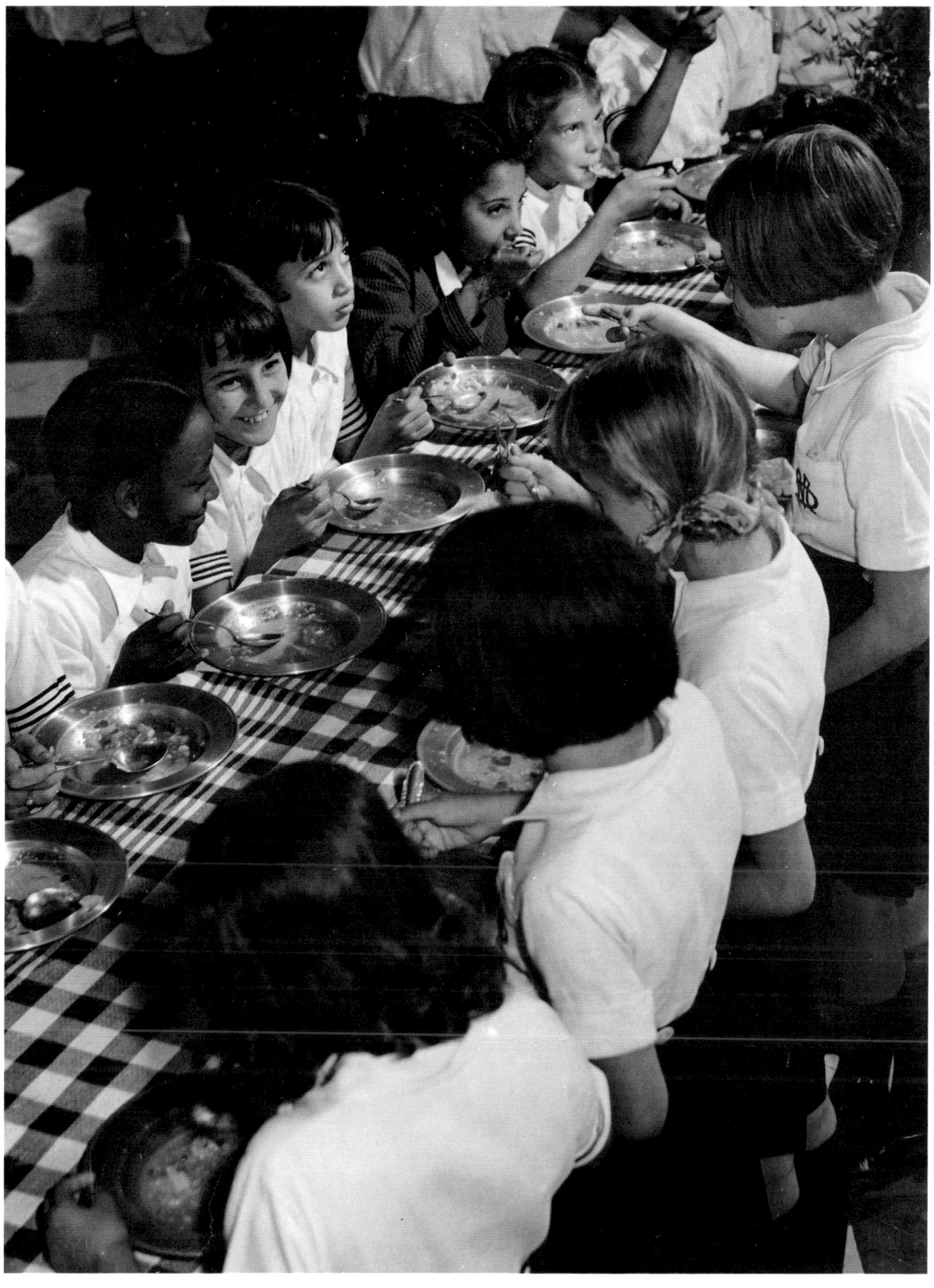

45 GIRLS AT A MEAL

These girls wear uniforms with the initials of their school or,
possibly, state institution.

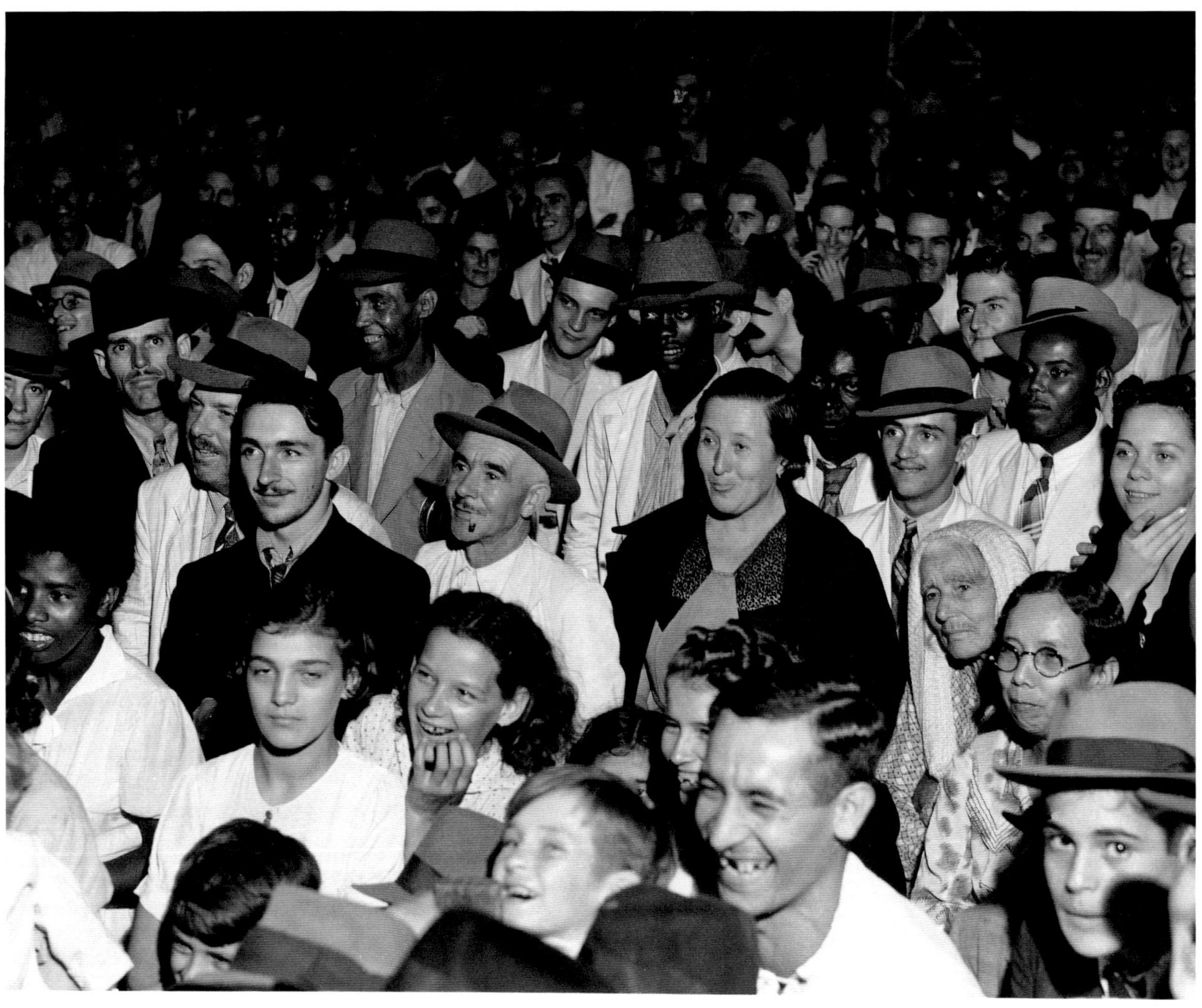

46 AUDIENCE AT OUTDOOR PLAY

The faces and gestures of this varied group of people express the sense of warmth and good feeling that Naylor tried to capture. There are blacks and whites and persons of mixed race in the scene. The picture is perfectly framed, although not in a pictorial sense, and its off-line composition adds a dimension to its energy. It is strikingly reminiscent of group photographs taken by the New York photographer Weegee during the 1930s and early 1940s.

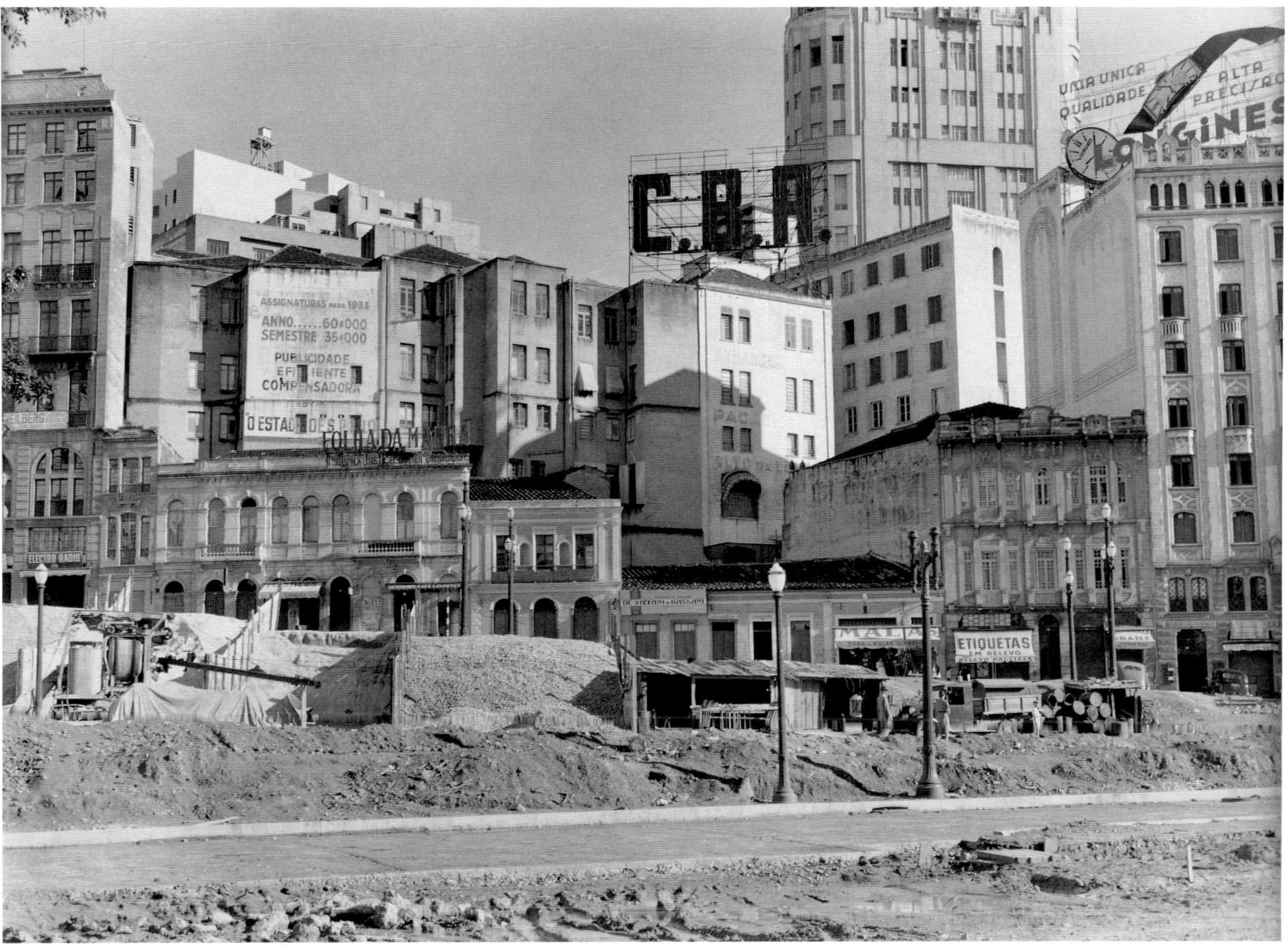

A huge construction project in downtown São Paulo, probably photographed on a Sunday, contains heavy trucks and sheds for supplies. Many of the older neighborhoods in Brazilian cities were torn down to make wider avenues and to facilitate commerce. A painted wall behind the *Folha da Manhã* letters atop the building on the left advertises subscription rates to the rival *Estado de São Paulo* for the year 1933, indicating that either the rates stayed the same during the entire Depression or that no one bothered to change the sign. The office buildings and single-level shops, some of them restaurants, stand across the street. These would remain untouched until the 1970s and 1980s, at which point they were leveled to make way for office buildings dozens of stories high.

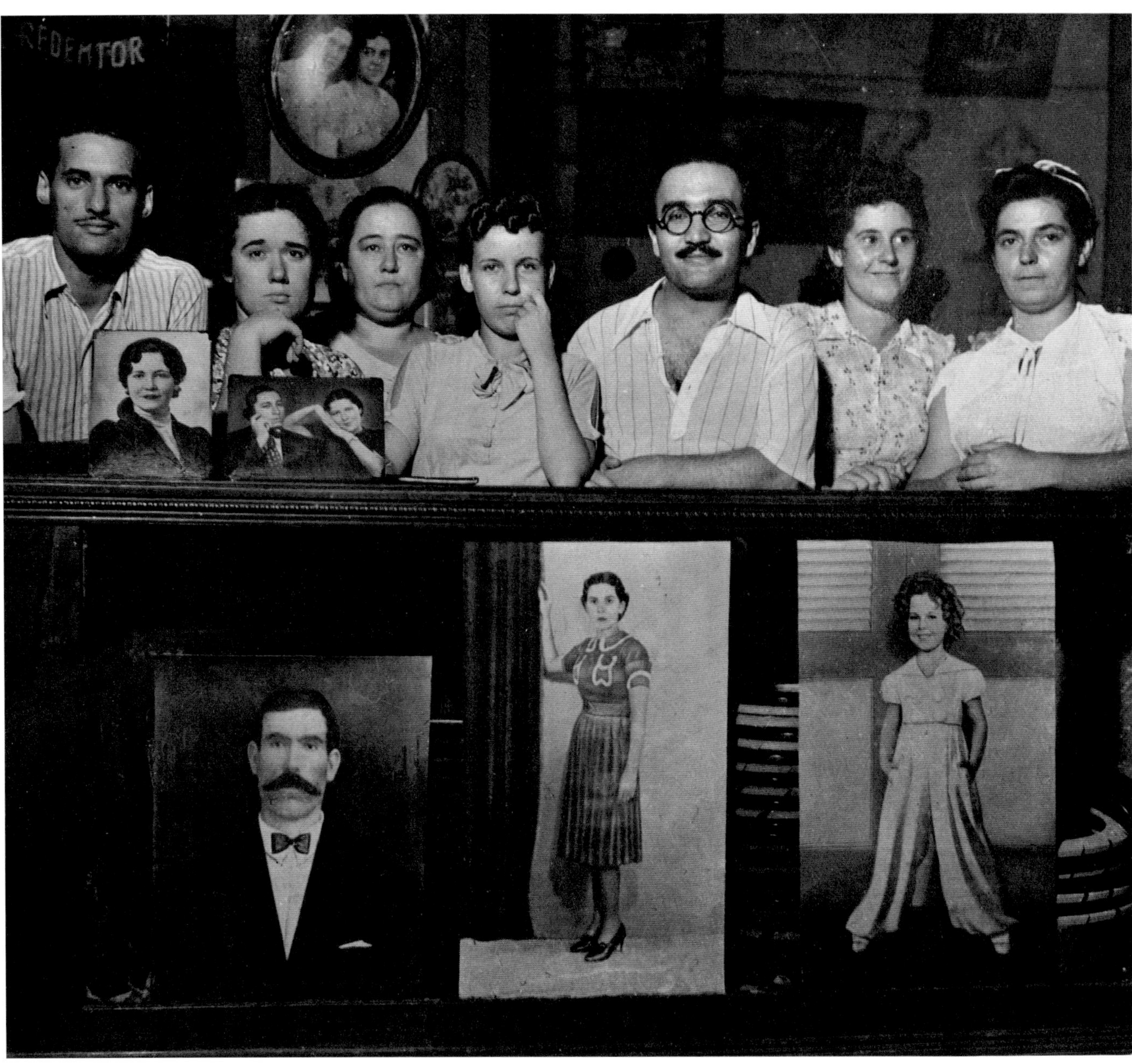

In this indoor group portrait bordering on the whimsical, the people pose not only with two photographs on the ledge (of absent or departed family members?) before them but against a backdrop of three larger photographs, one of which is the child actress Shirley Temple. The juxtaposition of her image on the right with the nineteenth-century portrait of a relative on the left produces a droll effect.

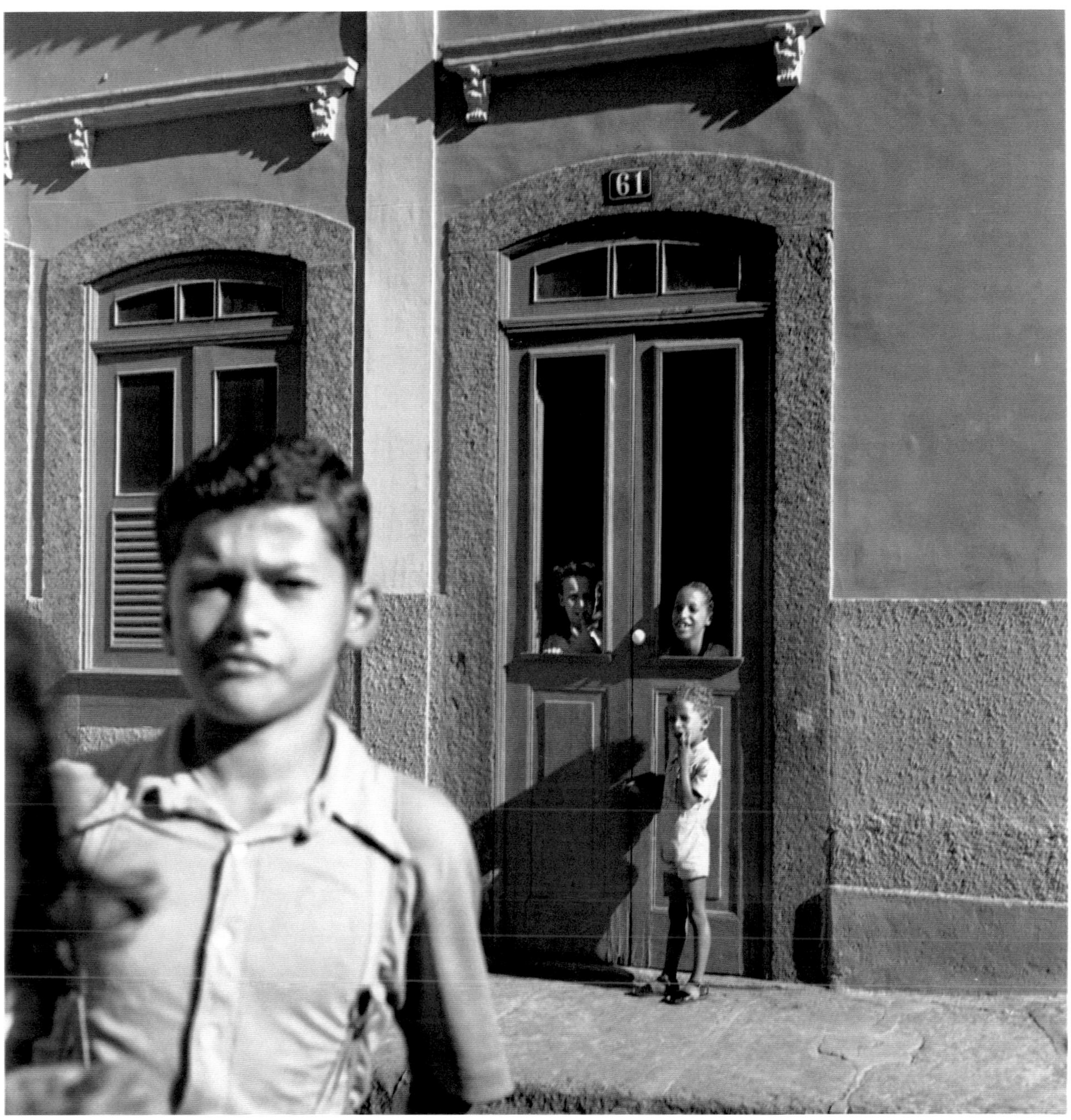

49 STREET SCENE

As a photographer who preferred formal compositions, Naylor rarely produced work that seemed spontaneous. Her turn after the war to commercial fashion photography reinforced her preference for formal positioning of her subjects. This is why this photograph, of a boy awkwardly placed close to the camera framed by twin doorways in which a mother (his mother?) and a small girl (his sister?) stand, is not like her other work. But it holds our interest, adding mystery (and verisimilitude) to Naylor's depiction of everyday life.

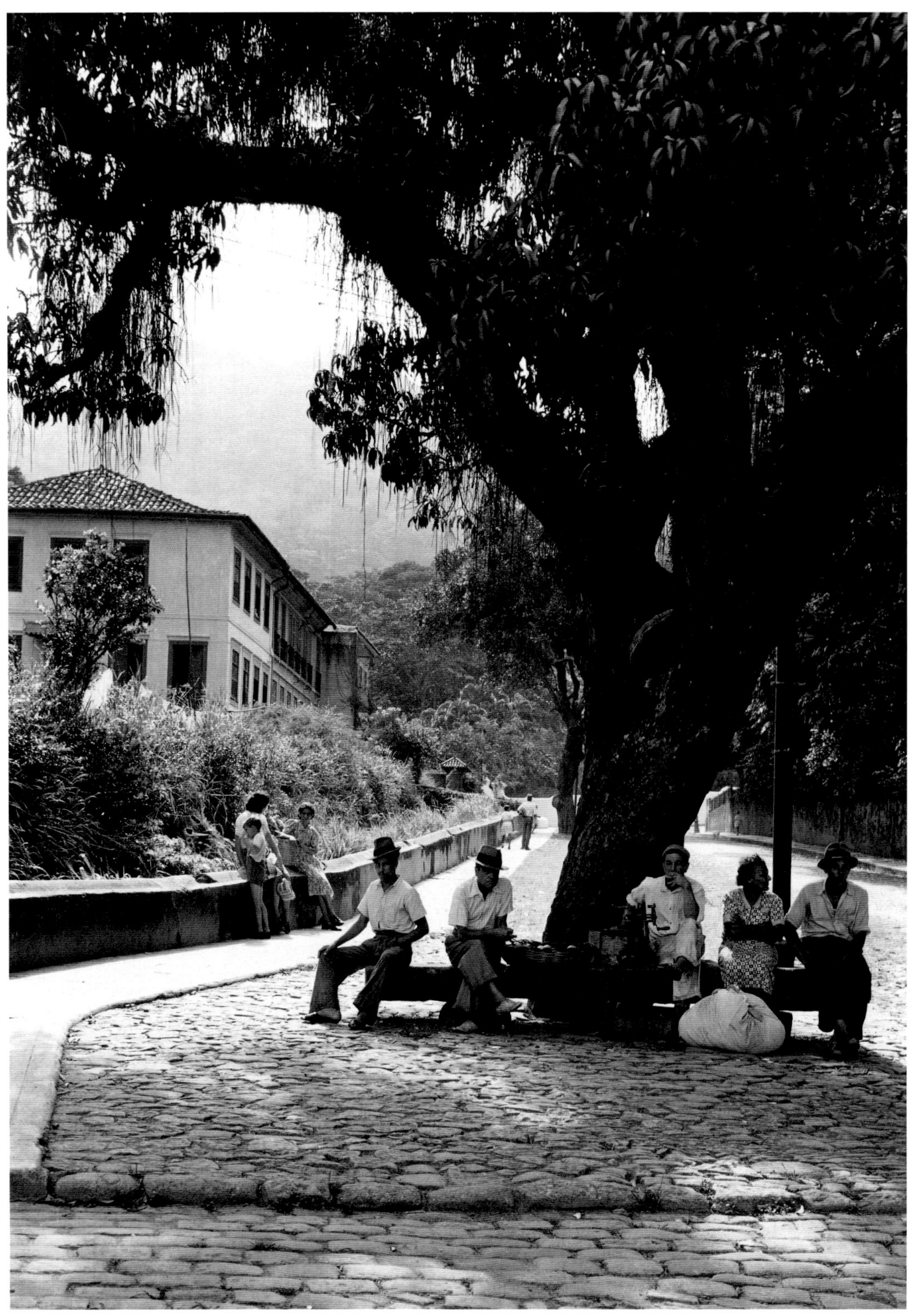

The woman with the bundle at her feet is a washerwoman delivering her laundry or taking it to her home to clean. The building in the background—possibly a school—blends in nicely to its affluent, wooded setting because of the angle of Naylor's lens.

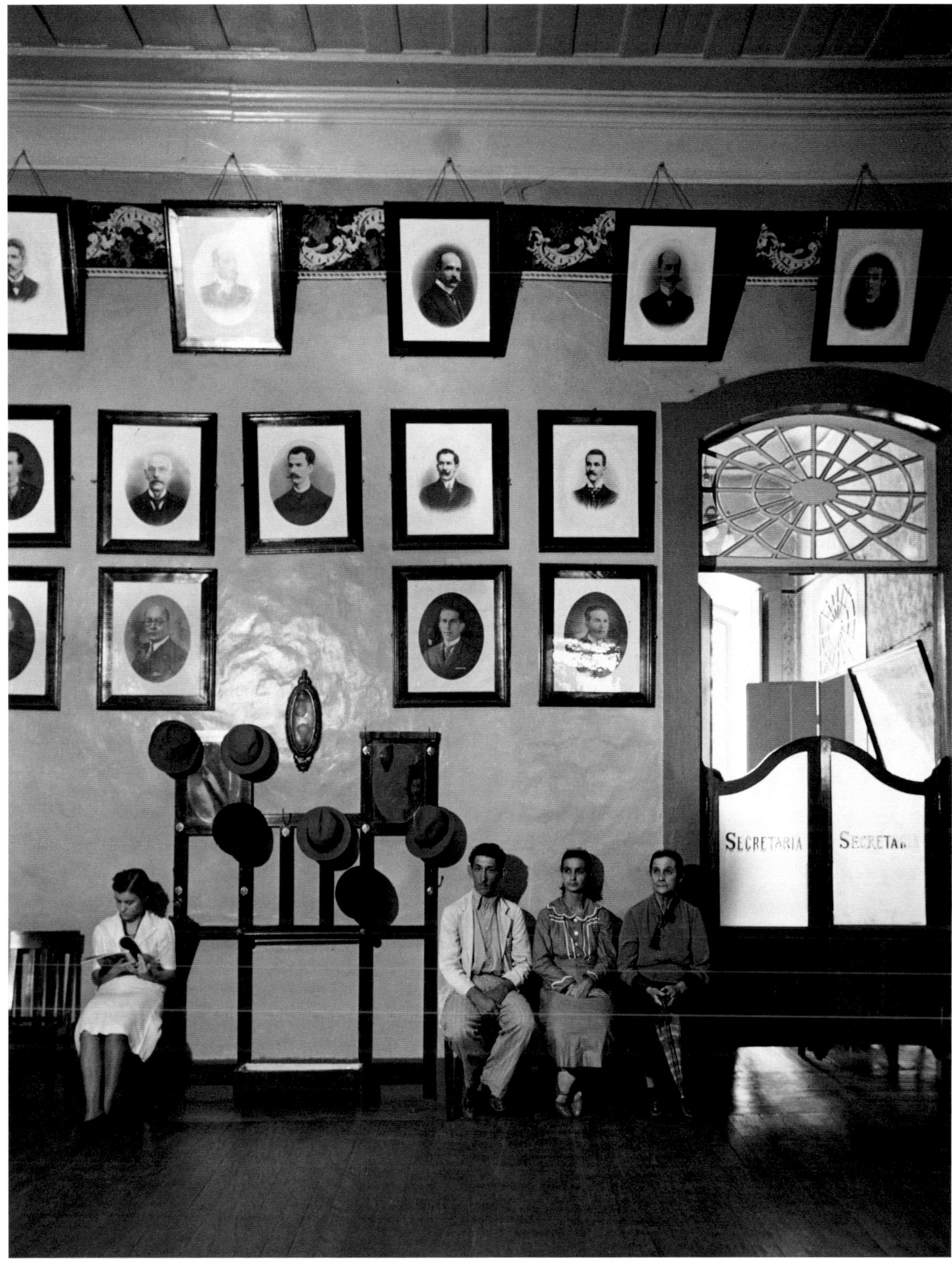

51 WAITING ROOM

During her 1941 trip to Minas Gerais, Naylor found four towns-people sitting patiently in the town hall of São João del Rei. From the wall peer the portraits of more than a dozen important officials; there are half a dozen hats on the rack, indicating either that more sat waiting outside of the picture or that some peti-tioners had been admitted to the inner sanctum. Brazil's political system, even under Vargas's centralization, thrived on interper-sonal relations. Ordinary people approached bureaucrats with individual requests—perhaps for a job, or an exemption from military service, or to petition for a street repair.

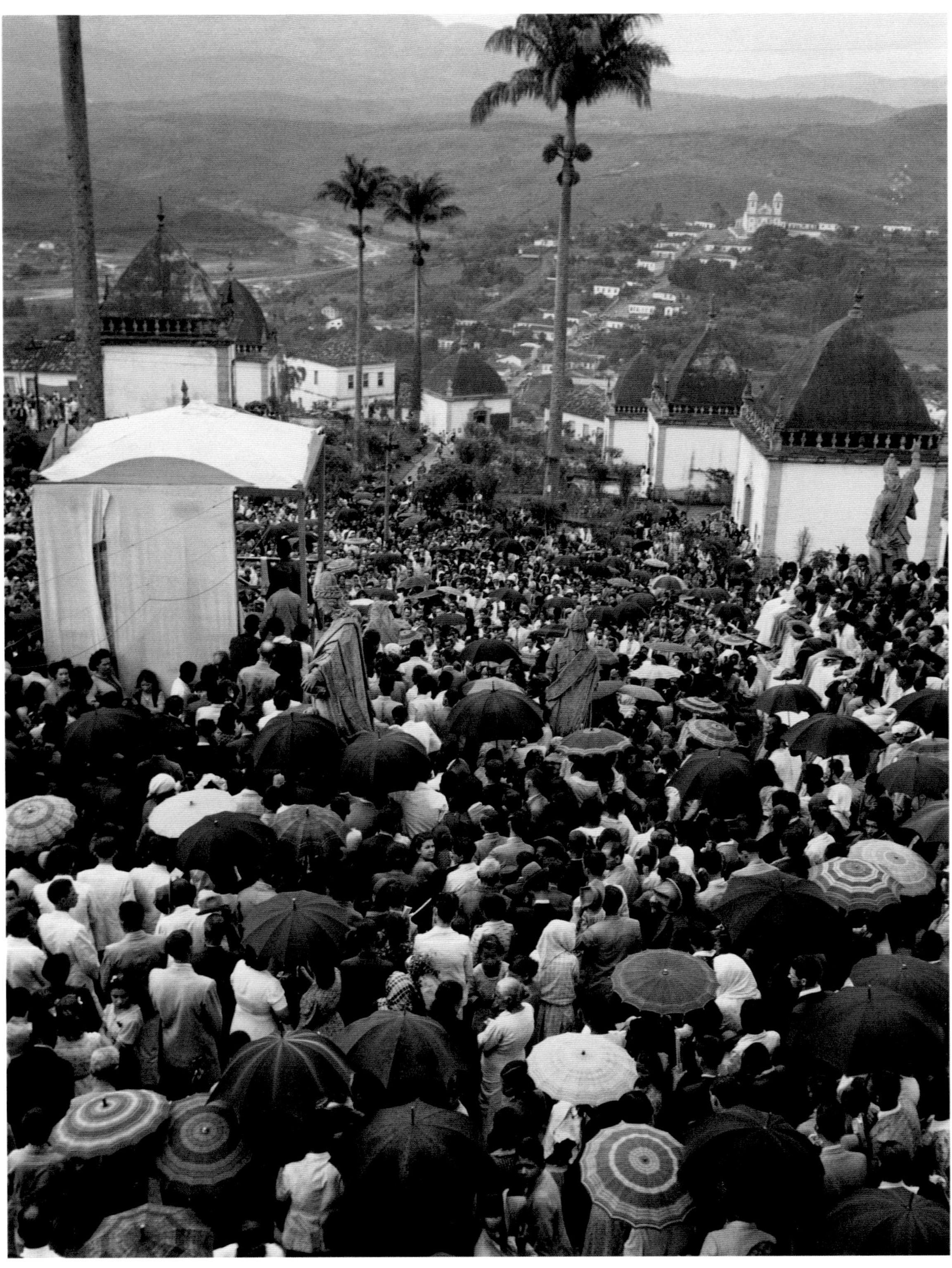

52 PILGRIMS

Photographed from above as a light rain falls on the crowd of religious pilgrims in the baroque city of Congonhas, Minas Gerais, the image captures the intensity of the occasion against the rich backdrop of the mountainous terrain, dotted by tall palm trees and the tile roofs of the city's residences and churches.

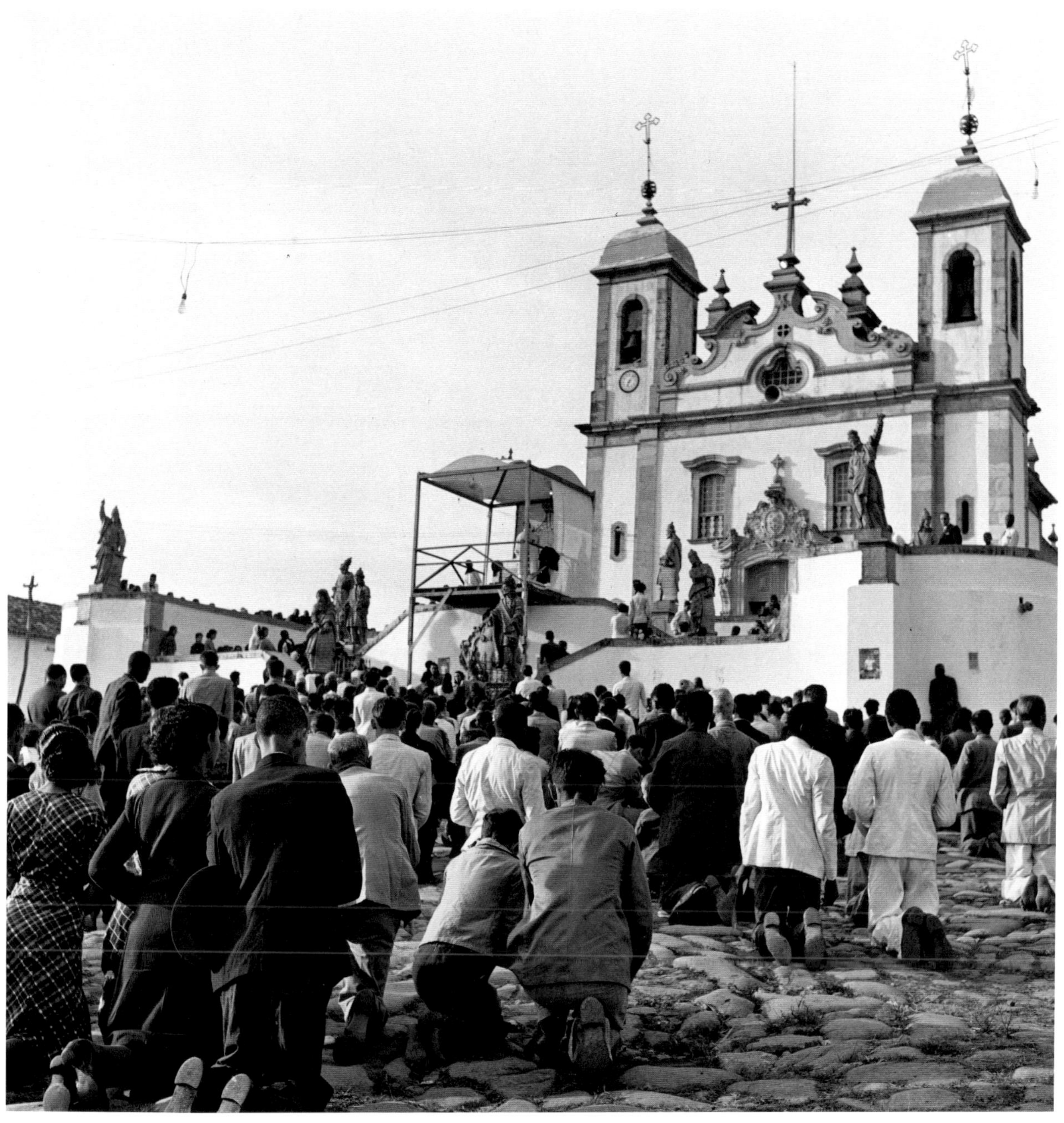

53 PENITENTS

Men and women slowly approach the church on their knees. By the 1940s, urban Brazil had become a mostly secular society, but in remote areas such as central Minas Gerais (and the backlands of Brazil's vast Northeast), religious expression was both tradi-tional and intense. It stressed penitence and *promessas*—vows by supplicants to perform acts of immense self-discipline in return for the right to ask for divine intervention.

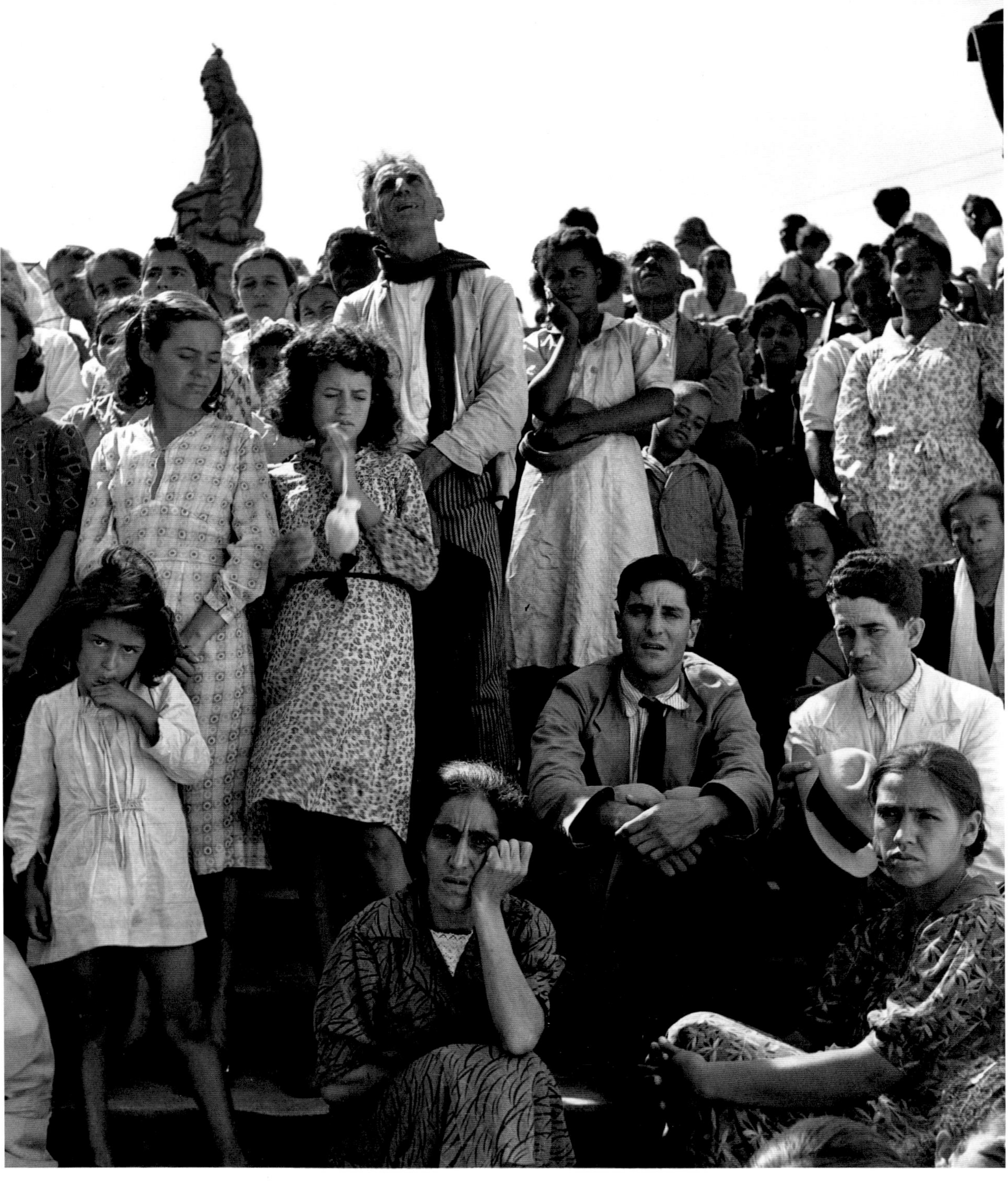

In this powerful image, Naylor renders the Aleijadinho statue a part of the crowd. The men, women, and children seem anguished, especially the woman seated at front center. She reminds us of the migrant workers photographed by Dorothea Lange. The man with striped trousers and scarf looks up to the heavens, but he does not seem expectant that anything good will happen. The photographs capture the tension of religious activities in a way reminiscent of the work of the Brazilian photographer Sebastião Salgado.

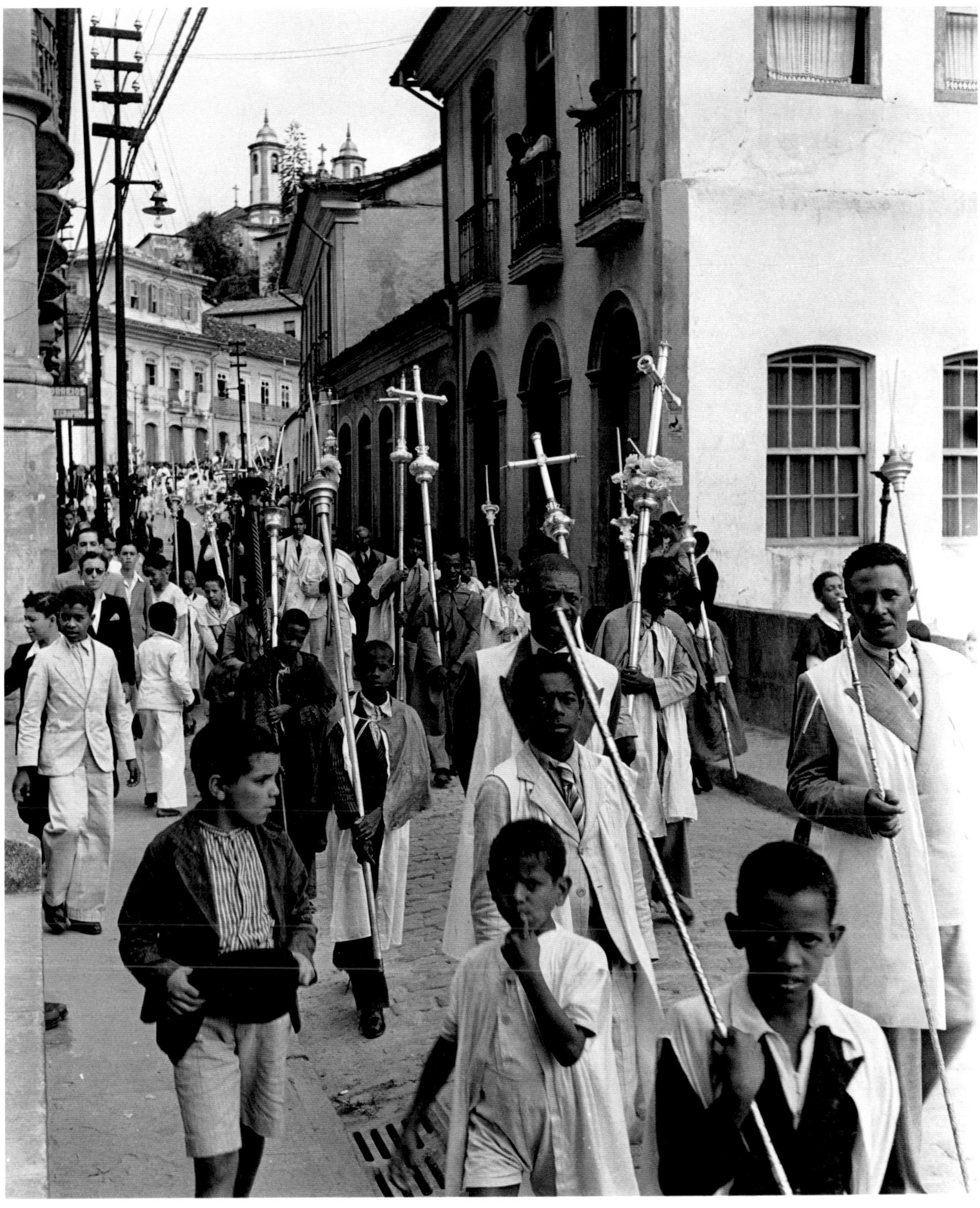

55 PROCESSION

A religious procession winds down a Congonhas street, with a
hilltop church in the background. The men are members of
Catholic brotherhoods.

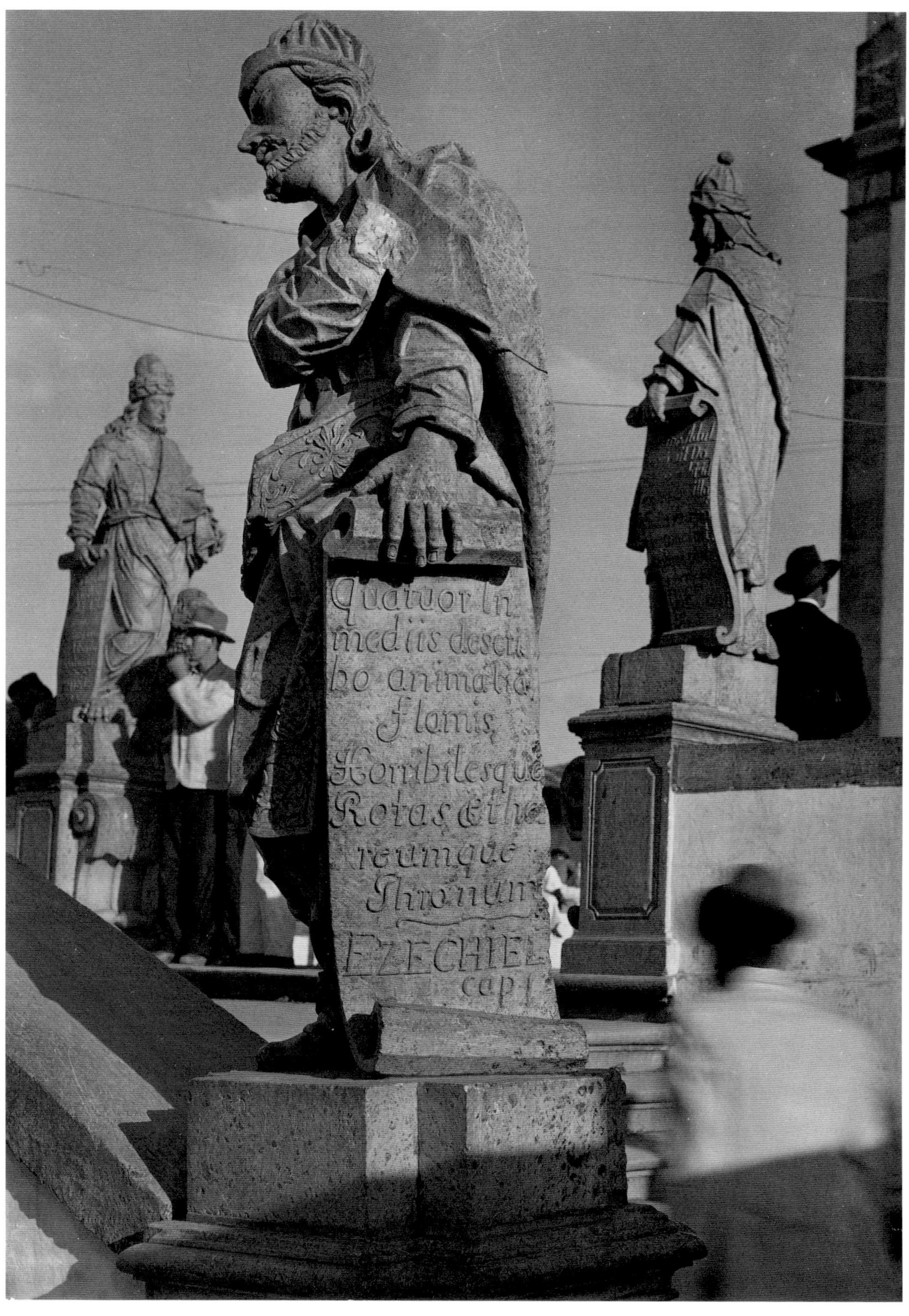

5 6 STATUES

This composition departs significantly from Naylor's usual straightforward depictions of everyday life. The towering statues by Aleijadinho are set off by three human figures, facing in different directions—like the statues—creating a surrealistic effect. This impression is heightened by the blurred (and shadowed) figure entering the composition from the lower right. The crisscrossing horizontal electric wires further lend a sense of contrast with the hulking statuary photographed from a low angle; they recall the film techniques of D. W. Griffith (and Orson Welles).

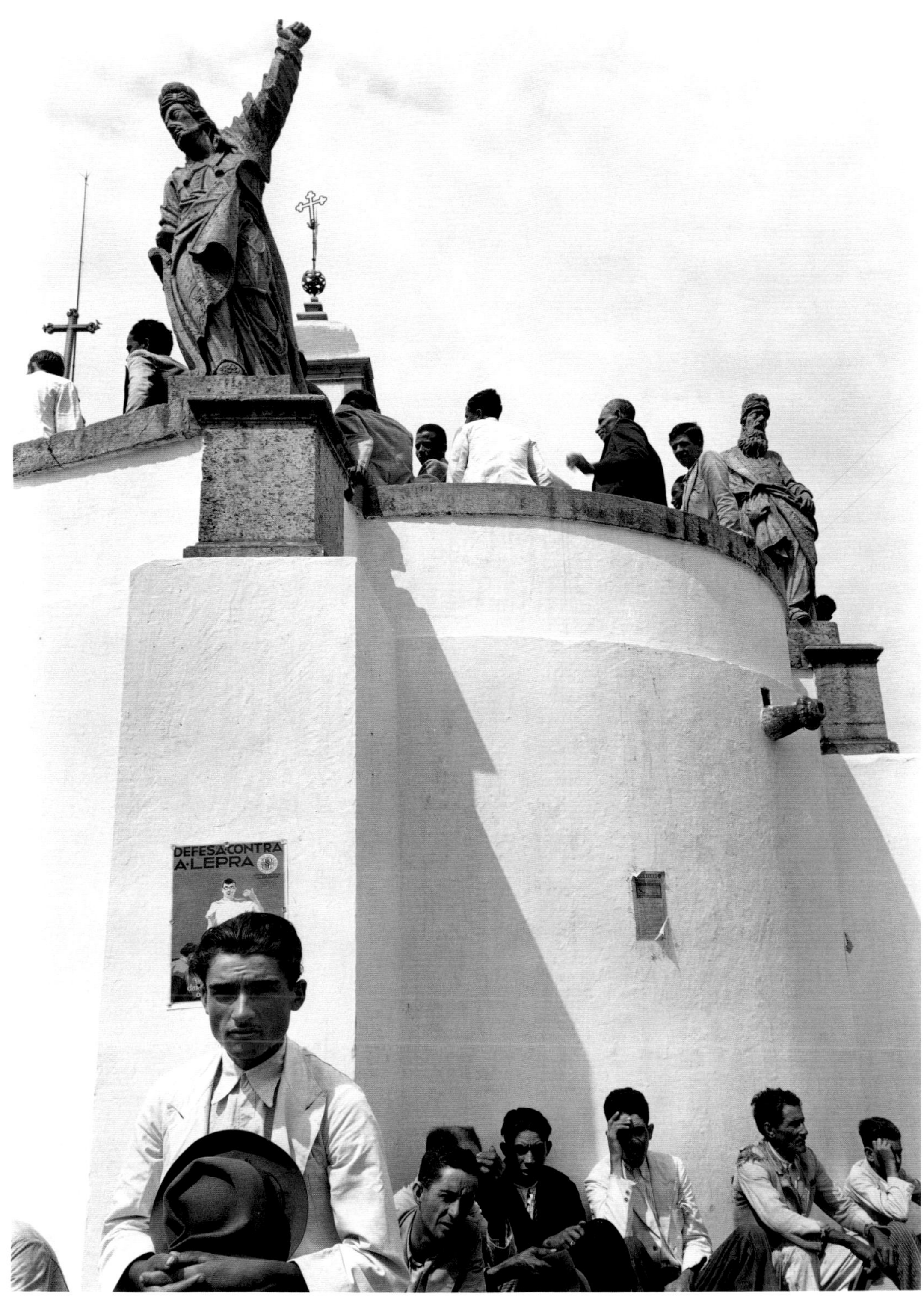

57 DURING A LULL

Several interesting elements are juxtaposed in this image. Naylor captures the stark presence of the Aleijadinho statue by photographing from below, depicting, as well, pilgrims to the church on two visual levels. The central figure at the bottom of the photograph stands hat in hand in front of a poster announc-ing the Vargas government's campaign to treat and cure leprosy, an apt (or ironic?) allusion to the fact that Aleijadinho was a leper. More than most of her other images, this one follows the photojournalistic device of freezing subjects into immobility during moments of tension.

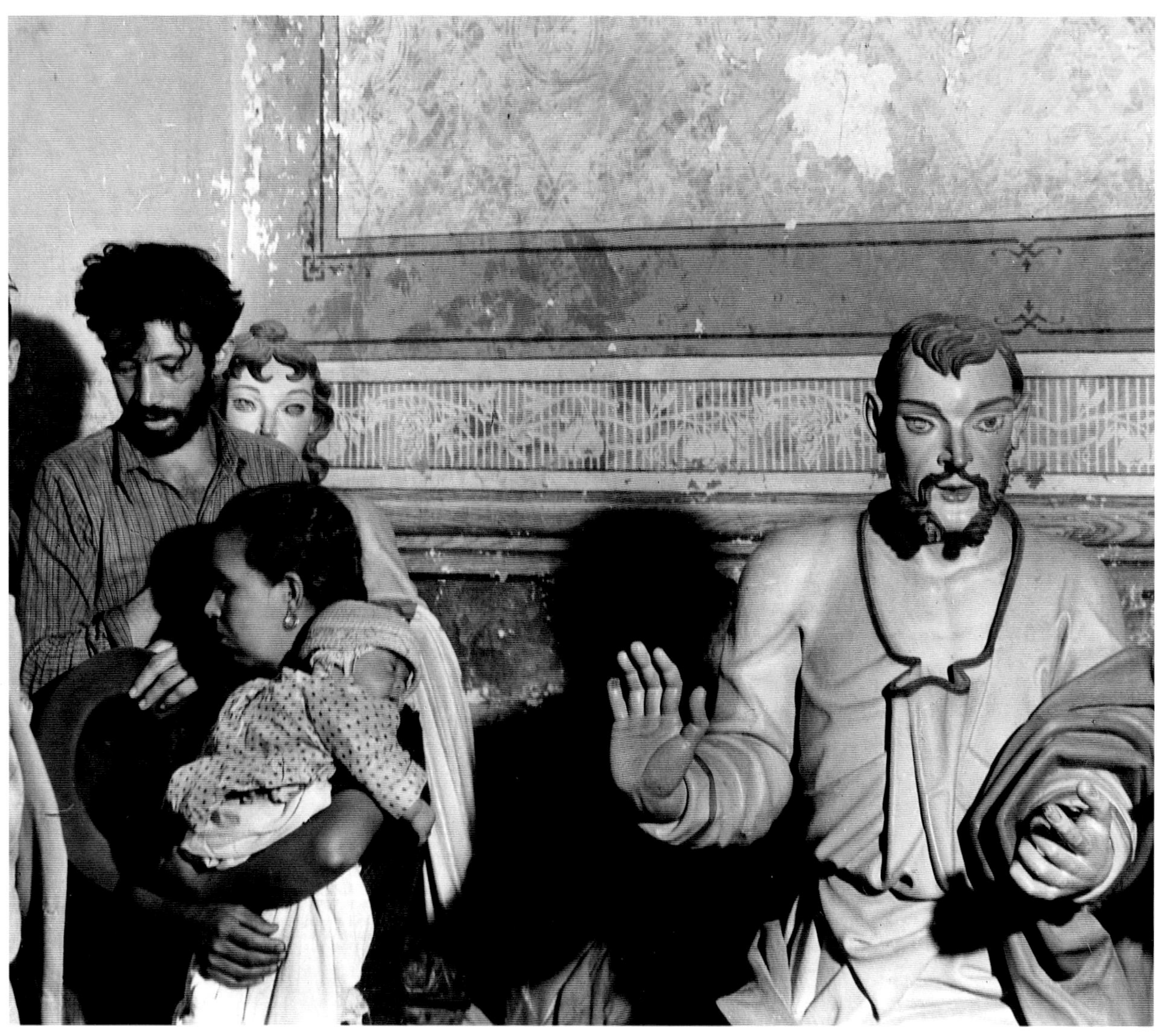

58 FAMILY GROUP

This photograph of a distraught family group standing before
two Aleijadinho statues is uncharacteristic of Naylor's work, but
it is a powerful image.

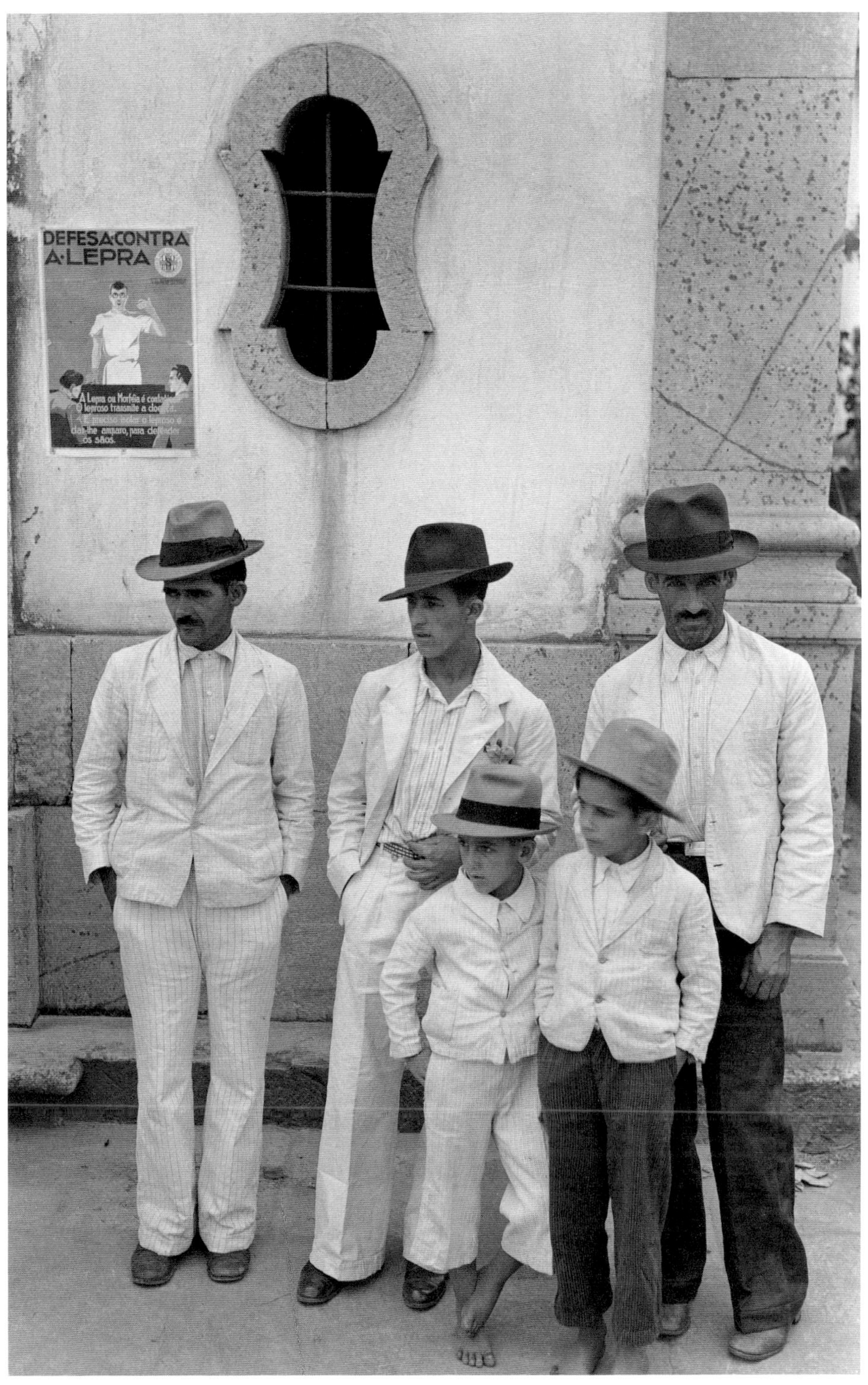

59 MEN AND BOYS

Naylor poses her five subjects in a classical triangle. On the
church wall is another antileprosy campaign poster, illustrating
the extensive presence of the national government under Vargas
and federal efforts to improve public health.

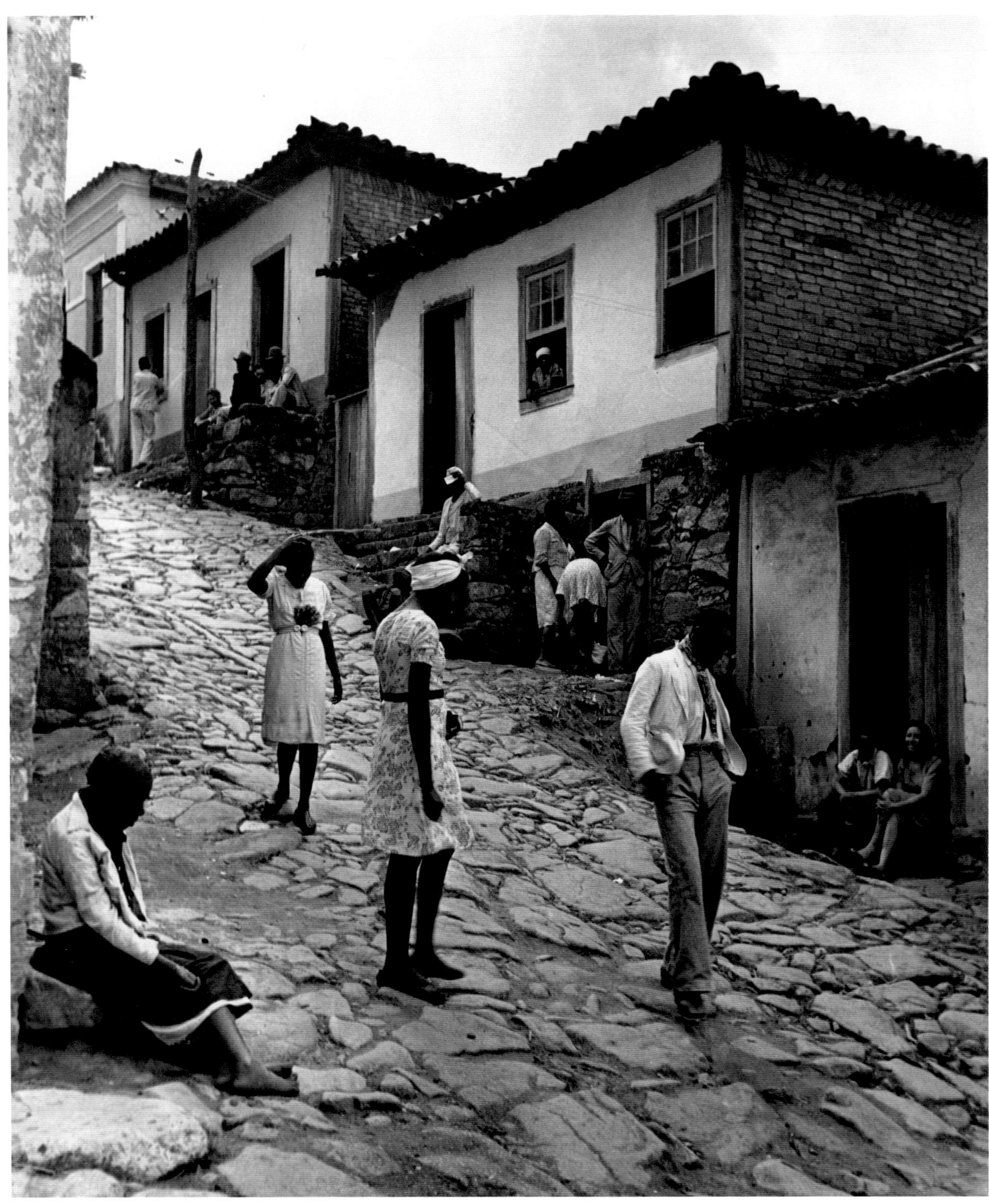

60 STREET SCENE, MINAS GERAIS

This panoramic view captures what in essence was a small neighborhood, a cluster of houses and open space winding down from the hills. It is probably a day of rest, because men are at home. Most of the people in the street seem carefree—a characteristic of Naylor's images—although the barefoot woman sitting at the lower left-hand corner does not seem very happy. These are not houses of the poor: the houses at the top of the street have electricity.

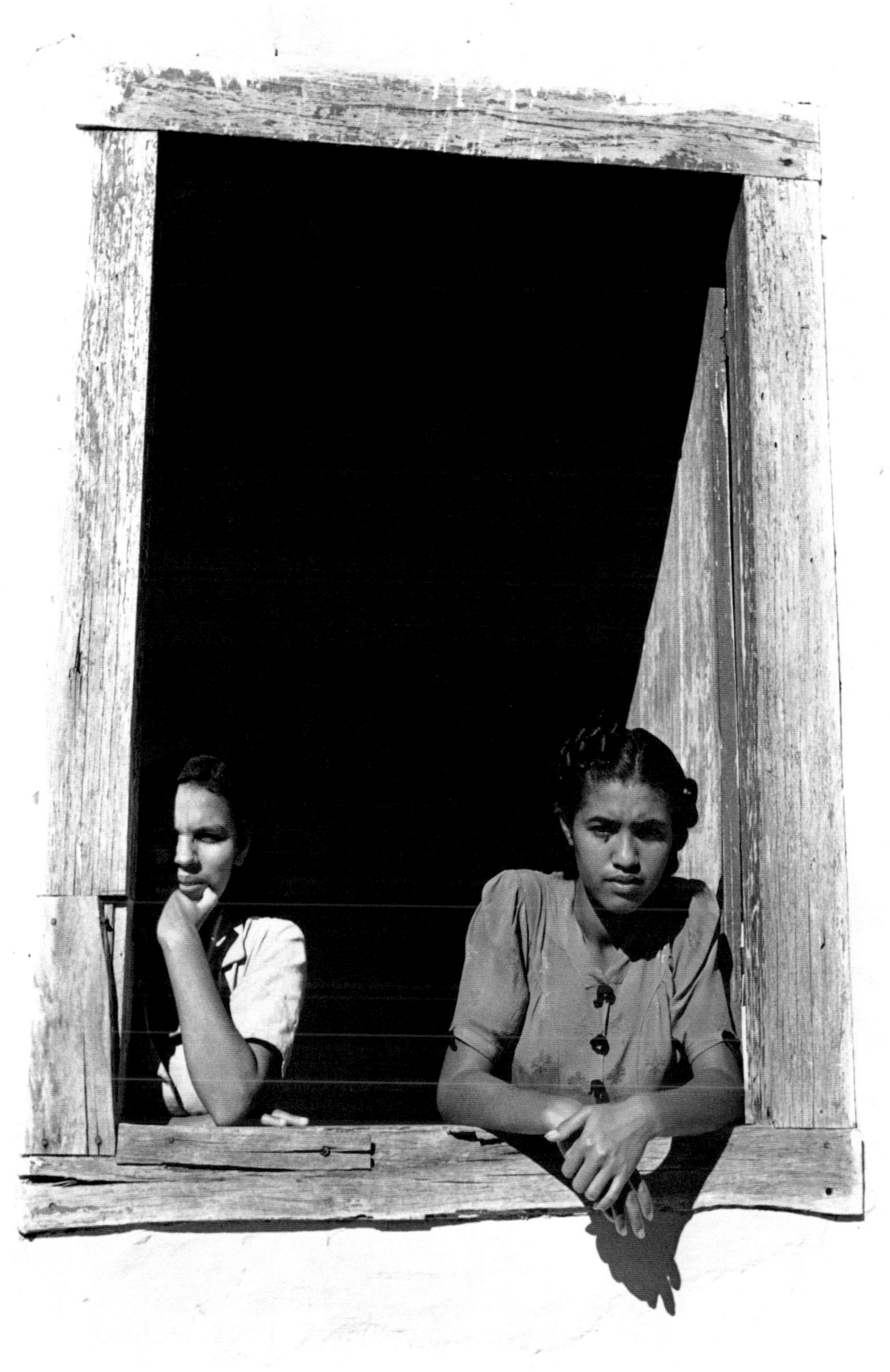

61 PASSING TIME

Two young women stand in their glassless window frame
watching the street.

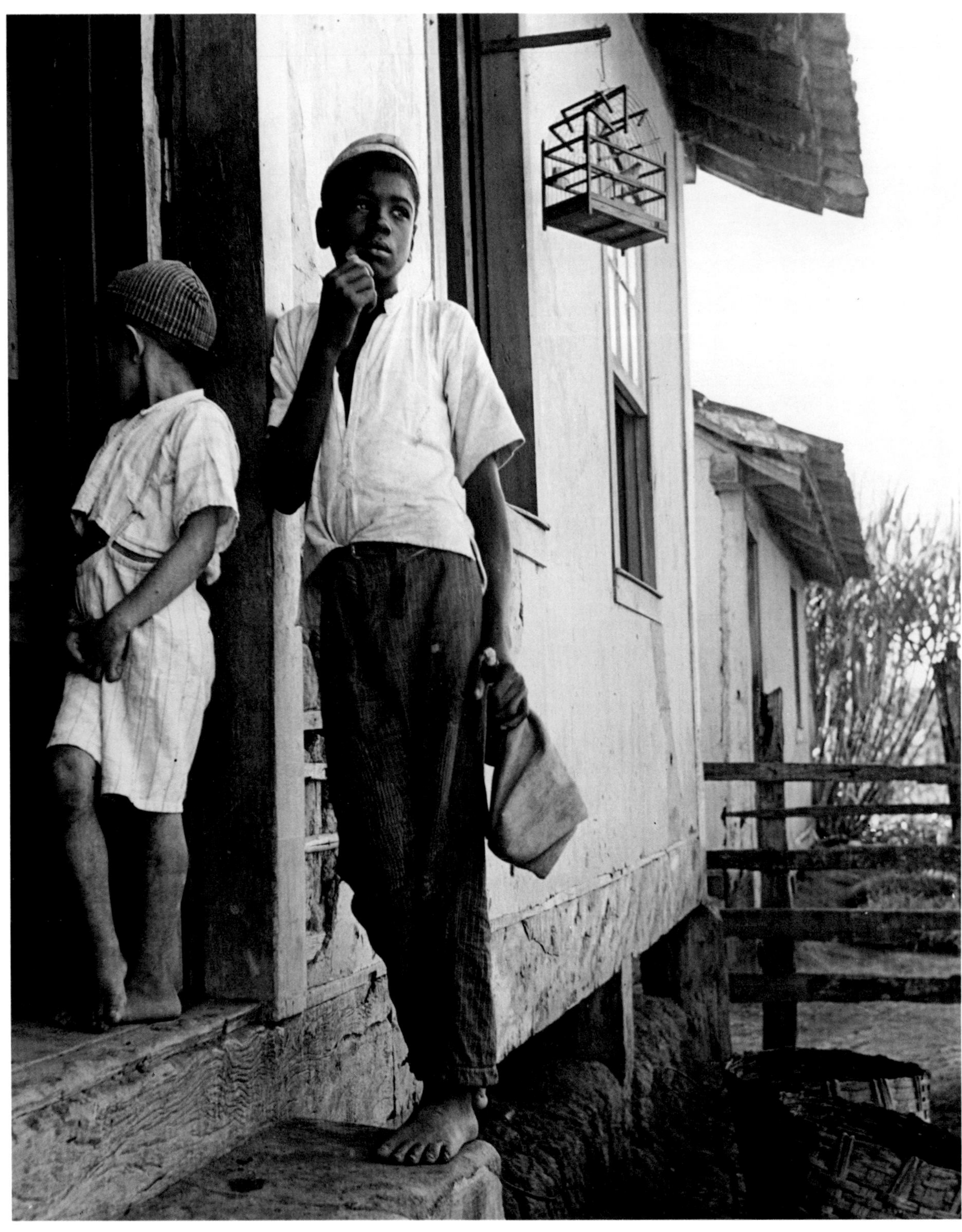

Two barefoot boys stand at the rear of their house, which is solidly constructed (although unfinished) and which has a small bird in a handcrafted cage affixed to the window frame. One of the boys holds a leather flask, which he will take to work with him. The empty baskets suggest that they will take goods to sell.

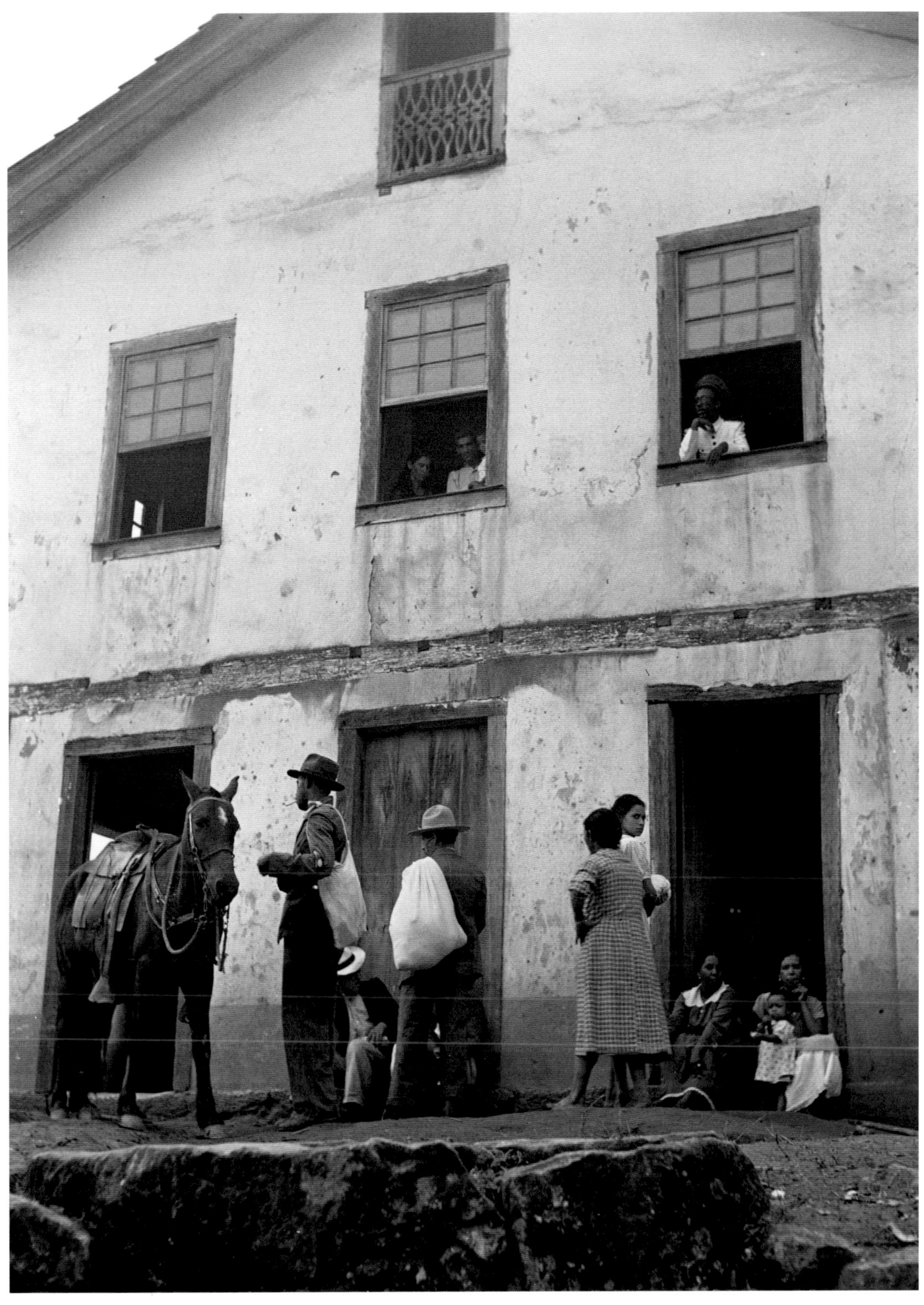

This family group has taken its horse up the narrow streets to a dry goods store, where they have either purchased provisions or brought items to sell. The building has windows with glass panes, a sign of its prosperity.

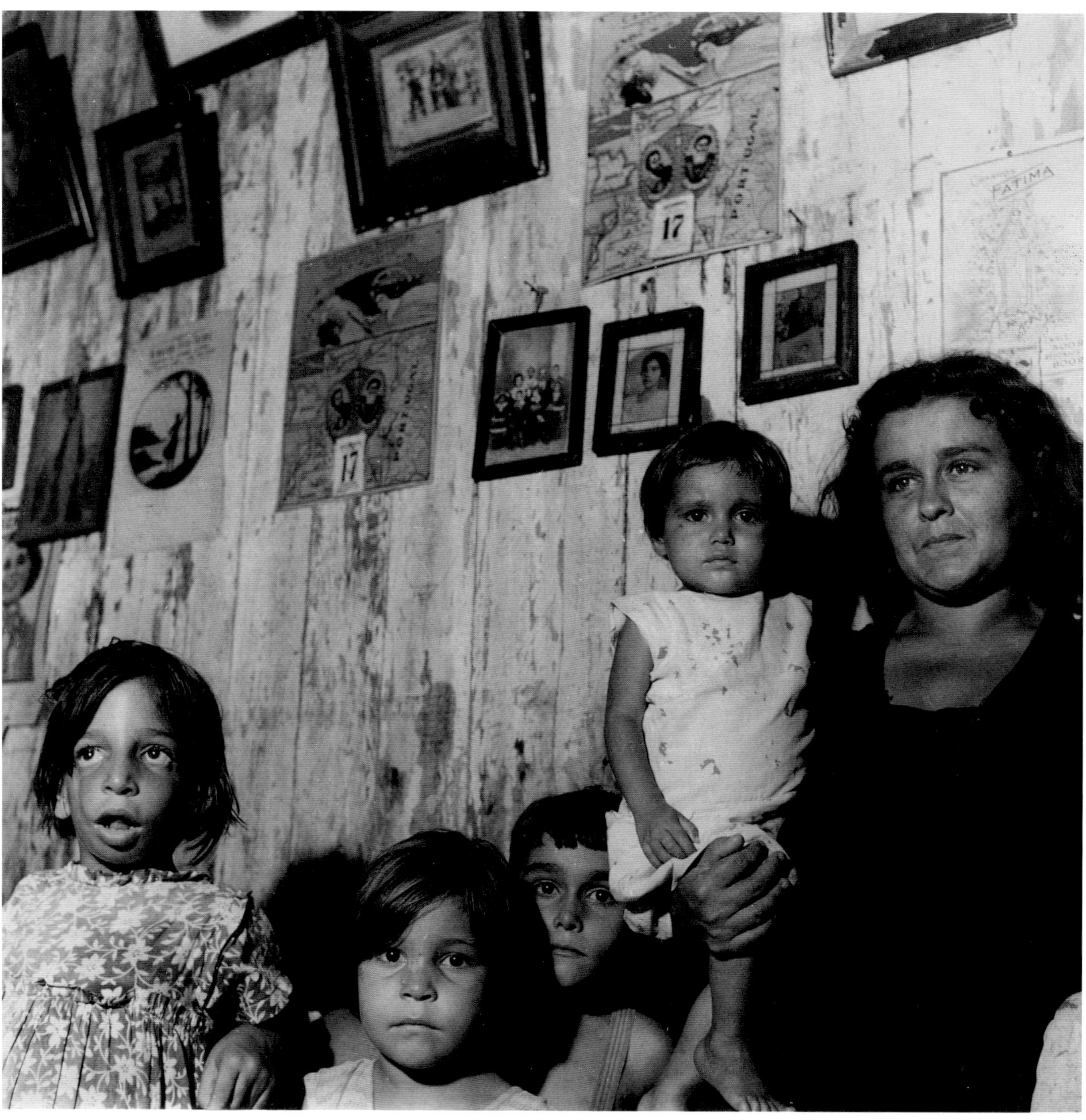

64 SEVENTEENTH OF THE MONTH

A woman, who is a descendant of Portuguese immigrants, stands with her children. On the wall hangs a collection of family photographs taken in a studio, fliers, and two calendars from Portugal. One of the souvenirs is from Our Lady of Fátima, the patron saint affiliated with Portugal's healing shrine.

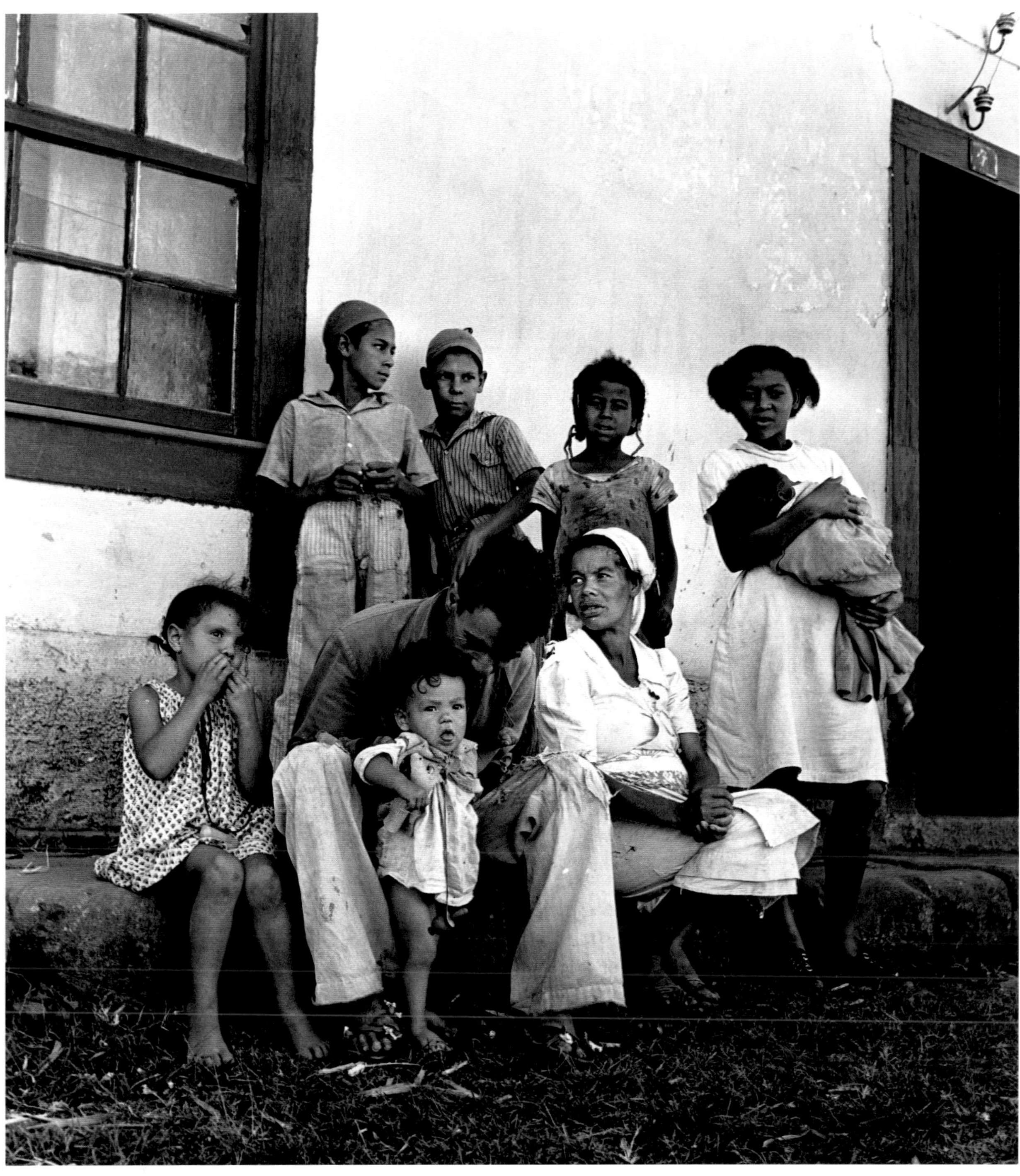

65 FAMILY GROUP

Here Naylor captures an image that reminds the viewer of the socially conscious Depression-era photographers in the United States working for the FSA and WPA. The father and mother are distracted, and the younger children are ill at ease. These are poor people, and their patched clothing is their best. Shooting from a low angle accentuates the starkness of the scene. The building, which has electricity, is not their home.

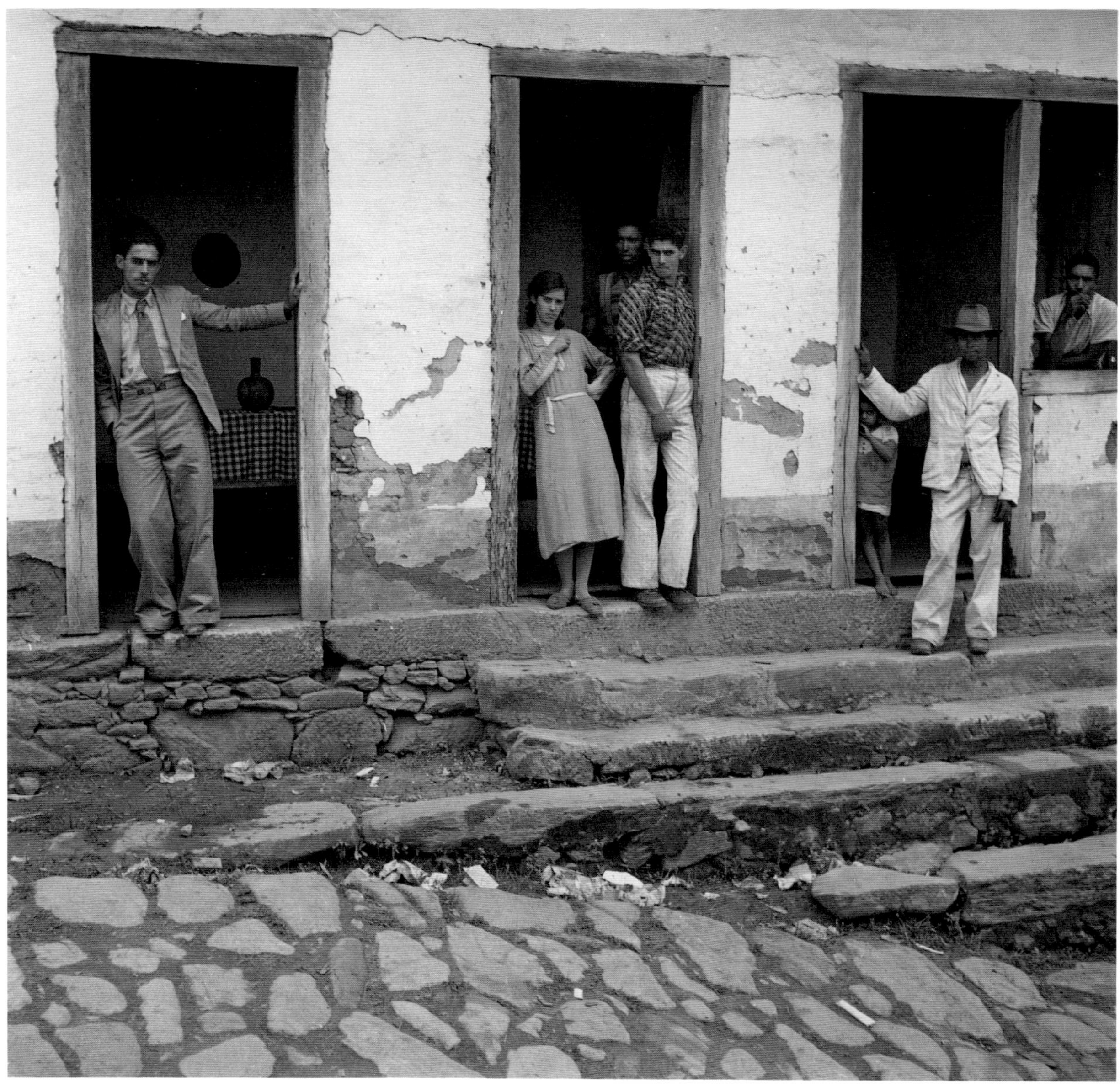

People stand in the entry doors of a restaurant, dressed in their best clothes. In this photograph the camera seems to have intruded: body language and facial expressions show this. The street has been swept clean, probably because of the festival going on. Usually one would find discarded paper and debris outside the door of such establishments. In the rainy season, the street would swell with rushing water cascading down to the bottom.

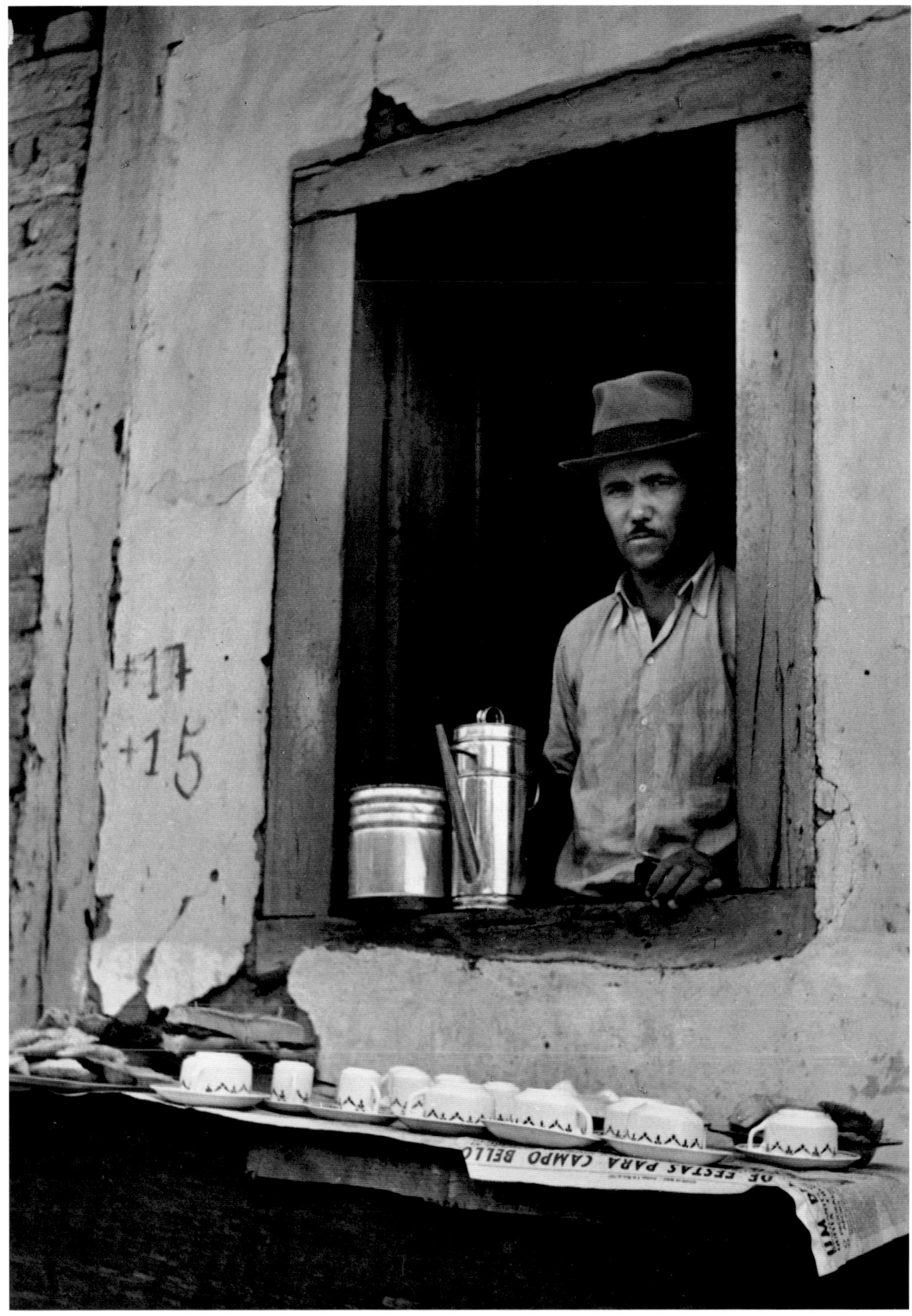

67 COFFEE VENDOR

A man uses a ledge outside his window and sells coffee and pastries as well as sandwiches. He uses a newspaper for a tablecloth. This is an excellent example of how Naylor's photographs depicted the material culture of everyday life—in this case, a creative strategy within the country's informal economy.

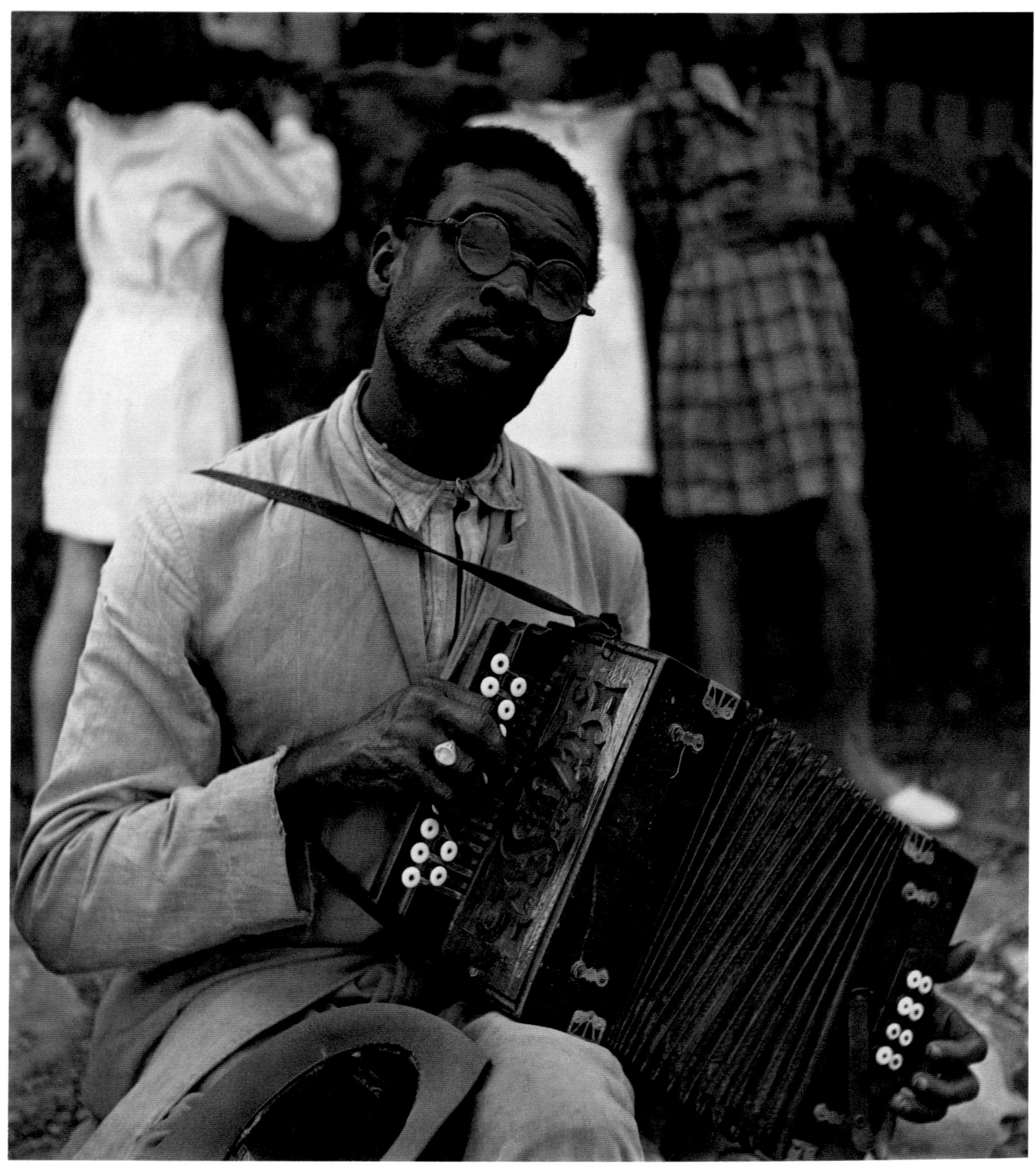

This man made his living playing his *sanfona* (accordion) for tips
at open-air markets.

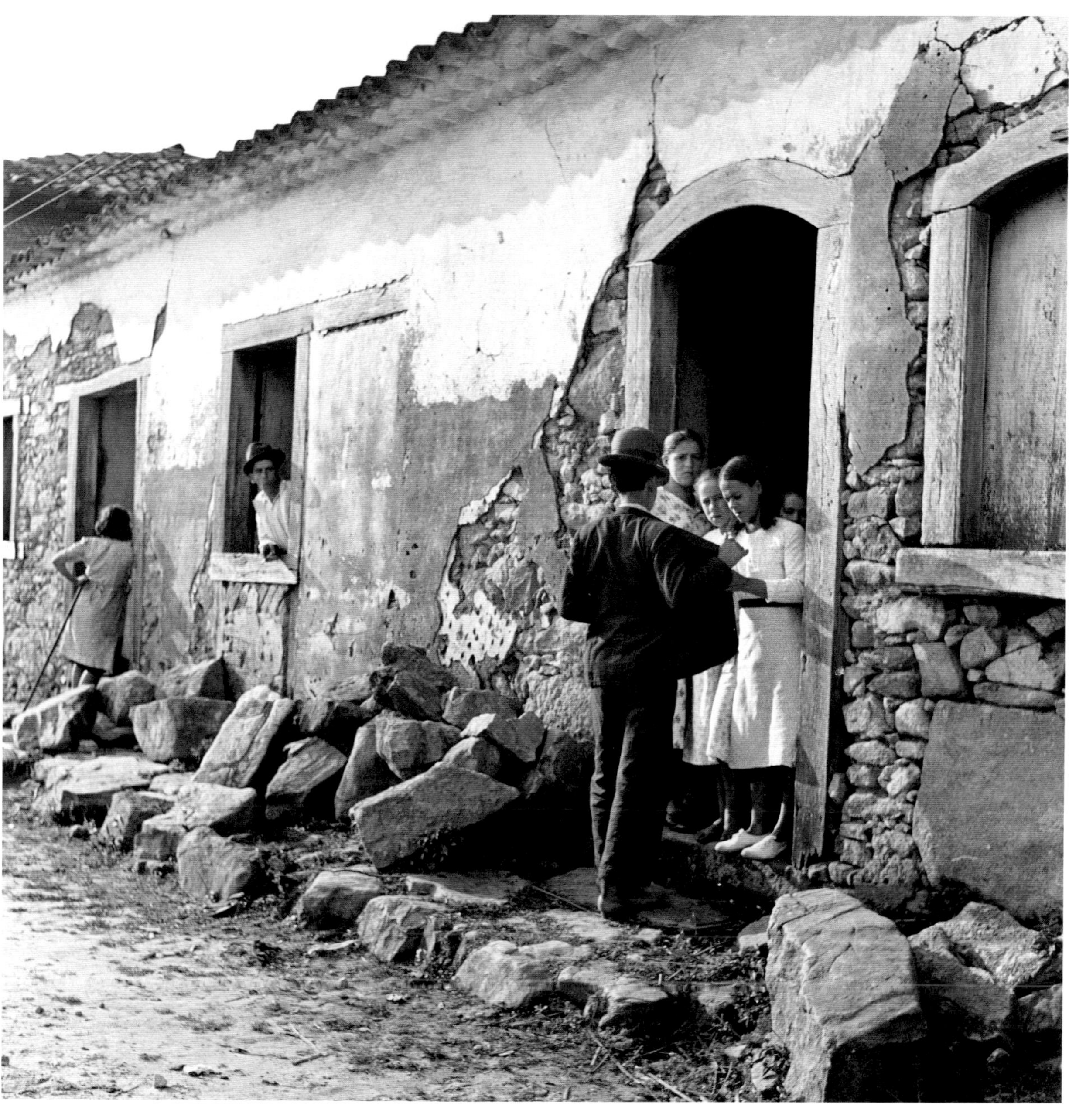

This may be an itinerant seller with his wares pinned to the inside of his suit jacket. Or he may be a local resident showing off a new vest or shirt. When sons came home on leave from military duty, for example, proud mothers often took them door to door to show off their uniforms to neighbors. Although humorous, the photograph also shows the house in a state of disrepair. It is possible that the man of the house had died; women were not expected to make repairs on their dwellings.

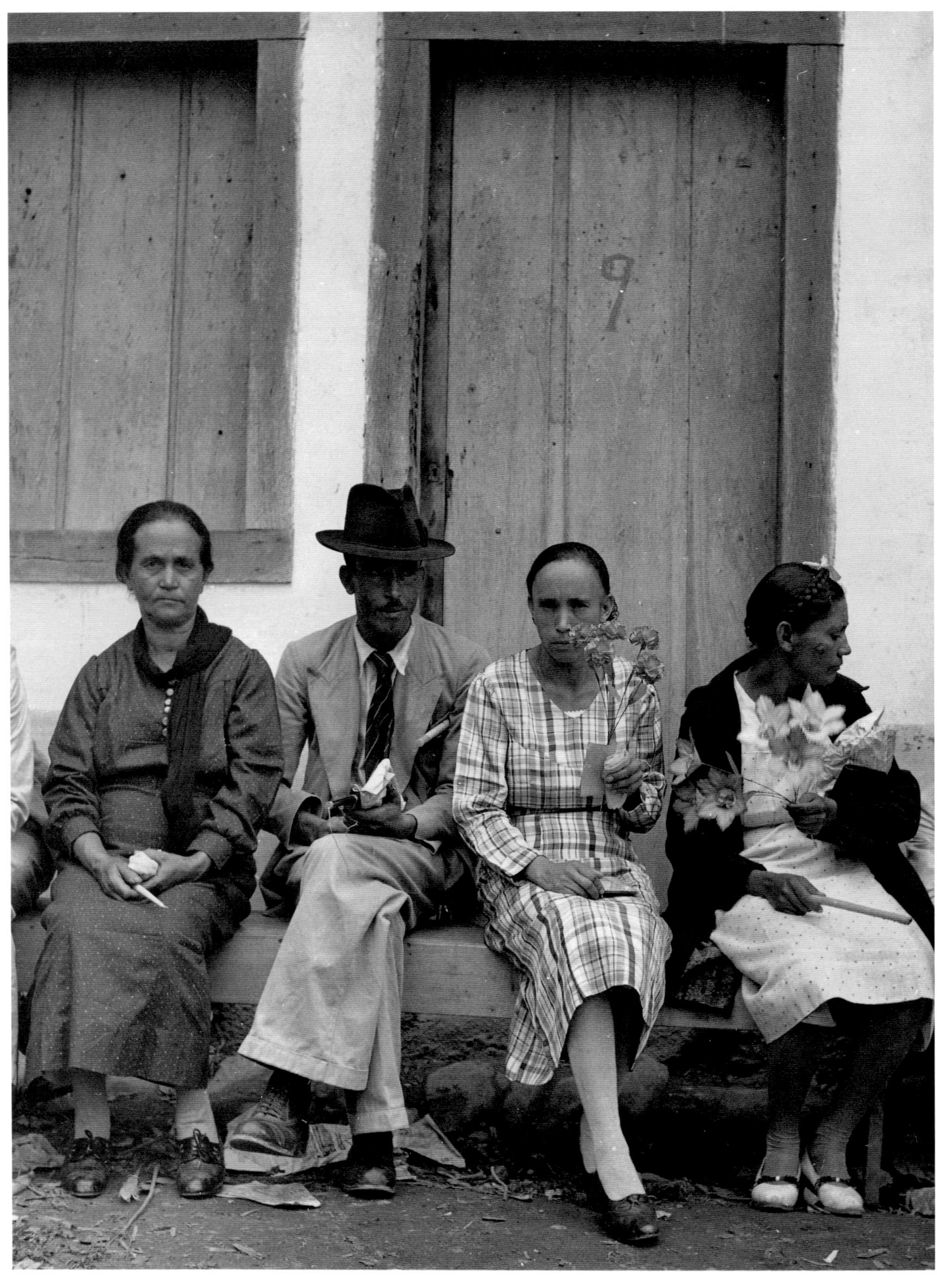

70 WAITING

A man and three women sit, somewhat uncomfortably, on a
bench.

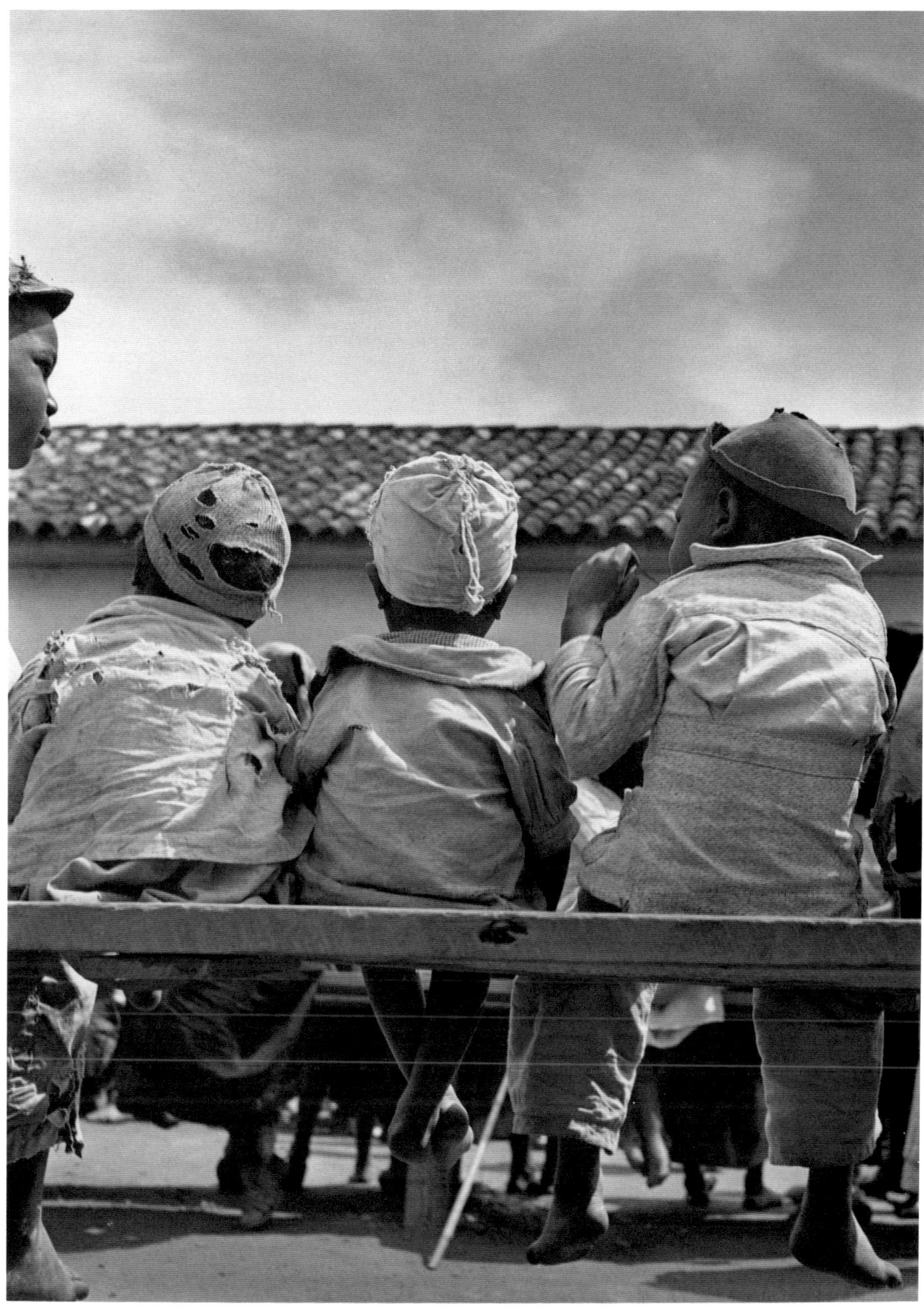

7I STREET CHILDREN

Naylor usually avoided sentimentality, but here she captures
four ragged and barefoot children, presumably beggars, on a
bench.

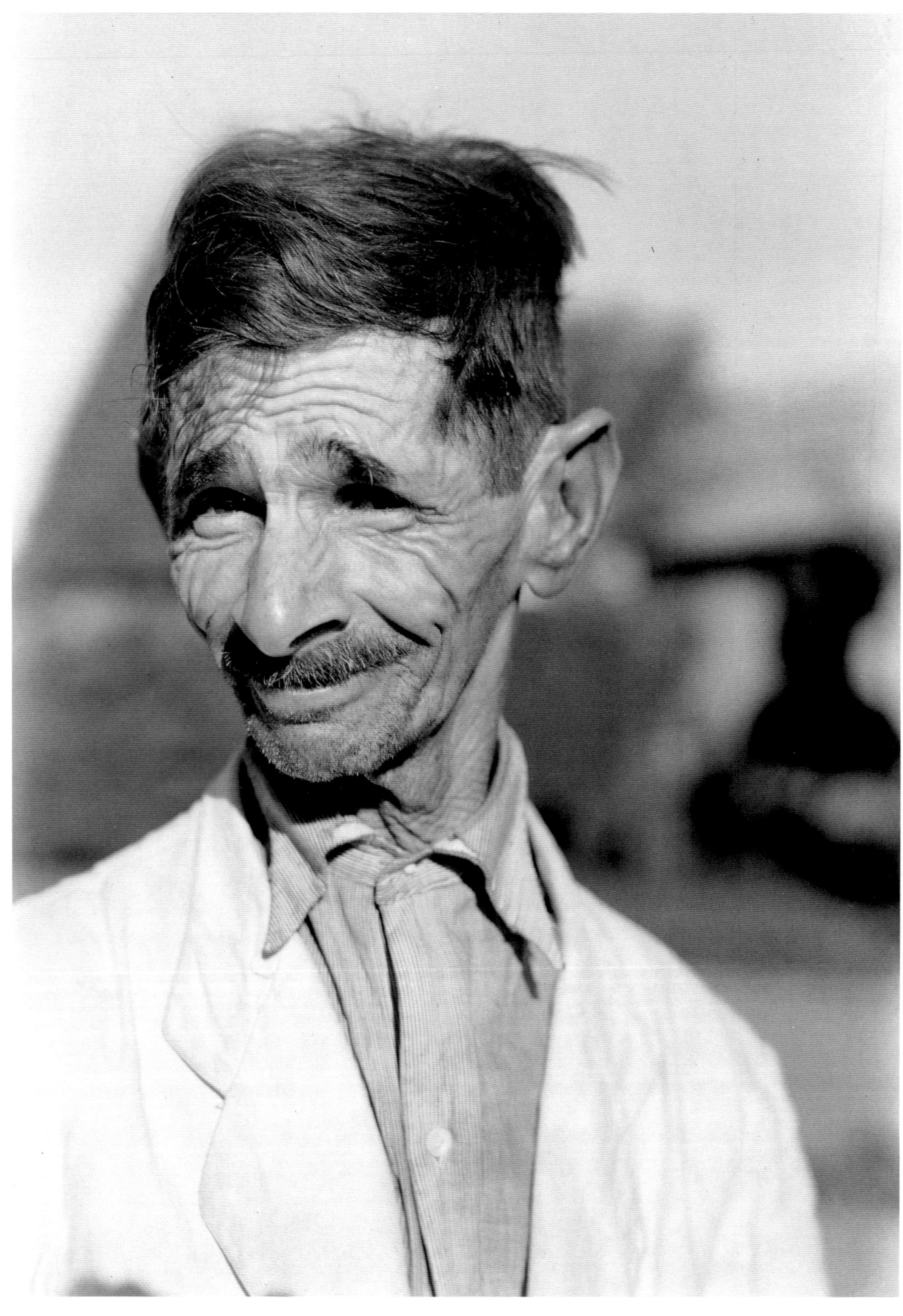

This man with leathery, wrinkled skin probably stands five feet two inches or less. Men and women from the interior and from the Northeast after generations of inadequate diet were shorter in stature and had a shorter life expectancy than people from the South.

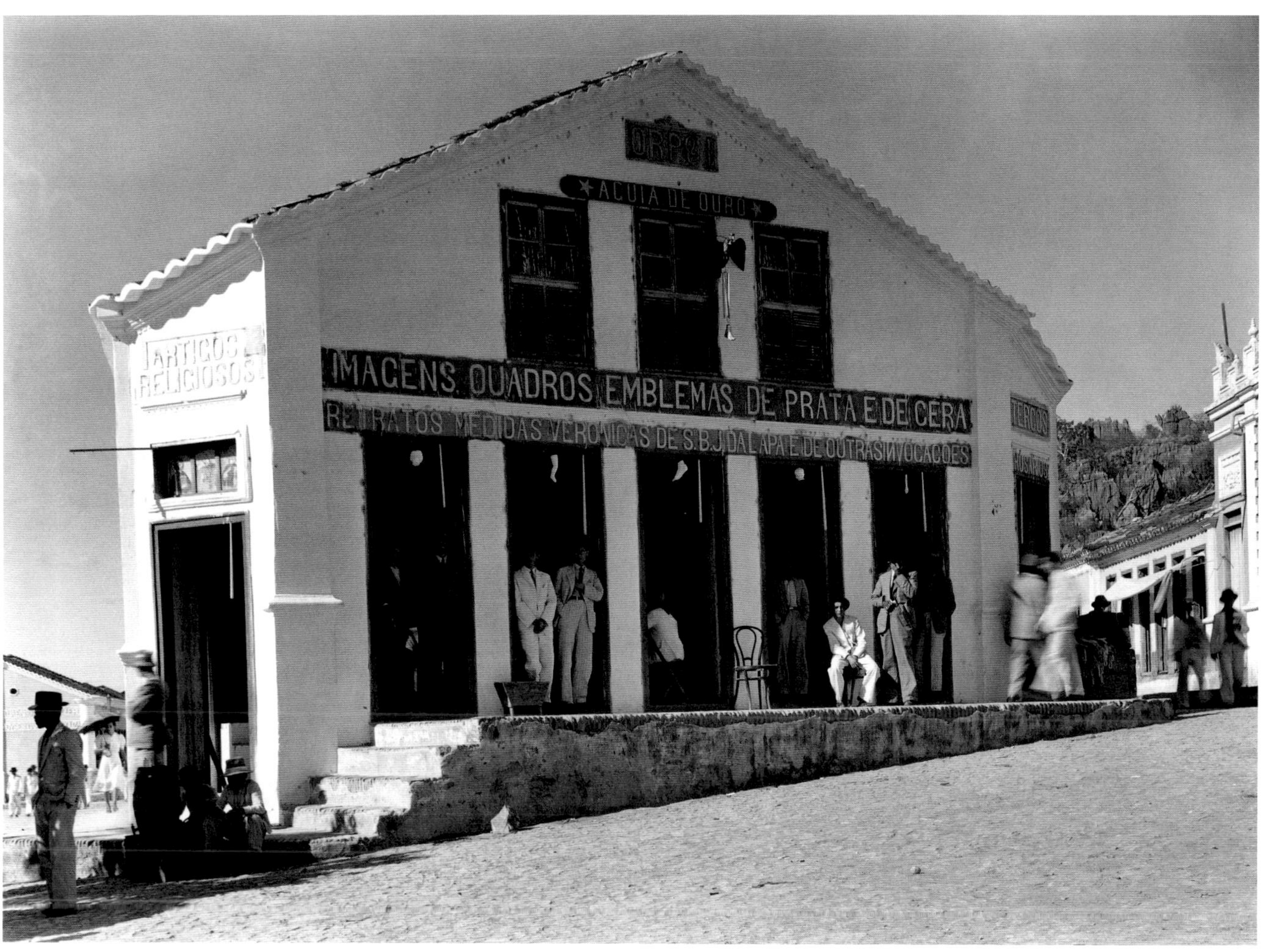

73 RELIGIOUS DRY GOODS

This large commercial establishment sells religious images and emblems in silver and wax. The people's clothing suggest that this was probably a Sunday or religious holiday.

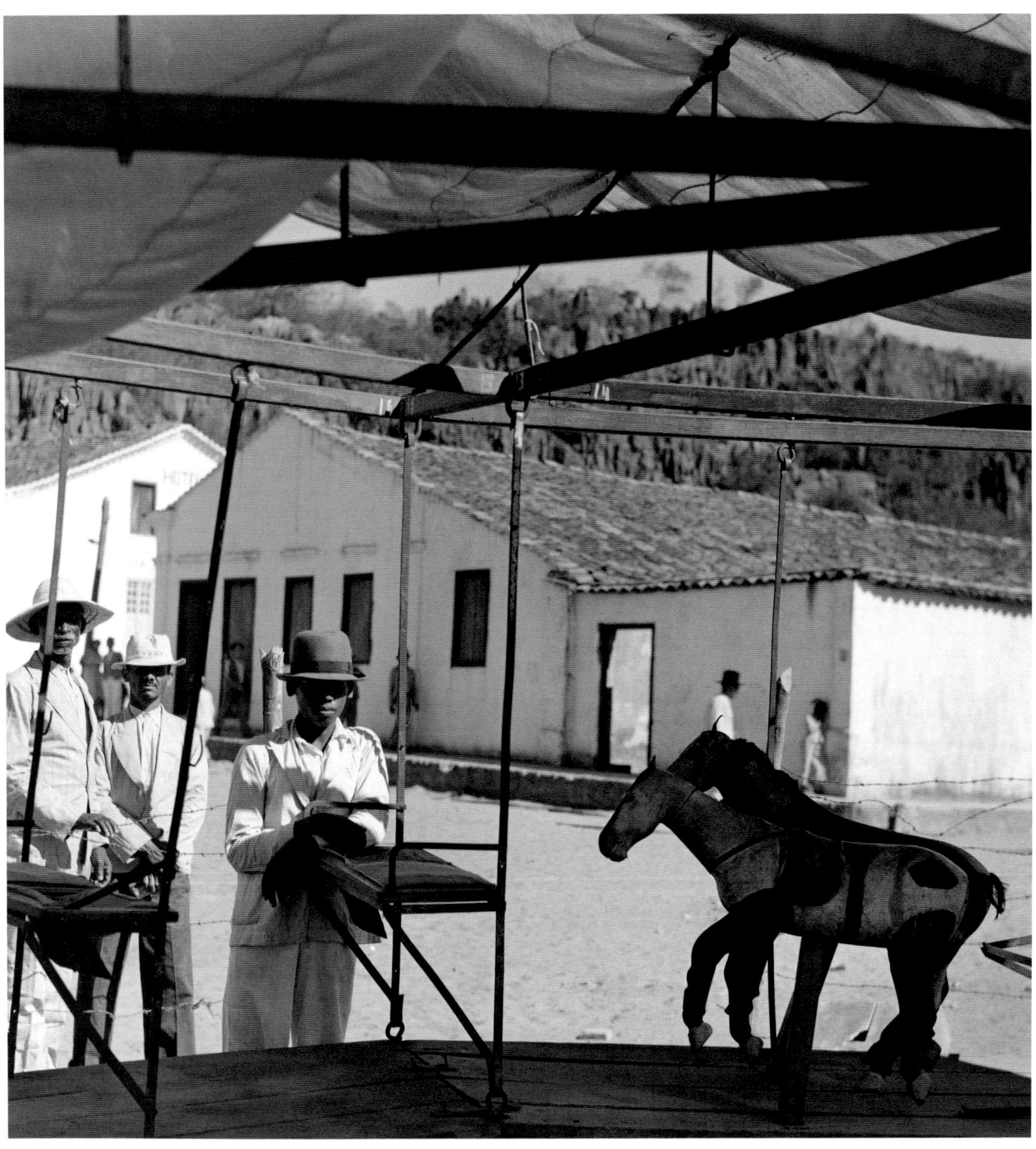

74 CAROUSEL

A boy and two men look at the camera through a rustic carousel
that has been erected in an open square. The perimeter of the
carousel is marked by barbed wire. Often circuses or other diver-
sions visited towns during religious festivals.

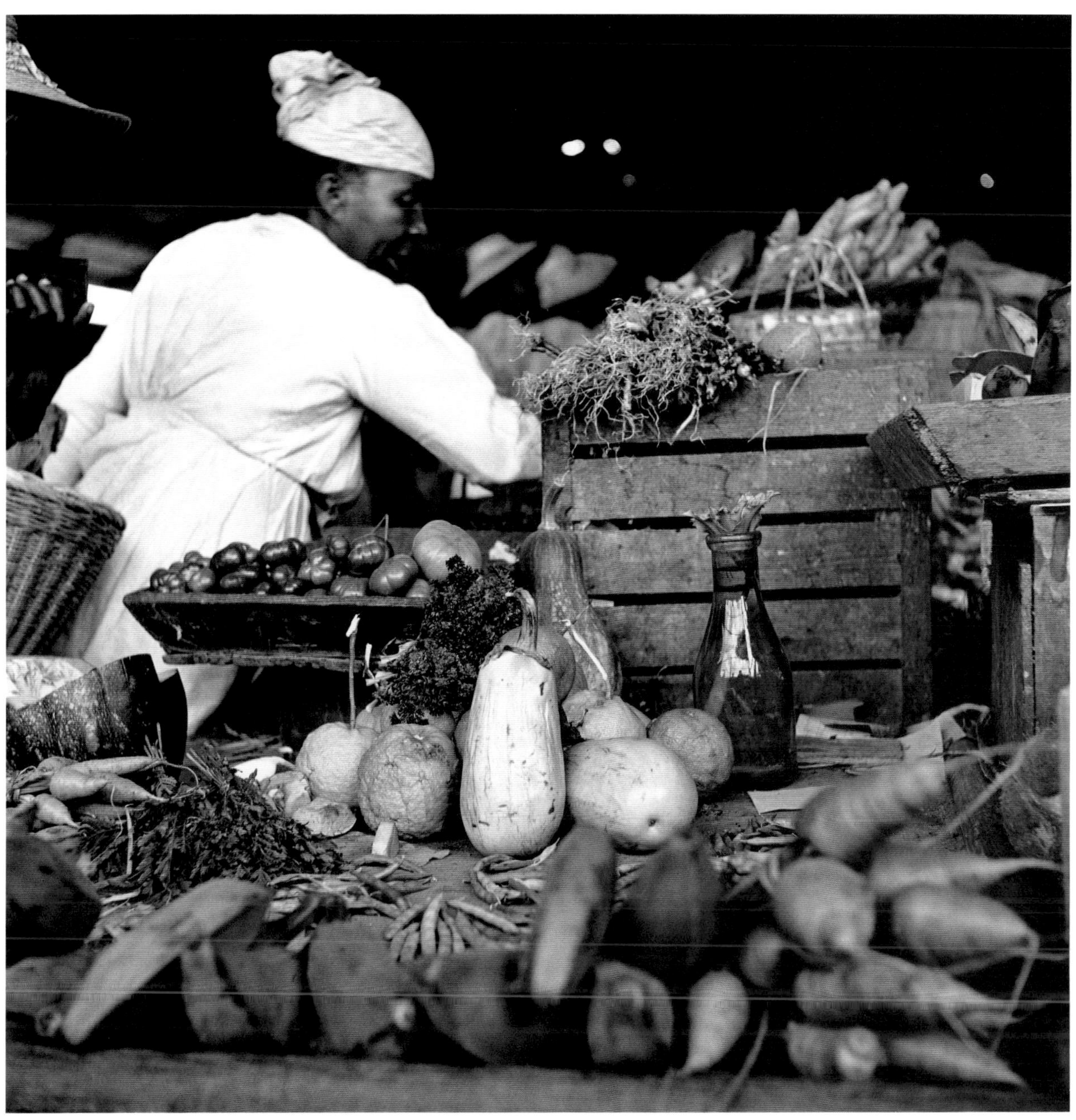

By the 1940s, some towns and cities had moved their markets—
held for generations outdoors one day a week on the town
square—to a permanent location indoors.

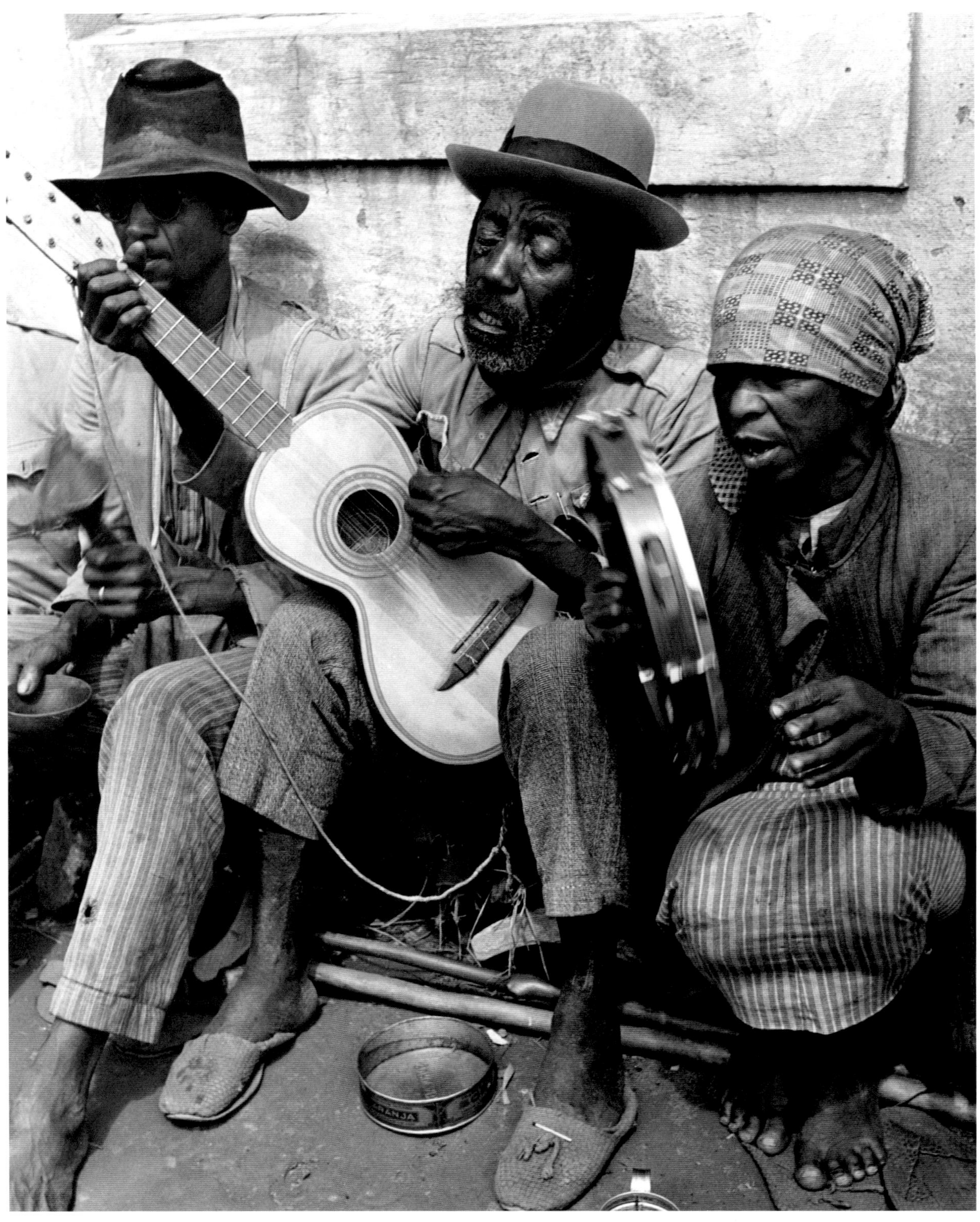

76 BEGGARS

The blind guitarist and his companions are beggars. In some places, beggars—who were required by the state to have licenses to beg—staked out the same place on the sidewalk for years at a stretch.

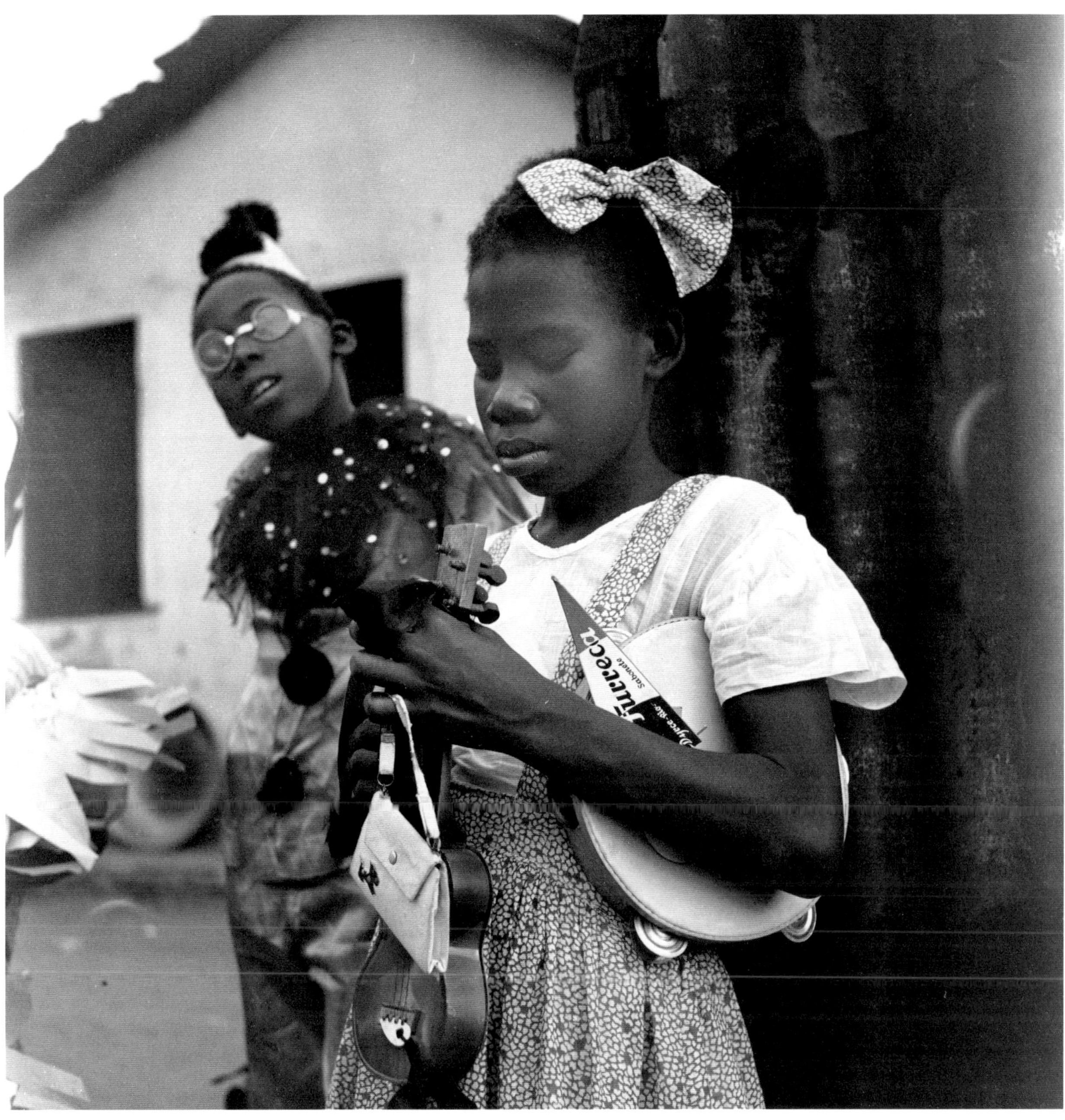

77 CARNIVAL

The child in the background wears a kind of goggles and a clown costume. His sister(?), who does not seem very happy, holds a small, rough-hewn wooden violin and a small handbag. Under her arm is a tambourine and a banner produced by a soap company.

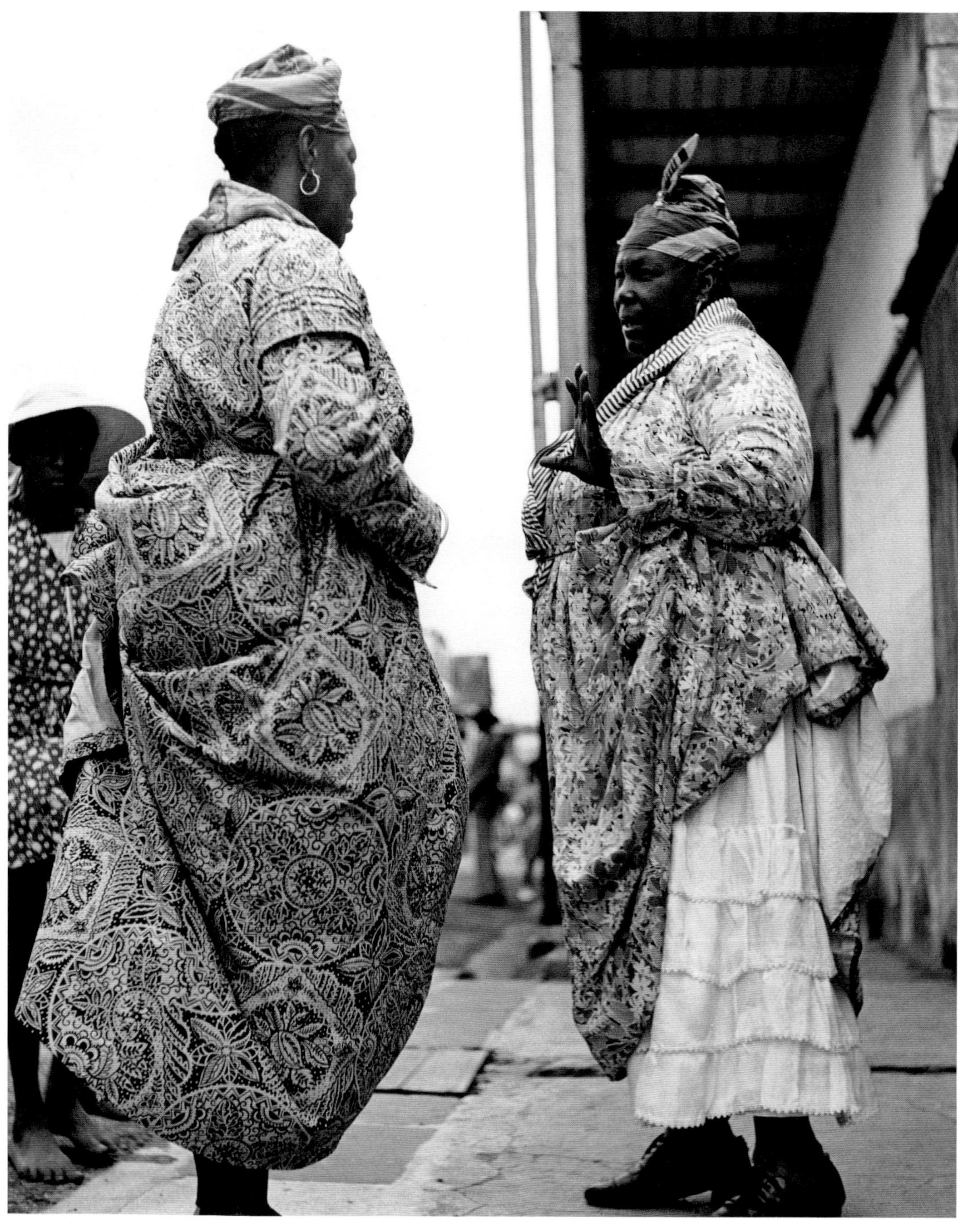

Afro-Brazilian women often dressed in traditional garb, especially in Salvador. Because Naylor probably did not visit that city, the photograph may have been taken in a riverfront town in the interior of the state of Bahia. The camera angle she chose accentuates their girth. They are wearing ornate leather shoes, indicating a certain degree of economic well-being.

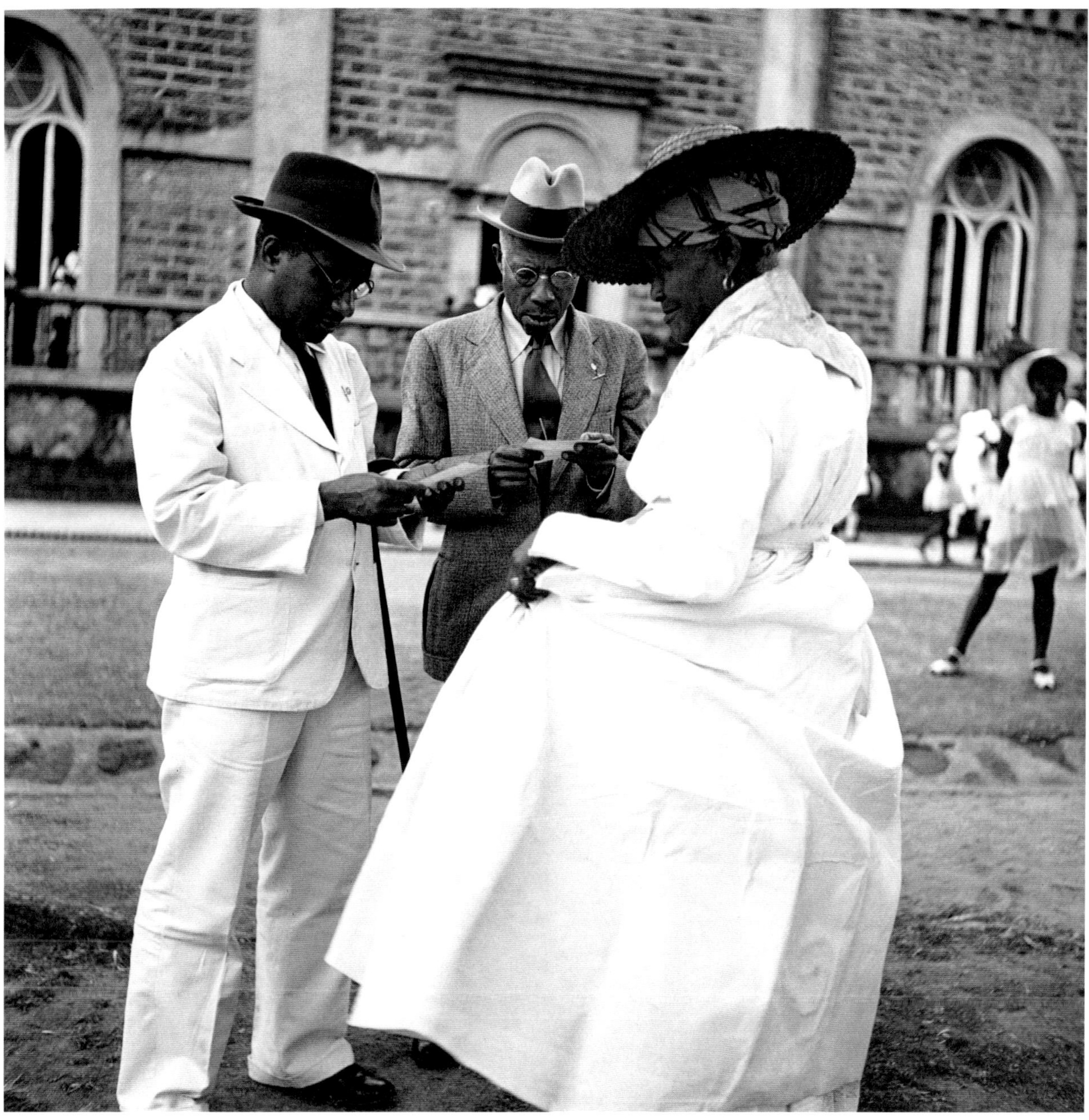

79 TWO MEN AND A WOMAN

This photograph challenges the stereotype of Brazilian blacks as impoverished. Both men have eyeglasses; one carries a walking stick. The men wear well-fitting and expensive tailored suits and jewelry; the woman wears a straw hat and a billowing white dress. Children in the background are equally well dressed. Perhaps they were attending a graduation ceremony or communion.

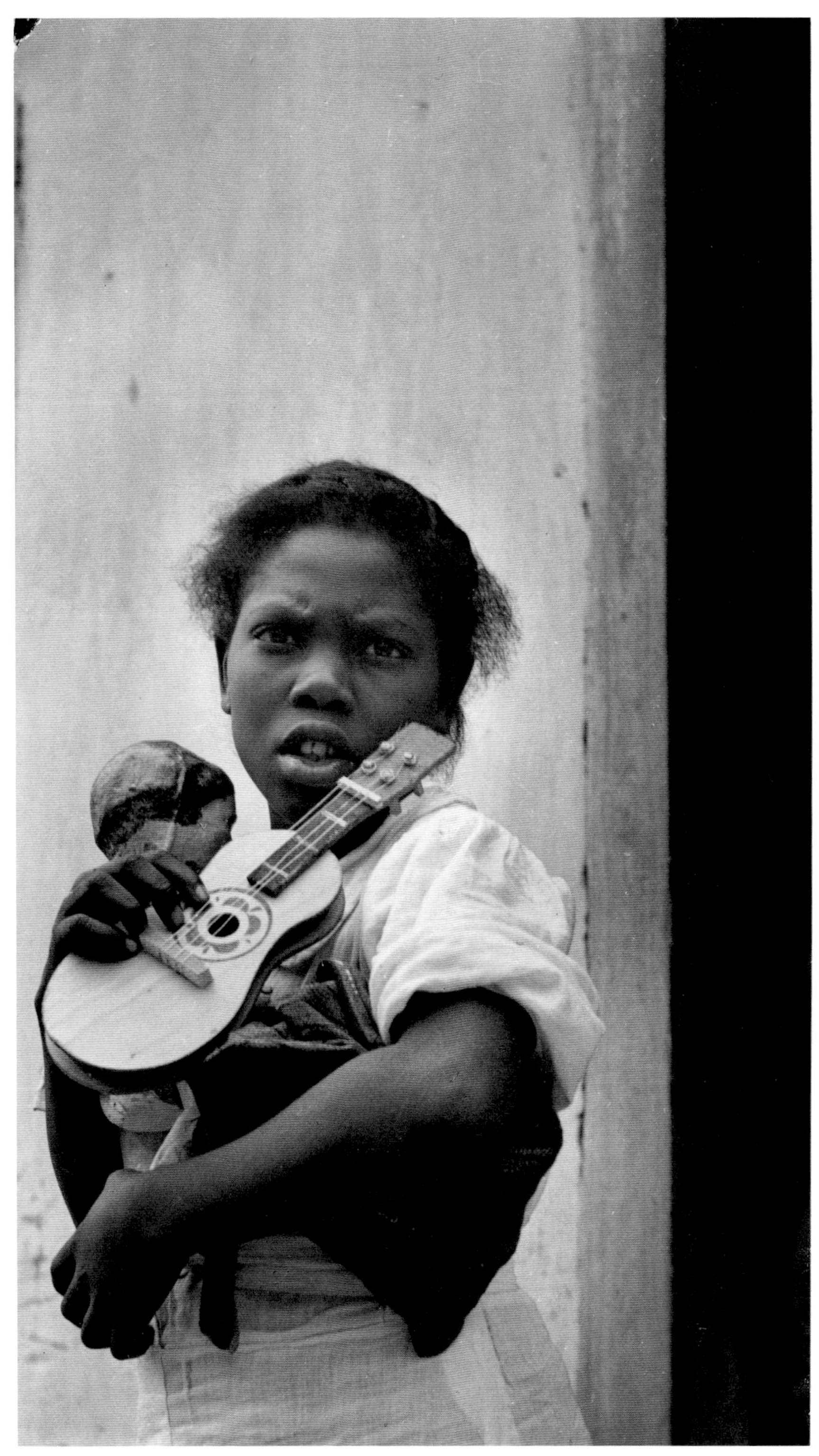

8 0 G I R L

The girl in her doorway holds not only her toy musical instrument but her doll.

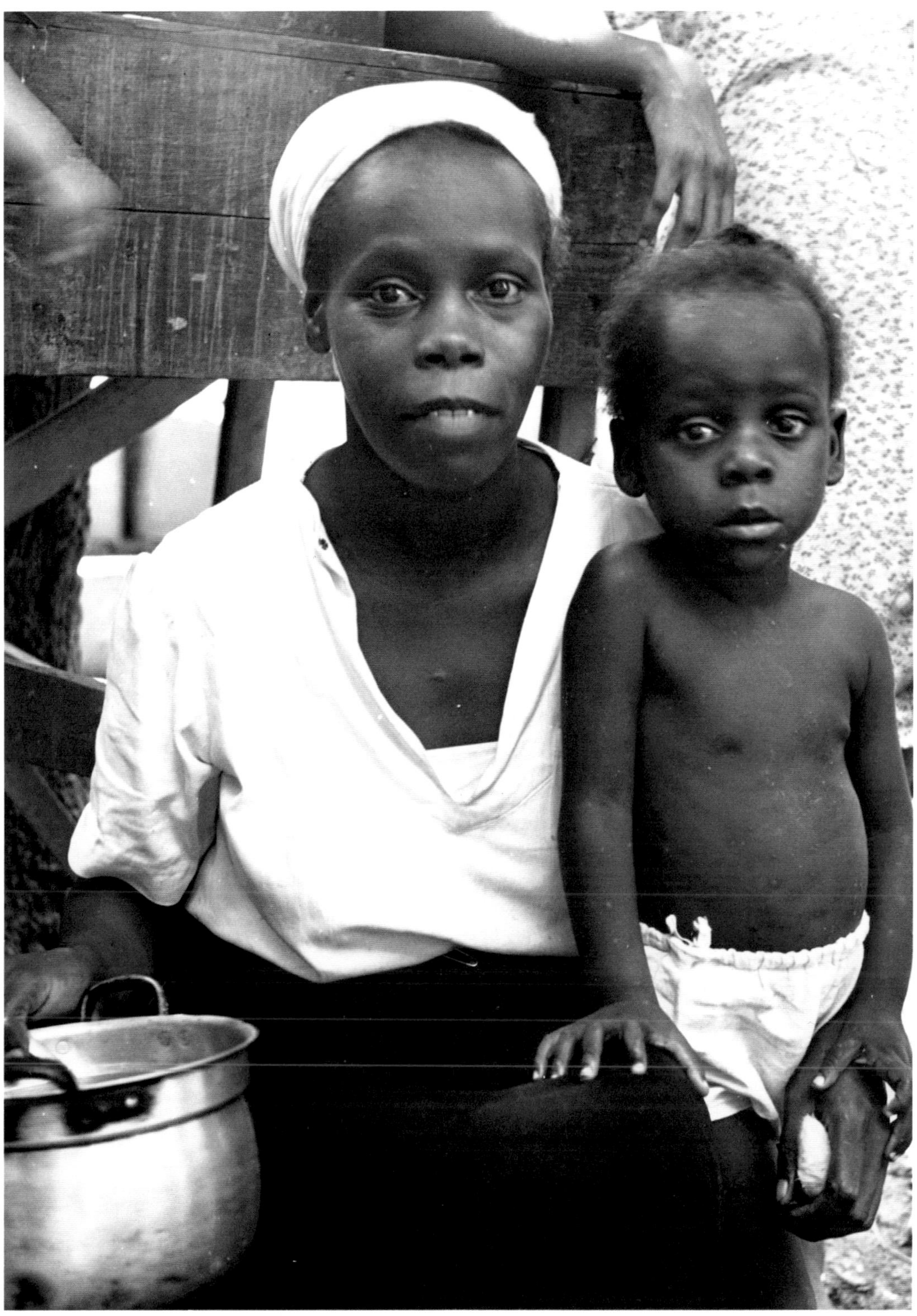

The woman sits with her child holding a pot in front of a wooden stand. She may be preparing food to sell. She may be poor, but the composition emphasizes her clean blouse and head covering; the pot is clean as well. The child looks at the camera with a sense of wary expectation.

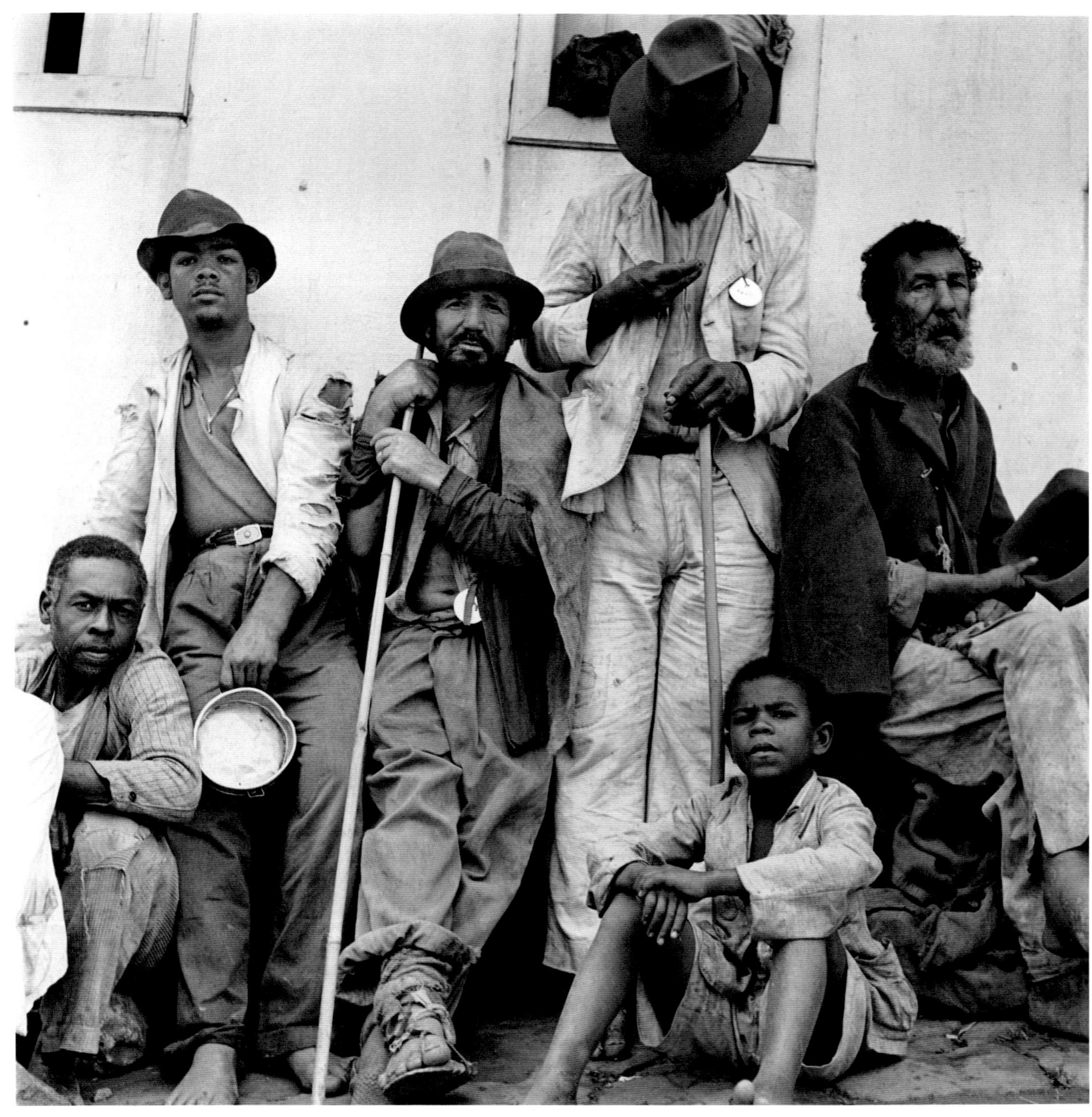

Naylor's portrait of five needy men and a boy awaiting distribution of food captures their individuality and does not deprive them of their dignity, although their clothing is frayed and at least one of them—the hatless man on the right staring at the camera, seems haggard.

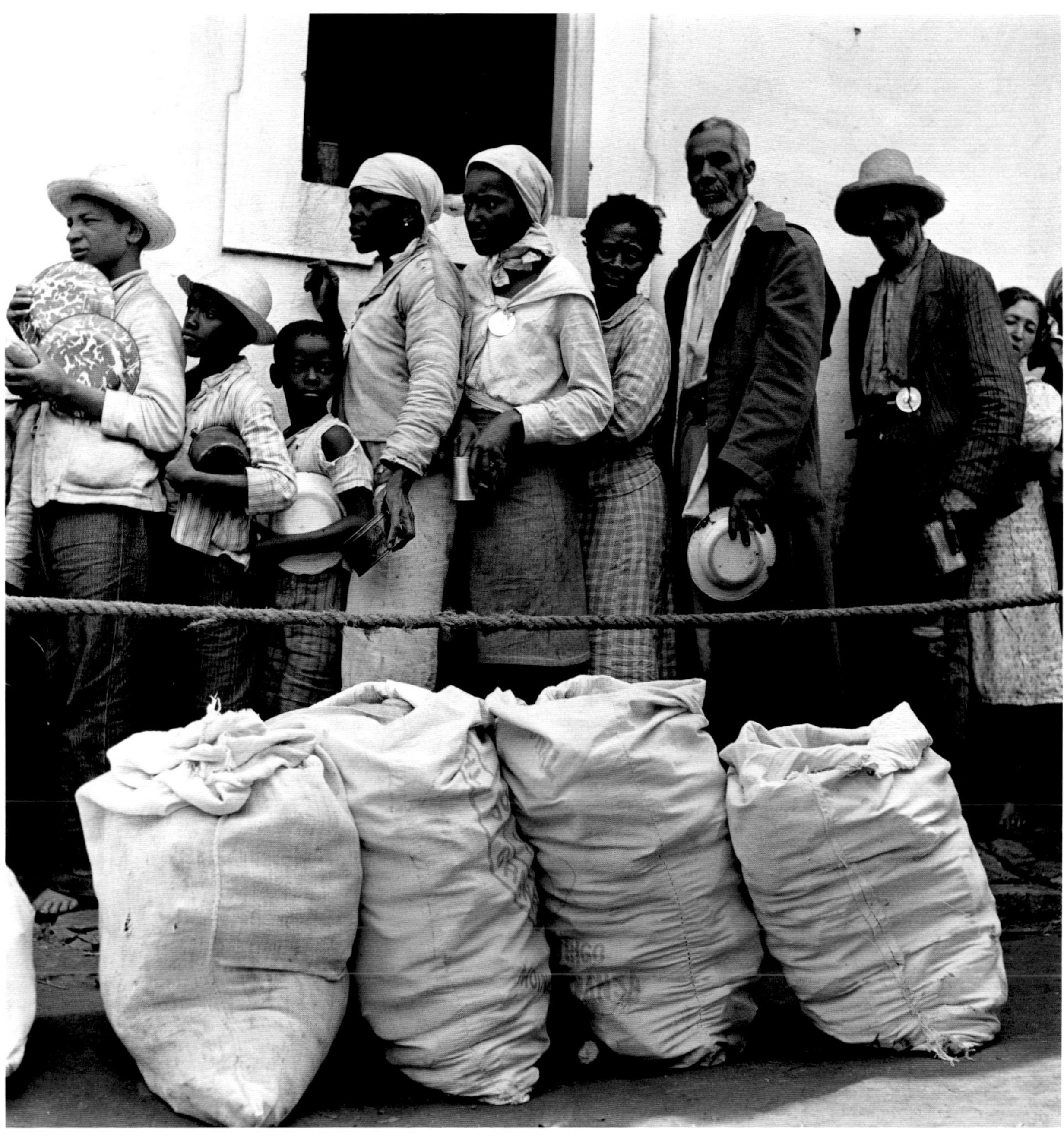

The states and the federal government usually did not give out food to indigents except during times of drought. These men and women lined up for a meal are probably migrants fleeing the drought region of the Northeast for the Center-South. Naylor's low camera angle emphasizes the dual rows of people and food sacks.

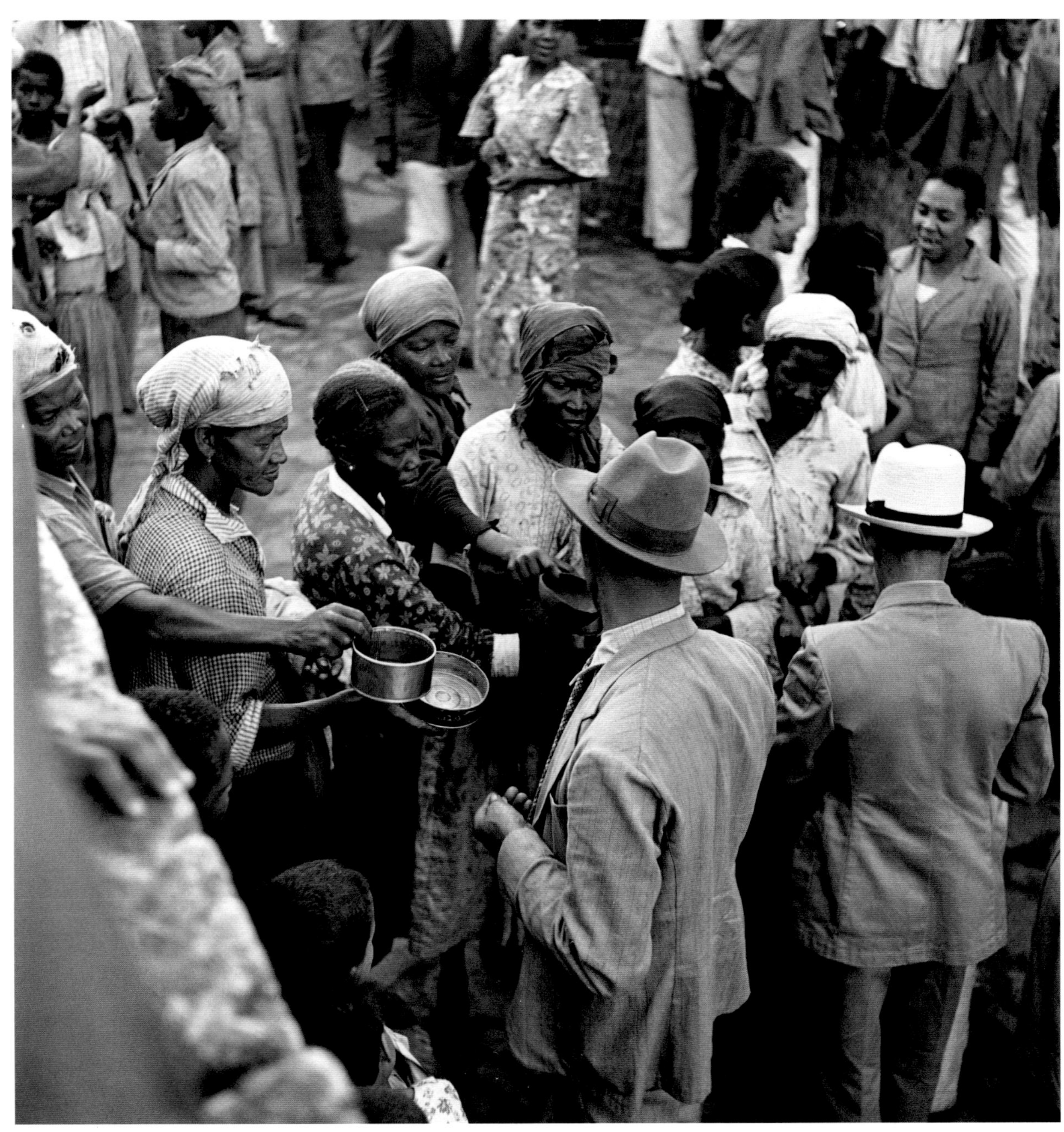

Even in this food line, Naylor captures some friendly exchanges;
in particular, among the three women in the upper right. The
two men in suits may be officials distributing tokens or coins.

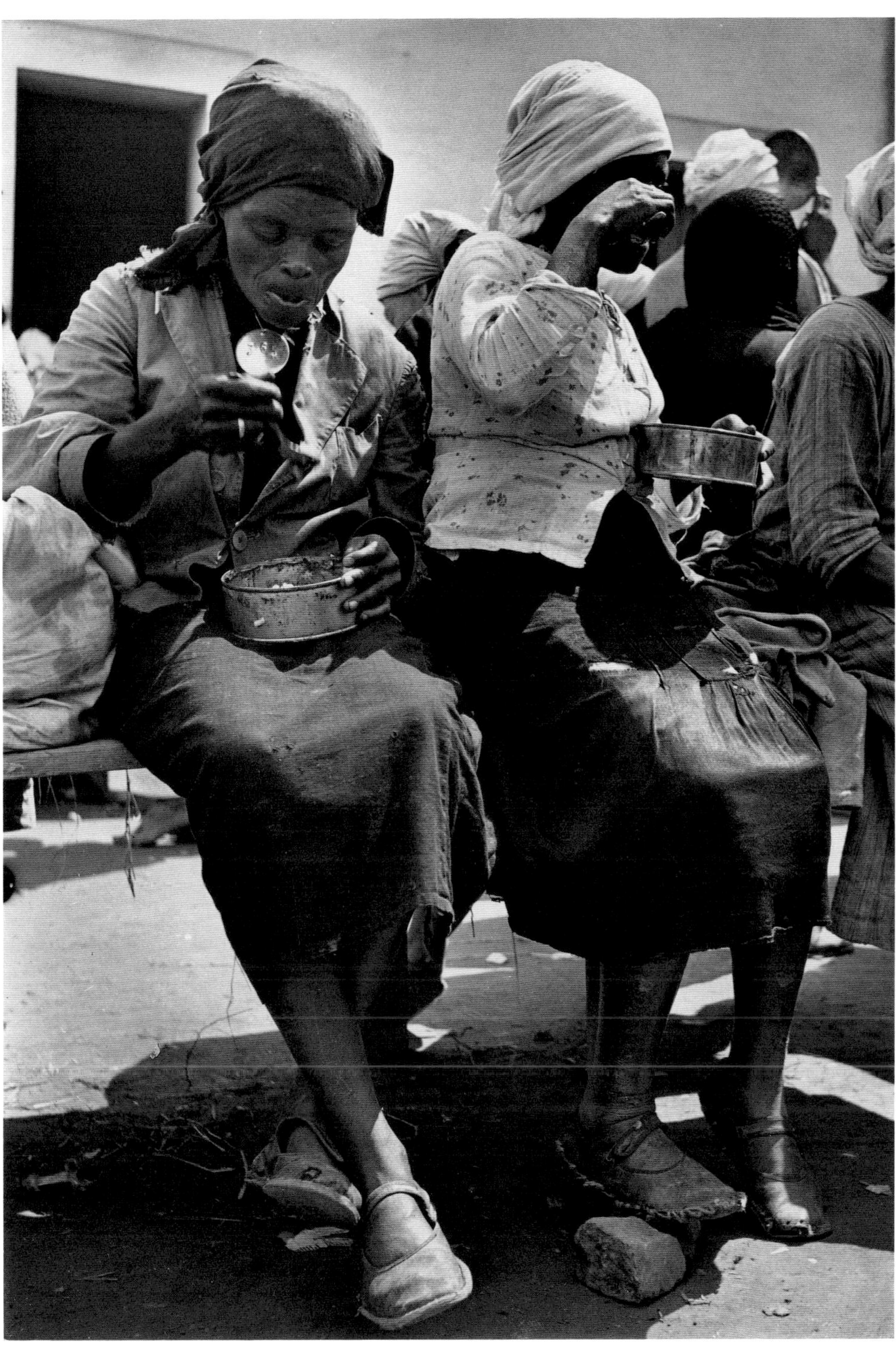

8 5 CHARITY

These women are eating a meal of rice and manioc meal (farina)
provided by the local relief agency.

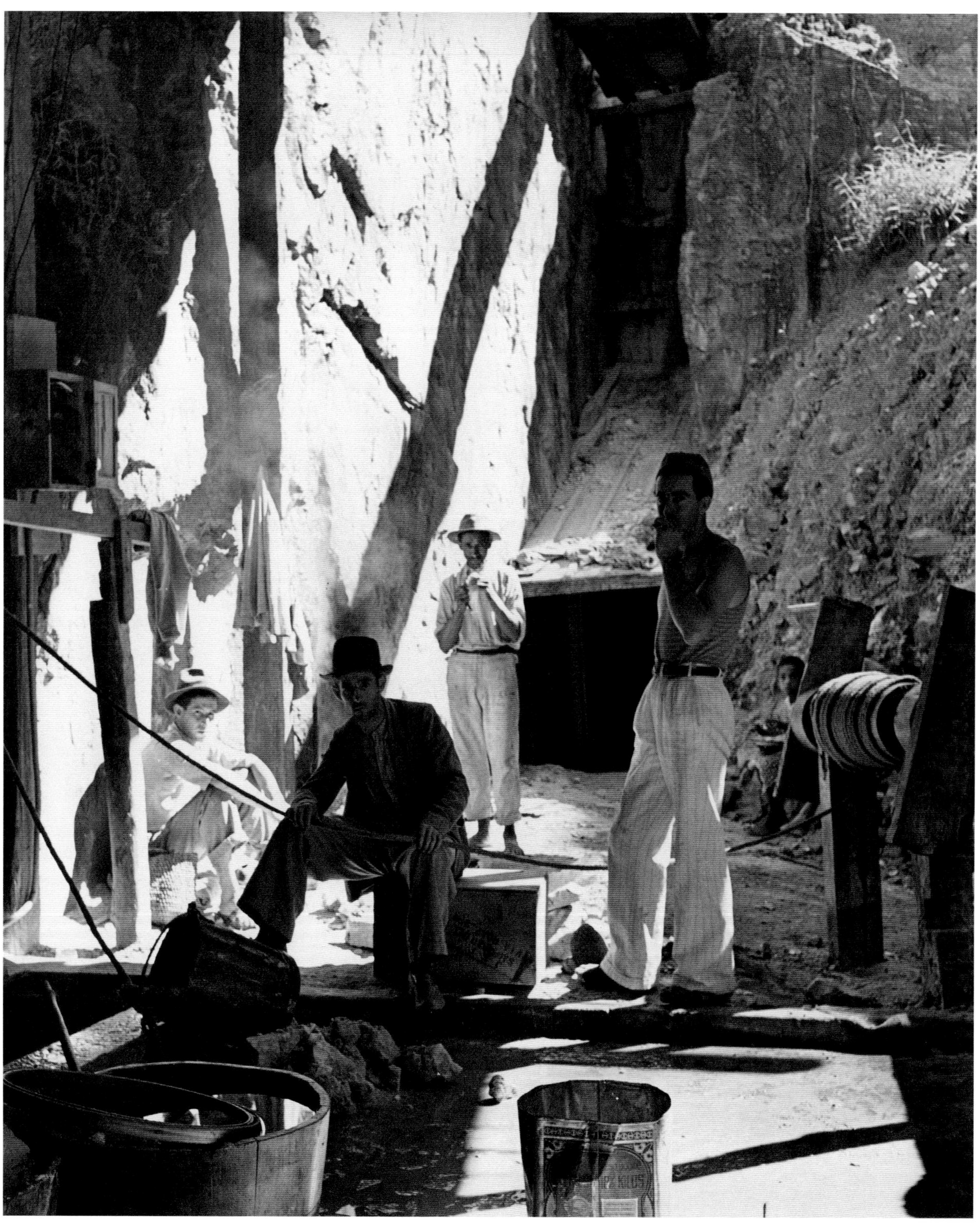

Naylor journeyed far inland, to the Baroque cities of the mountainous state of Minas Gerais, the site of the gold boom of the
seventeenth century. Men and boys at the entrance to a mine
shaft are taking their break.

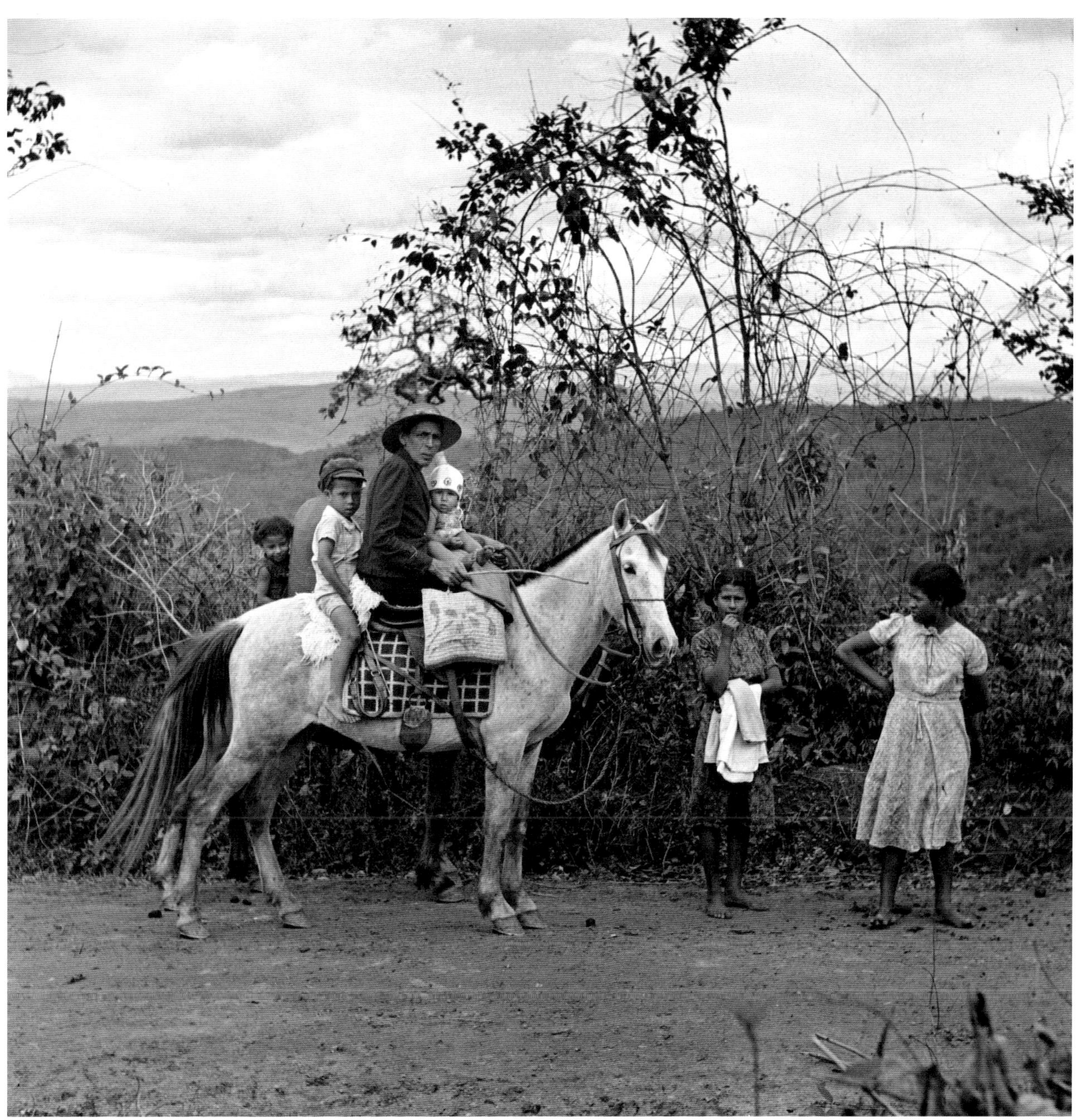

87 FAMILY ON HORSEBACK

The vegetation is sparse and conditions are semiarid. All of the
children walk barefoot.

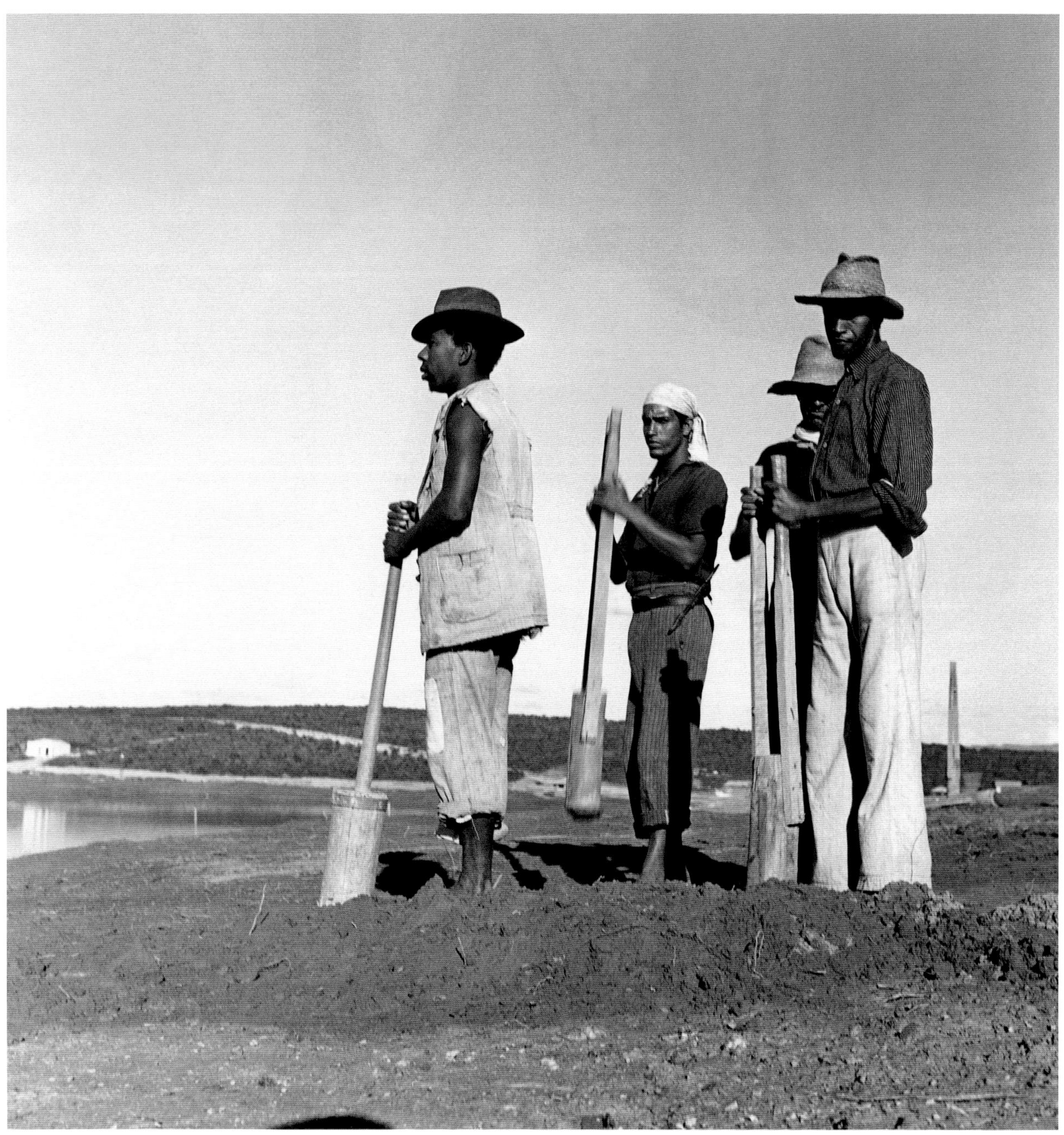

88 RURAL WORKERS

The men with their primitive tools stand with the tall smoke-
stack of a sugar refinery in the distance. The low camera angle
and the long shadows emphasize their weariness.

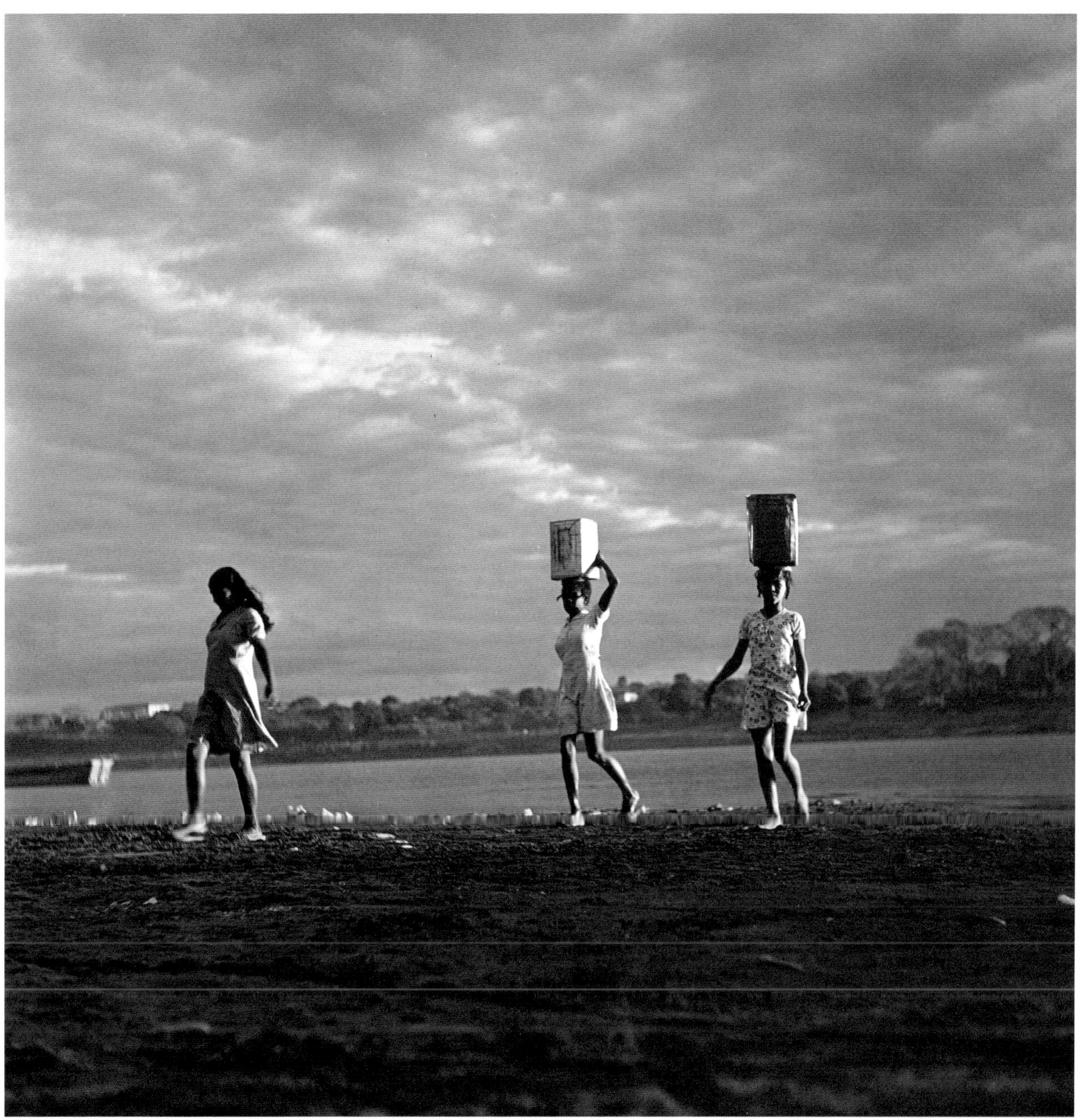

These girls are carrying metal containers of water on their heads. Many places in Brazil lacked running water. This photograph is powerful because of its simplicity: it records the difficult task of fetching water, but it does not add elements that ask the viewer for sympathy.

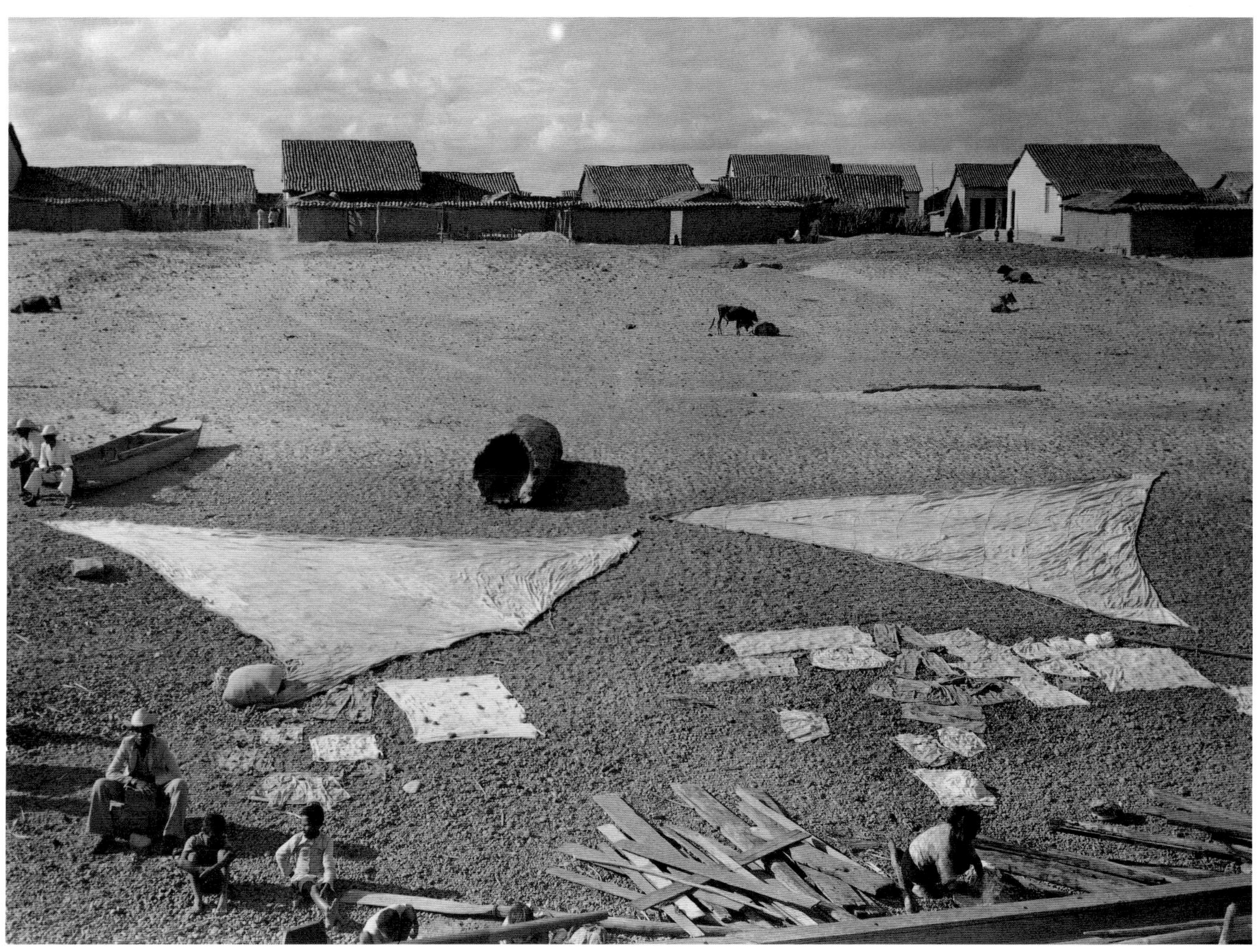

Balsa raft fishermen along the banks of the São Francisco River wait while their canvas sails are stretched on the shore to dry. In the background is a substantial town with houses of adobe-like mud-and-wattle bricks. Goats wander the area; their droppings were used for fertilizer.

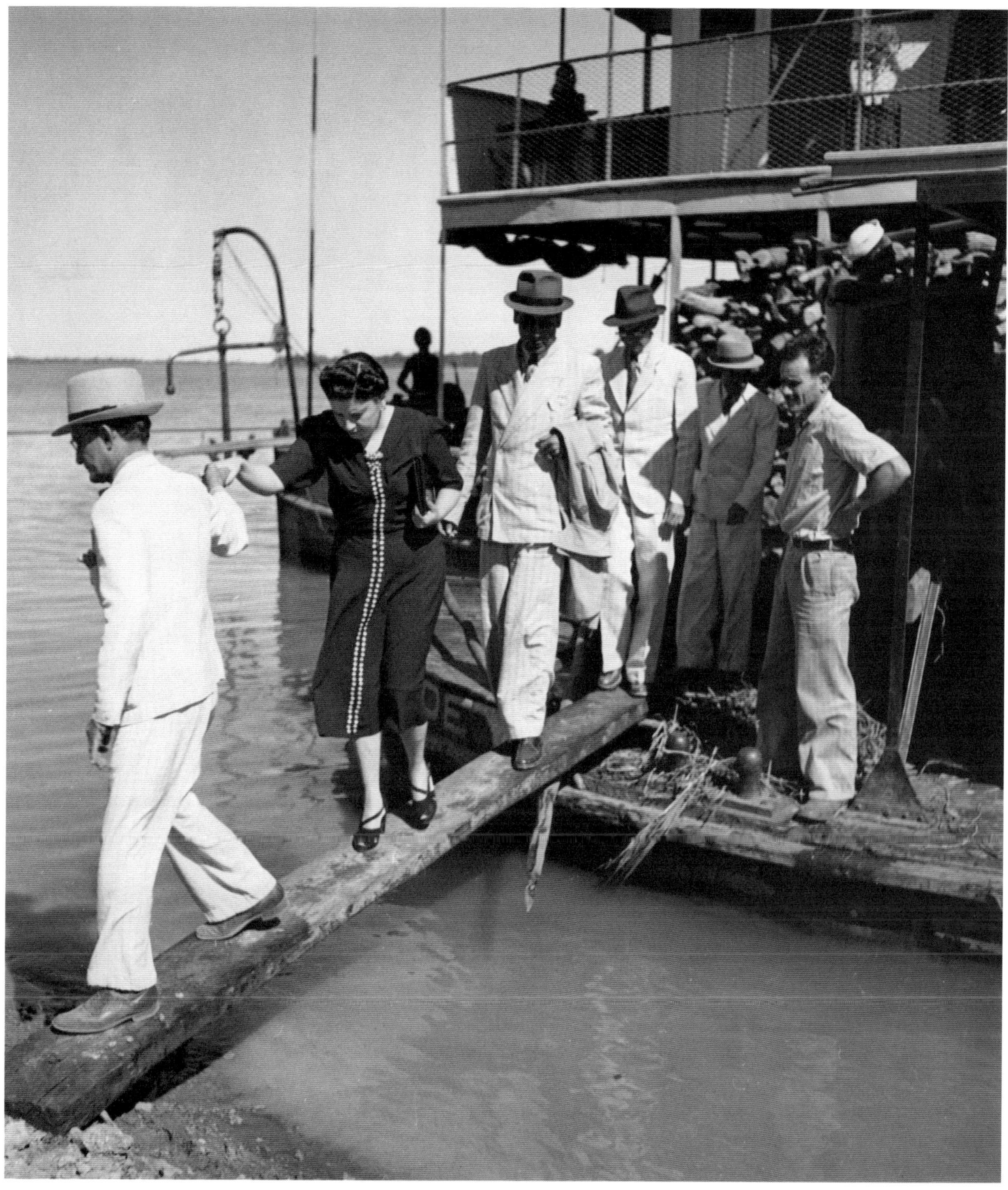

91 PASSENGERS WAITING TO DISEMBARK

Many of the small towns along the São Francisco River did not
have permanent dock facilities, so makeshift landing ramps—in
this case a single board—were used.

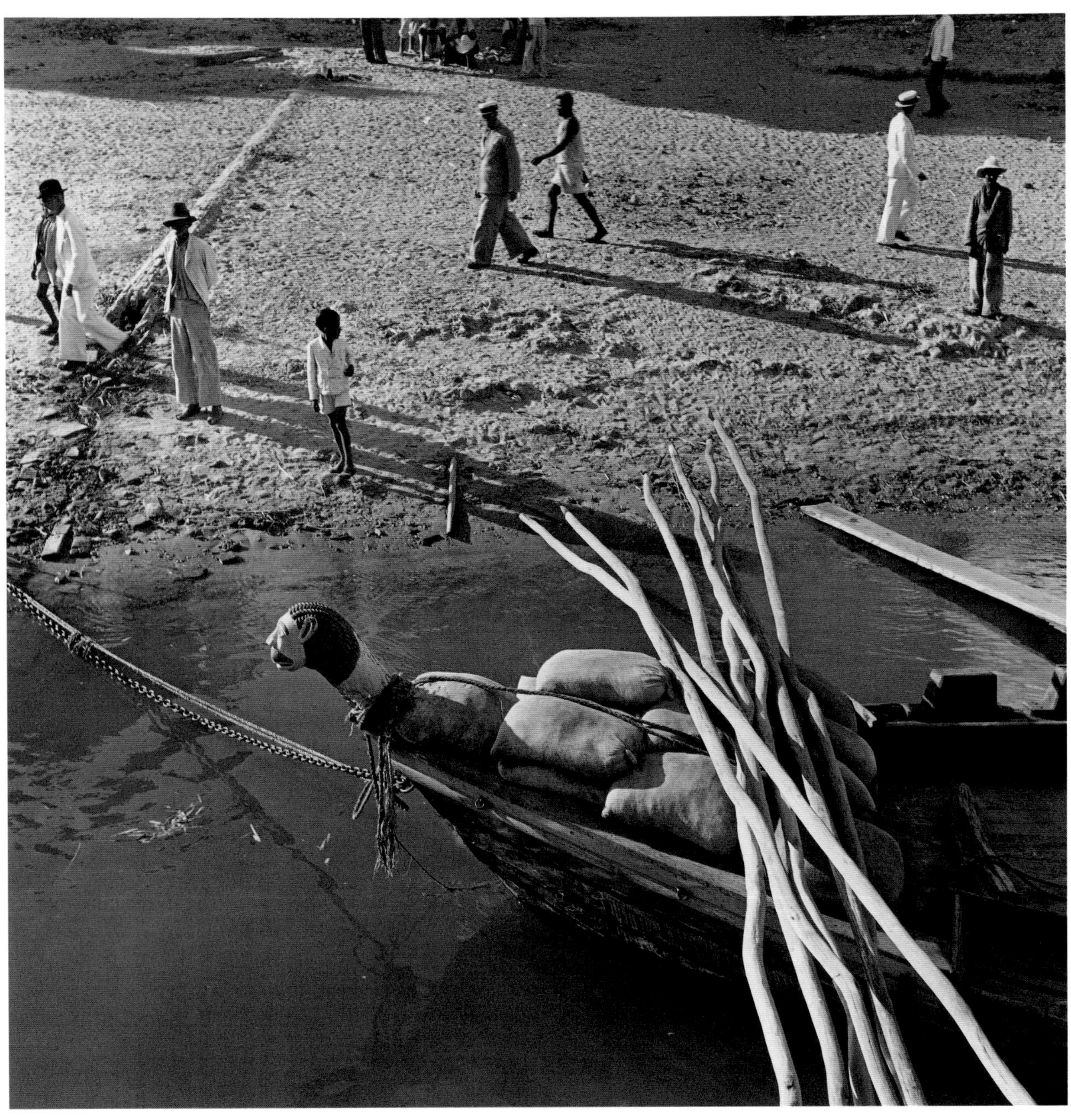

92 RIVER BOAT FIGURE

The ornate carved wooden head at the prow of the boat was believed to ward off harmful spirits.

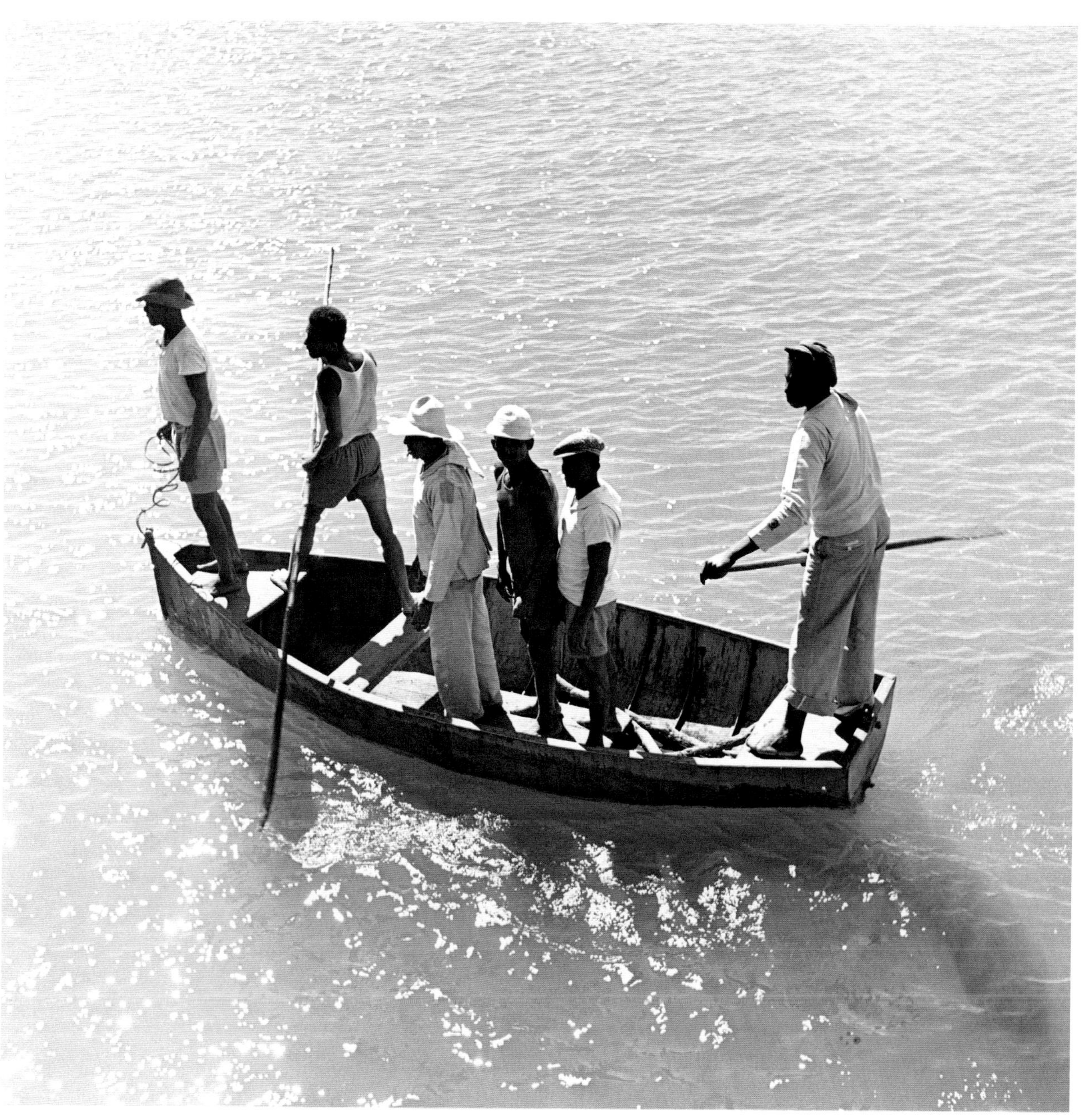

93 CARRYING PASSENGERS

Guiding a small boat while standing in the rear requires significant skill.

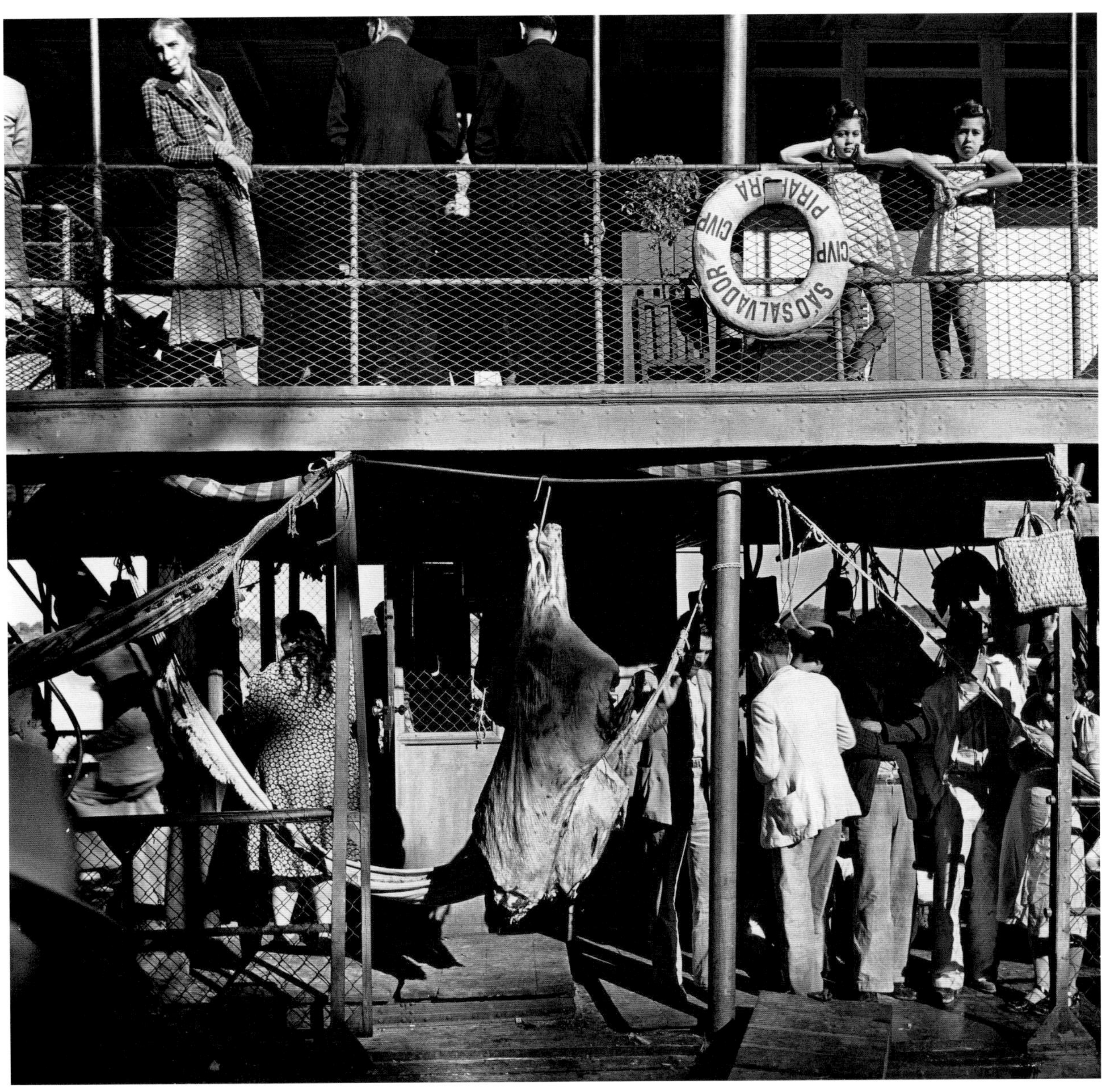

Some passengers on the Pirapora-Juazeiro riverboat have hung up their hammocks in which they will sleep. An assortment of other things are also strung up on the deck, including an entire side of beef covered with a tarpaulin. The lower deck was a kind of steerage; more prosperous passengers occupied the upper deck.

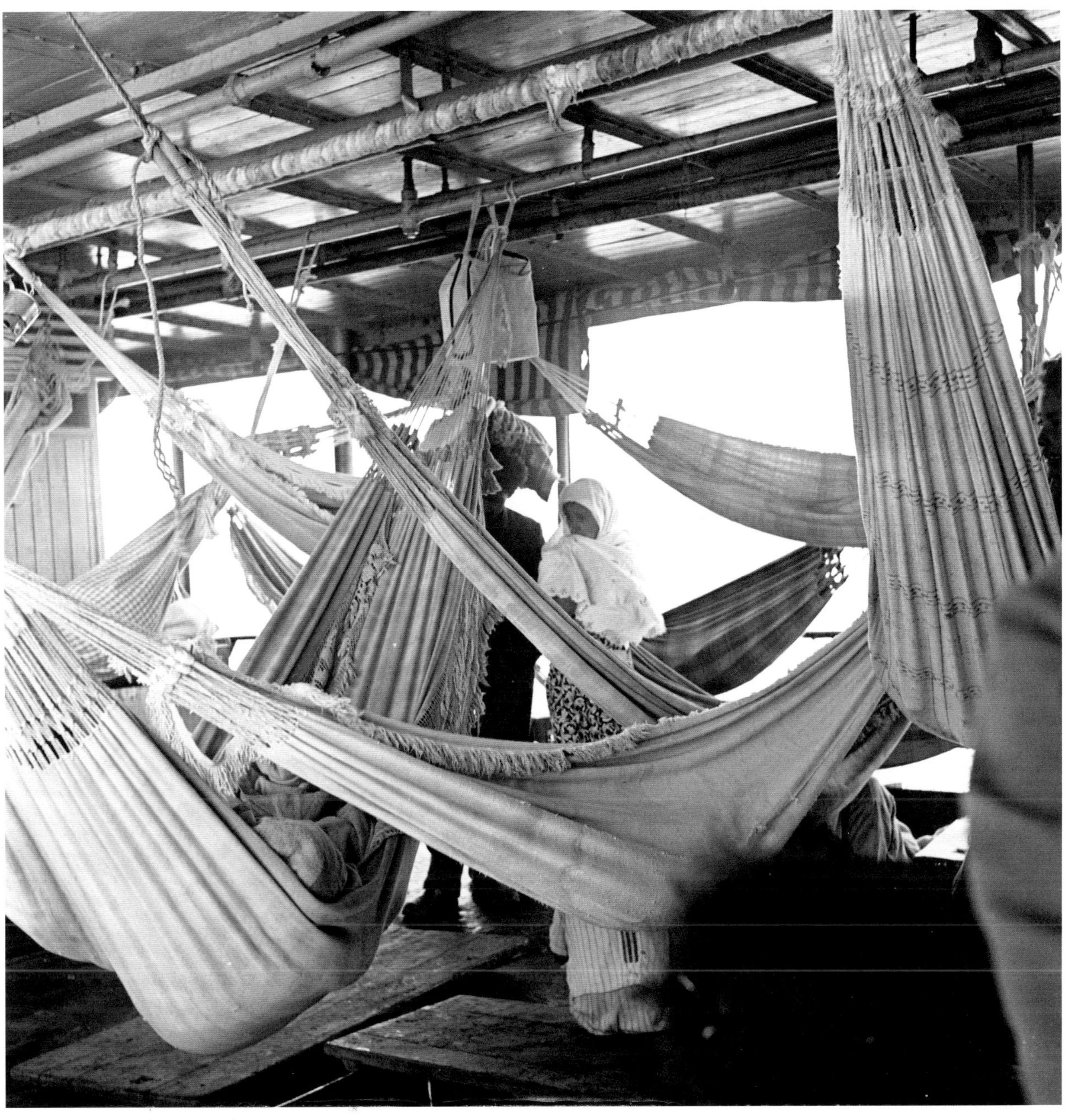

95 HAMMOCKS

A woman standing on deck is surrounded by hammocks, most
of them filled with sleepers. Her head is covered, giving her the
aspect of a woman wearing Muslim garb.

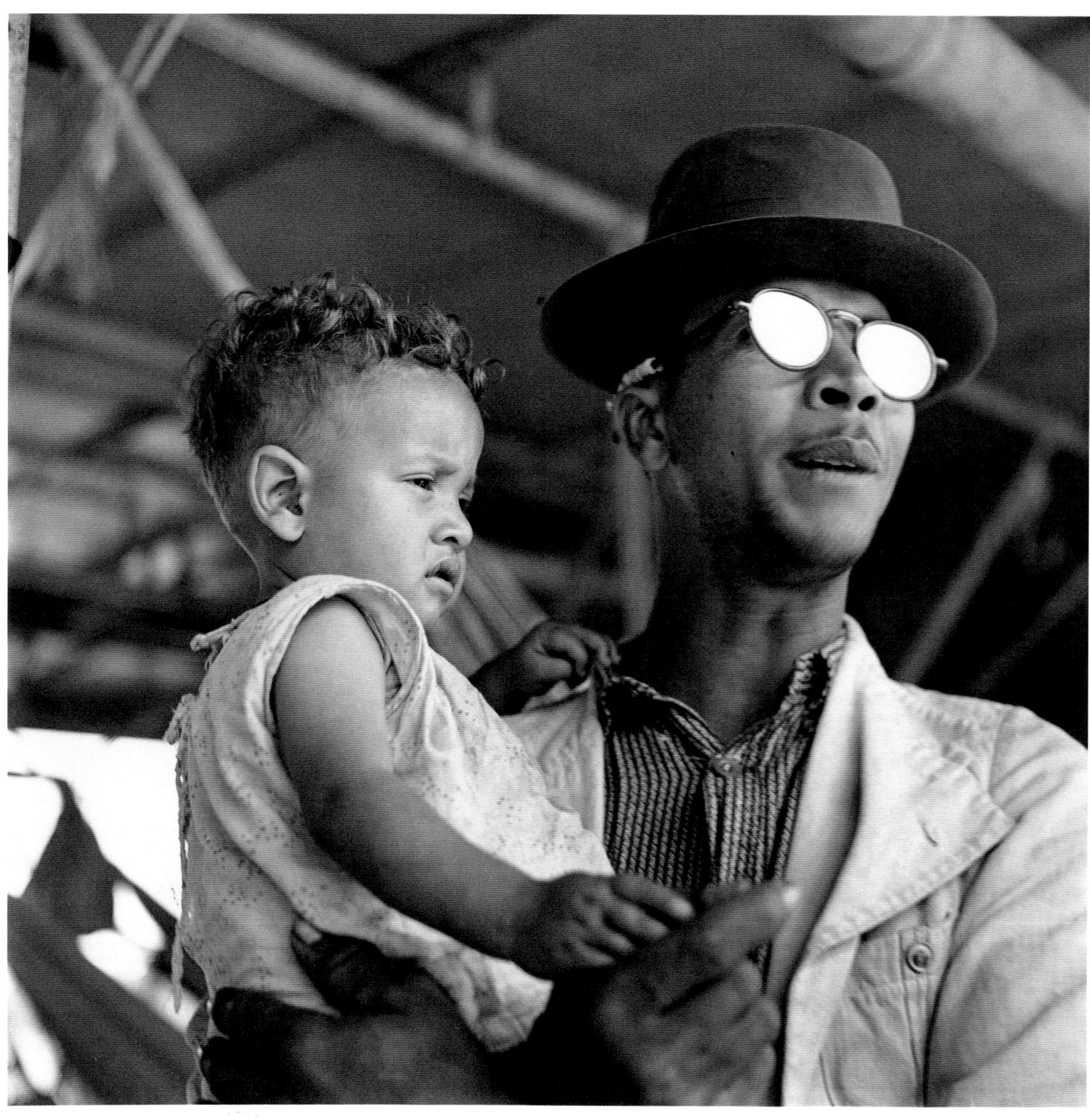

The two passengers were photographed from a low camera angle with the sun reflecting in the man's glasses. We know little about the man's social standing, but there is a radiant quality to the way he looks and the tender manner in which he holds his child.

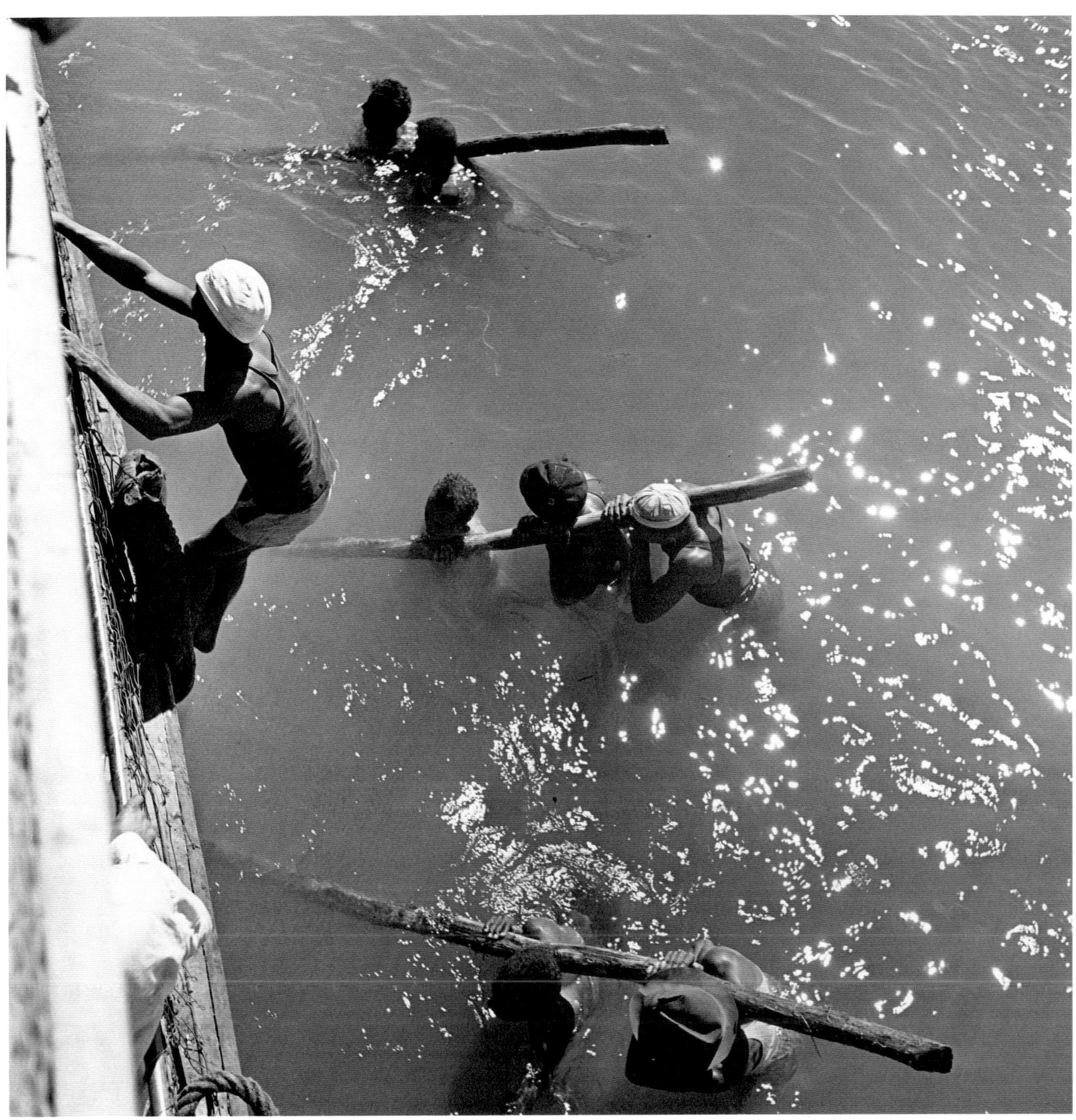

97 PUSHING OFF

Manual laborers stand in the muddy water up to their heads to
free the riverboat from a sandbar. Riverboats traveled only by
day but, even so, frequently got stuck.

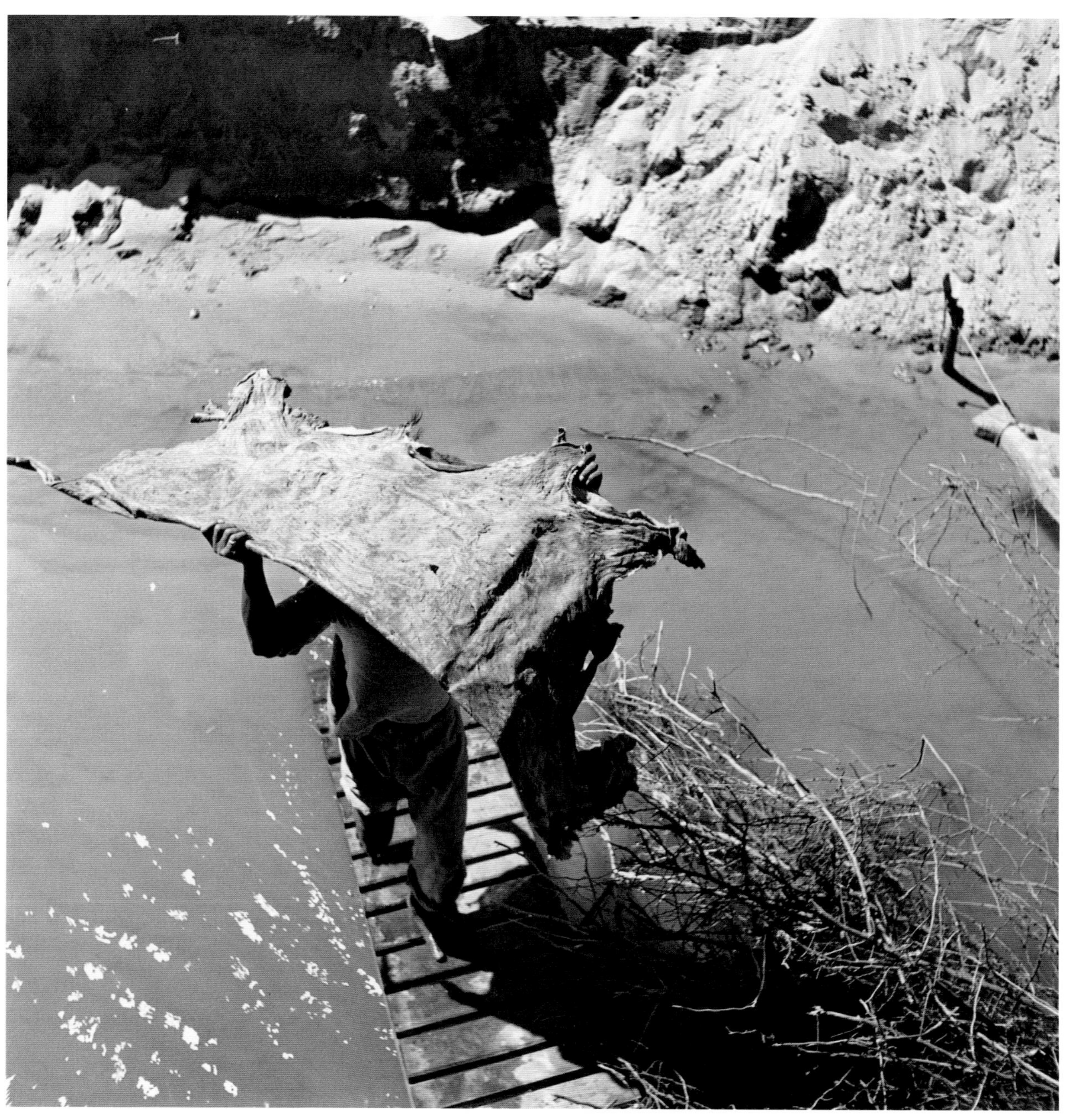

A man boarding a riverboat is hidden by a large dried animal
skin balanced on his head, in a scene reminiscent of the documentary films of Robert Flaherty.

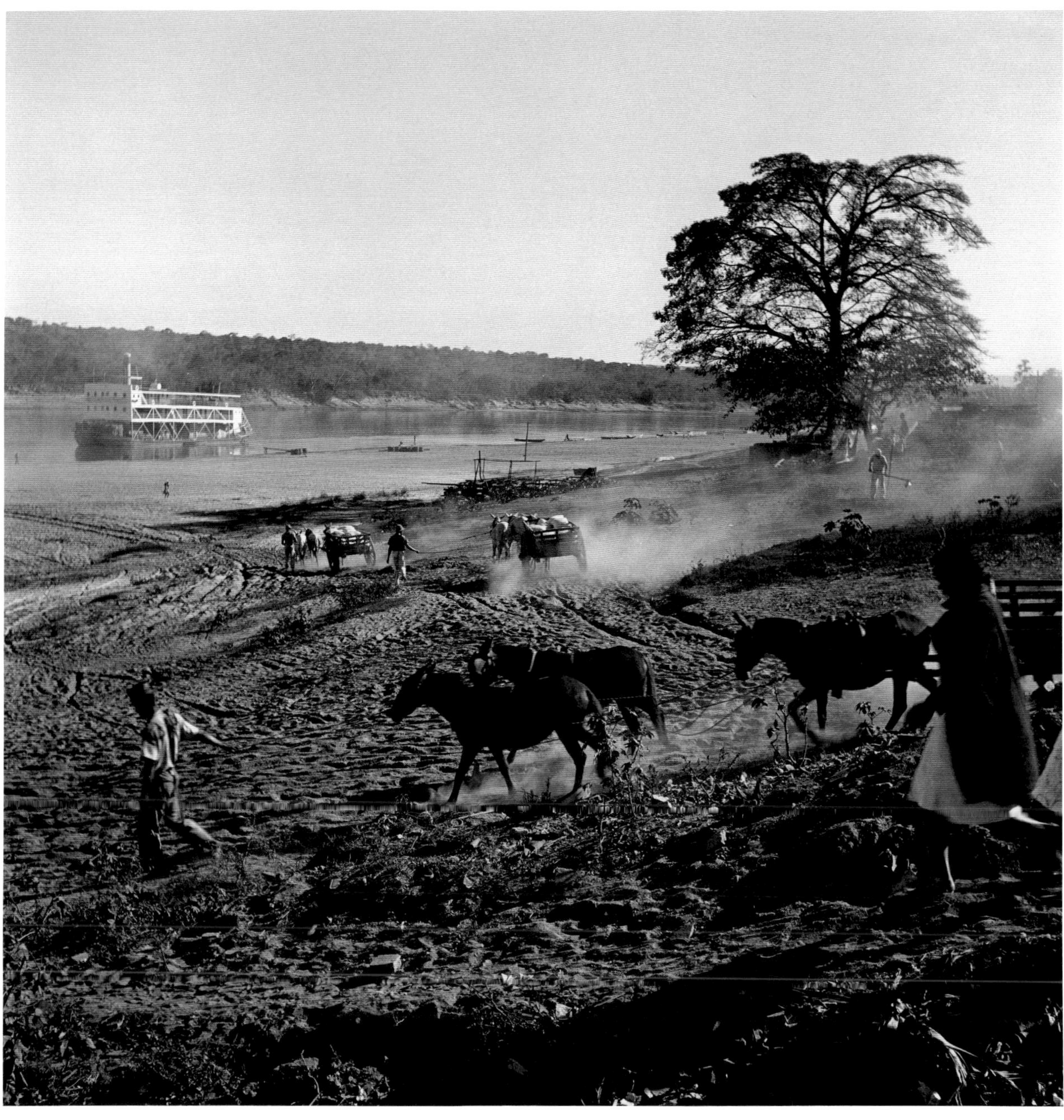

Several wagons are shown approaching the riverside dock where the paddle-steamer awaits to ship the goods to their destination. The scene is beautiful; at the same time it shows the difficulties of transport under such conditions. The high cost of transportation in rural areas is one reason that agricultural yields were often not profitable unless farmland lay adjacent to railroads, which were few and far between. This was a factor in the exodus from the countryside to the large cities during and after the 1940s.

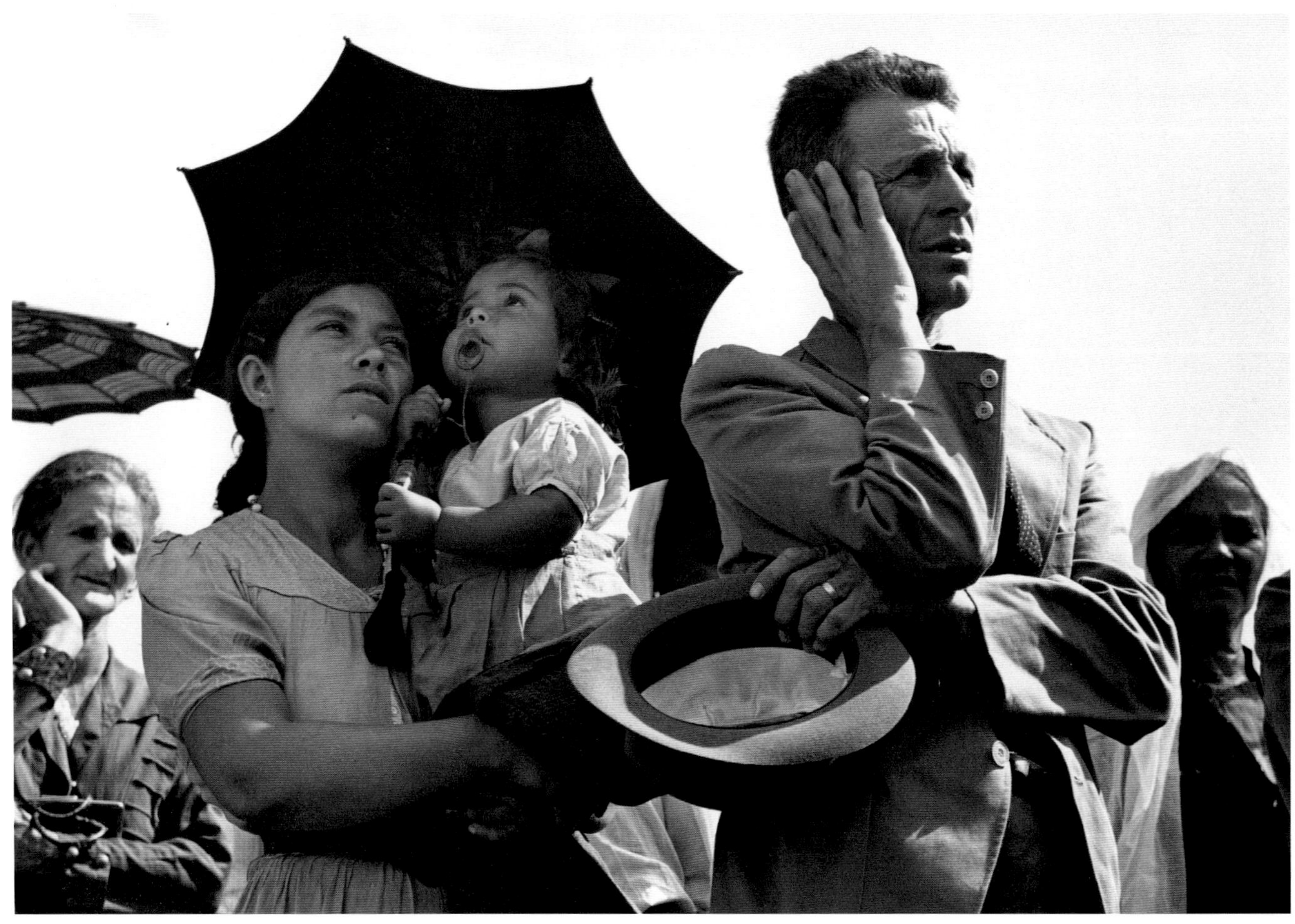

100 FAMILY GROUP AT RELIGIOUS FESTIVITY

The father's stance in the hot sun mirrors the old woman standing behind his wife. They are a modern family—the child has a pacifier in her mouth, but their expression is timeless. Perhaps they are listening to a speech or oration over a loudspeaker. The child watches something in the other direction. Her father's wedding band is prominently displayed. This emphasis on family life is a theme the DIP liked, but there is a bit too much tension in the adults' faces to make this a conventional Estado Novo–era image.

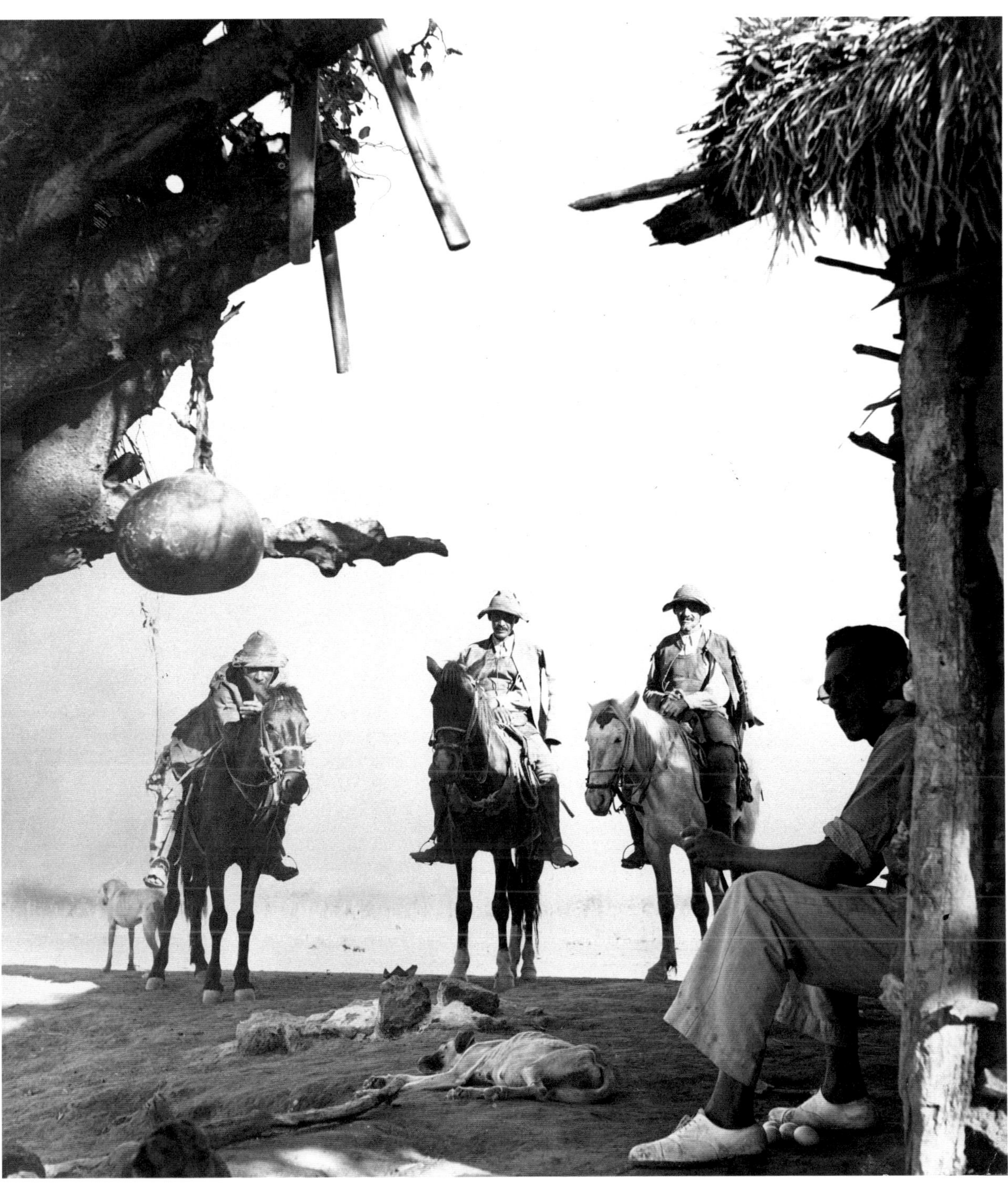

Naylor photographs the three leather-clad cowboys and their emaciated dogs next to a nattily dressed visitor. The men on horseback are framed by the tree and by their hut, an arrangement that gives the setting the look of a stage. The image was probably composed in a humorous vein, but it demonstrates the material and psychological distance between life in Brazil's interior and its modern coastal cities.

ROBERT M. LEVINE is Professor of History and Director of Latin American Studies at the University of Miami, Coral Gables. He has published seventeen books on Latin American history, including *Windows on Latin America: Understanding Society through Photographs, Bitita's Diary, Images of History,* and *Father of the Poor? Getúlio Vargas and His Era.* Several of his books have been translated and published in Brazil, and several of his original videotaped documentaries have been televised on the Arts and Entertainment Network's History Channel. He is the former chair of the Columbia University Seminars on Latin America and on Brazil, and the past national chair of the Conference of Latin American History's Committee on Brazilian Studies. He is the coeditor of the *Luso-Brazilian Review,* published at the University of Wisconsin.

As a young woman, GENEVIEVE HAY NAYLOR (1915–1989) was one of the first women to be hired by a newspaper wire service (Associated Press), and she also worked as a photographer for the New Deal's Works Progress Administration. In 1940 she and her husband, the painter Misha Reznikoff, were sent to Brazil by Nelson Rockefeller, the head of the Office of Inter-American Affairs. Her photographs document the texture of Brazilian life in ways not seen before in published photographs. After her return from Brazil she was only the second woman to have a one-woman show at New York's Museum of Modern Art. She then turned to high-fashion studio photography, becoming a leader in her profession.

Library of Congress Cataloging-in-Publication Data
Levine, Robert M.
The Brazilian photographs of Genevieve Naylor,
1940–1942 / Robert M. Levine.
ISBN 0-8223-2160-2 (cloth: alk. paper). —
ISBN 0-8223-2189-0 (pbk.: alk. paper)
1. Documentary photography—Brazil.
2. Naylor, Genevieve, 1915–1989.
3. Brazil—History—1930–1945—Pictorial works.
4. Brazil—Social life and customs—20th century—
Pictorial works.
I. Naylor, Genevieve, 1915–1989.   II. Title.
TR820.5.L5   1998   779'.9981—dc21   97–41666 CIP